WHAT TO KNOW BEFORE YOU GO

A Tourist's Guide to New York City
Expert Advice on When to Visit, How to Get There and Around, Where to Stay, What to Do, Local Customs, and more.

Ronald N. Chambers

Copyright © 2024 by Ronald N. Chambers.
All rights reserved.

No part of this book may be reproduced, distributed, or transmitted in any form or by any means, including photocopying, recording, or other electronic or mechanical methods, without the prior written permission of the publisher, except in the case of brief quotations embodied in critical reviews and certain other non-commercial uses permitted by copyright law.

The information in this book is for educational and informational purposes only. While the author has made every effort to ensure the accuracy and completeness of the information provided, the author assumes no responsibility for errors, inaccuracies, omissions, or any consequences arising from the use of the information. The content is provided on an "as-is" basis, and the author does not offer any warranties of any kind, either express or implied.

Readers are advised to seek professional advice or consult relevant authorities for specific travel, legal, or health-related matters. The author and publisher shall not be liable for any loss or damage, including but not limited to indirect or consequential loss or damage, arising out of or in connection with the use of this book.

Trademarks
All trademarks, service marks, trade names, and logos mentioned or used in this book are the property of their respective owners. The use of any trademarks, service marks, trade names, or logos does not imply any affiliation, endorsement, or sponsorship by the trademark holders unless otherwise noted.

TABLE OF CONTENTS

INTRODUCTION 9
HOW TO USE THIS BOOK 12
WHY NEW YORK CITY IS A MUST-VISIT DESTINATION 15
CHAPTER 1 21
PREPARING FOR YOUR NEW YORK CITY ADVENTURE 21
   Visa and Entry Requirements 21
   Travel Insurance 26
   The Best Time to Visit New York City 31
   Packing Guide 35
CHAPTER 2 41
GETTING TO NEW YORK CITY 41
   How to Get There 41
   How to Get Around 45
   Public Transportation 51
   Local Transportation Apps 56
CHAPTER 3 63
MANAGING YOUR MONEY IN NEW YORK CITY 63
   Currency Exchange Locations 63
   Money Matters 67
   Currency Symbols and Denominations 73
CHAPTER 4 79

STAYING CONNECTED AND POWERED UP 79
   Electricity and Plug Adapters 79
   Internet and Communication 83
   Public Wi-Fi Availability 88
   Important Applications and Tool 93
CHAPTER 5 101
UNDERSTANDING LOCAL RULES AND CULTURE
.... 101
   Local Customs and Laws 101
   Local Etiquette 106
   Cultural Etiquette and Taboos 112
   The Language and Key Phrases 116
   Local Language Learning Resources 122
CHAPTER 6 129
STAYING SAFE AND HEALTHY 129
   Health Care and Safety 129
   Emergency Contacts and Numbers 134
   Weather-Related Safety Tips 138
   Responsible Tourism 143
   Travel Scams and How to Avoid Them 149
CHAPTER 7 155
WHERE TO STAY IN NEW YORK CITY 155
   Accommodations (by traveler type, price, and location)
.... 155

CHAPTER 8 181

EXPLORING NEW YORK CITY 181

  Activities for Different Types of Travelers 181

  Free Tourist Attractions 204

  Paid Tourist Attractions 211

  Off the Beaten Paths 223

  Hidden Gems 229

  Historical Landmarks and Monuments 234

  Self-Guided Tours and Walks 240

CHAPTER 9 247

EXPERIENCING LOCAL CULTURE AND EVENTS 247

  Festivals and Celebrations Throughout the Year 247

  Local Festivals Calendar 253

  Public Events and Parades 260

  Traditional Festivals Celebrating Seasons 265

  Cultural Performances and Theater 271

  Local Myths, Legends, and Folklore 276

  Religious Sites and Pilgrimages 281

CHAPTER 10 287

FOOD AND DINING IN NEW YORK CITY 287

  Dining (for different travelers) 287

  Local Cuisine and Must-Try Dishes 293

  Street Food Guide 298

CHAPTER 11 305

SHOPPING AND ARTS 305
   Shopping Guide 305
   Shopping Districts and Malls 309
   Local Art and Music Scene 314
   Local Artisans and Crafts 319
   Local Crafts Workshops 323
   Local Street Art and Graffiti 327
   Local Architecture and Building Styles 331
CHAPTER 12 337
NATURE AND OUTDOOR ACTIVITIES 337
   Local Wildlife and Nature Reserves 337
   Guided Nature Walks 341
   Local Adventure Sports 345
   Popular Walking and Hiking Trails 350
   Fishing Spots and Regulations 354
   Local Boat Tours and Cruises 358
   Scenic Lookout Points 362
CHAPTER 13 367
TRAVELING WITH SPECIAL NEEDS 367
   Accessible Travel Tips 367
   Transportation for Remote Areas 371
   Bike Rentals and Cycling Routes 375
OPERATOR GUIDE 381
   Public Restrooms and Facilities 385

Health and Fitness Facilities 389
CHAPTER 14... 395
PHOTOGRAPHY TIPS AND BEST SPOTS..................... 395
    Photography and Drone Regulations............................... 399
    Road Trip Routes and Scenic Drives................................ 403
CONCLUSION 413
CREATING YOUR OWN ITINERARY........................... 414
HOW TO ACCESS AND USE YOUR FREE TRAVEL PLANNER 417
SCAN THE QR CODE BELOW 418

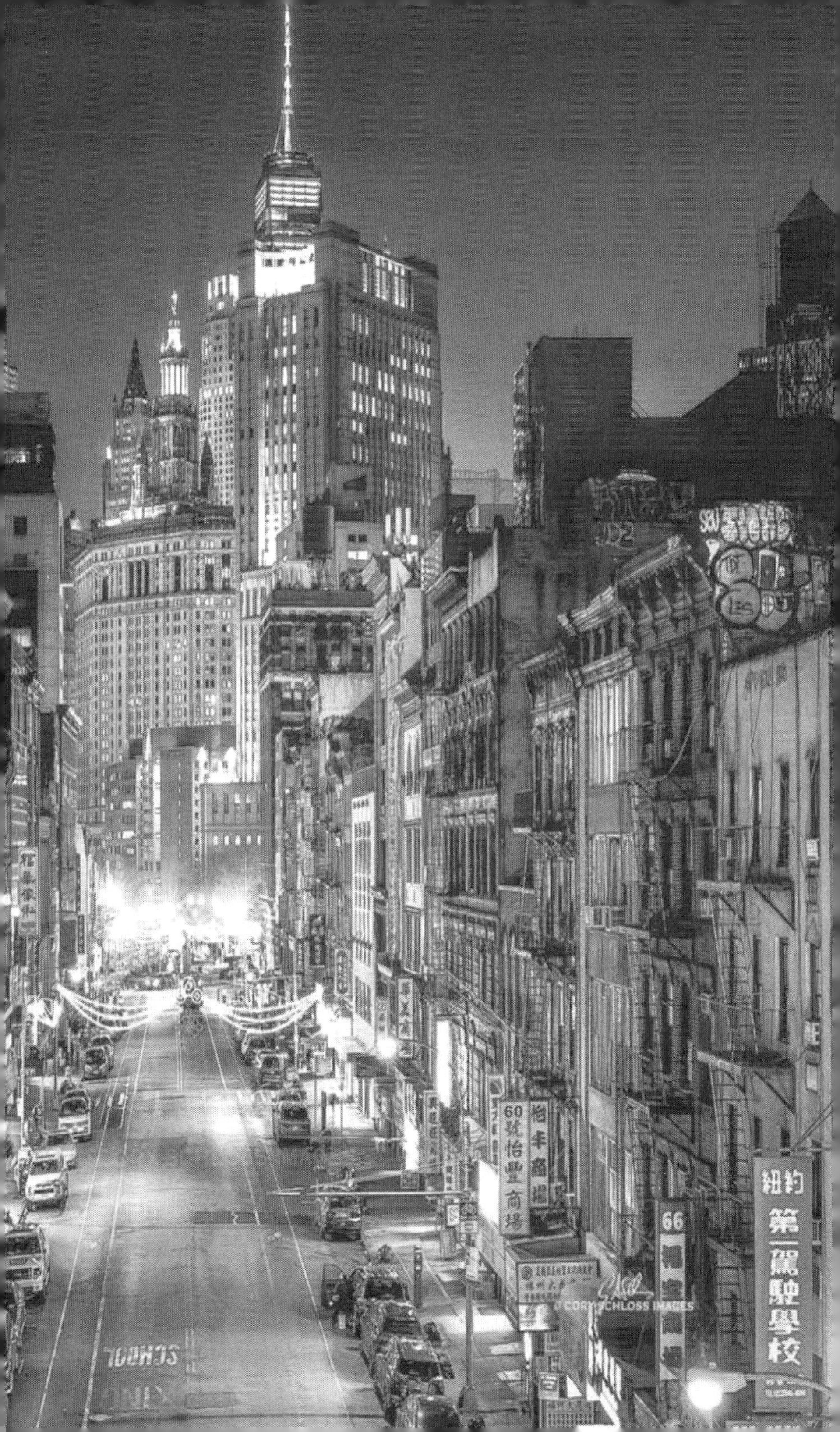
60號
怡豐商場
紐約
第一駕駛學校
66
© CORY SCHLOSS IMAGES

INTRODUCTION

New York City is often referred to as "The City That Never Sleeps," and for good reason. The rhythm of life here is fast-paced and constant, with endless activities and sights that cater to every type of traveler. From the towering skyscrapers that define the skyline to the small, tucked-away corners that only the locals know about, the city is full of contrasts and surprises. Each neighborhood has its own unique character, and exploring these different areas will give you a richer understanding of what makes New York City such a fascinating place.

As you prepare to embark on your journey, this guide aims to be your trusted companion, providing you with all the information you need to navigate the city with ease. Whether you're wondering where to stay, how to get around, what to eat, or which landmarks are worth your time, we've got you covered. This guide will help you avoid the common pitfalls that can befall travelers, ensuring that your experience is as smooth and enjoyable as possible.

One of the first things you'll notice about New York City is its incredible diversity. People from all walks of life and from every corner of the world call this city home, bringing with them a rich tapestry of cultures, languages, and traditions. This diversity is reflected in every aspect of the city, from the food you'll eat to the festivals you'll encounter. The city's cultural richness is one of its greatest strengths, and exploring this aspect of New York will give you a deeper appreciation of its global significance.

As you delve into the pages of this guide, you'll find practical advice on everything from obtaining the necessary travel documents to understanding the city's public transportation system. We've included tips on how to navigate the often-overwhelming choices of accommodation, so you can find a place to stay that fits your budget and preferences. The guide also covers the city's wide range of attractions, from the iconic landmarks like the Statue of Liberty and Central Park to the lesser-known gems that offer a quieter, more intimate glimpse into the city's life.

But this guide is not just about the logistics of travel. It also seeks to enrich your experience by giving you a sense of the local customs, etiquette, and even some key phrases that might come in handy. Understanding the cultural nuances of New York City can make your interactions with locals more meaningful and your overall experience more rewarding.

Safety and health are also important aspects of any trip, and this guide offers advice on how to stay safe while you explore the city. Whether it's dealing with the hustle and bustle of crowded streets, navigating public transportation, or knowing what to do in case of an emergency, you'll find helpful tips that will give you peace of mind.

New York City is a city of stories. Every street, building, and park has a history that contributes to the larger narrative of the city. While it's impossible to cover every aspect of New York in one guide, this book aims to highlight the most important and interesting parts, giving you a solid foundation upon which to build your own New York story.

As you turn the pages of this guide, you'll discover that New York City is not just a destination—it's an experience. From the moment you arrive, you'll be swept up in the city's energy, and every day will bring new adventures and discoveries. Whether you're here for a weekend or an extended stay, this guide is designed to help you make the most of every moment, ensuring that your trip to New York City is one you'll remember for a lifetime.

HOW TO USE THIS BOOK

Planning a trip can be an exciting yet overwhelming experience, especially when visiting a bustling and dynamic city like New York. This guide has been crafted to help you navigate the city with ease, providing you with all the essential information needed to make the most of your visit. Here's how you can make the best use of this guide:

1. **Start with the Basics:** Before diving into the details, take some time to familiarize yourself with the introductory sections of the book. These sections cover key information about New York City, including its neighborhoods, local customs, transportation options, and tips for navigating the city efficiently. Understanding these basics will help you feel more confident as you plan your trip.

2. **Customize Your Experience:** One of the unique aspects of this guide is its flexibility. Instead of offering pre-made itineraries, this book empowers you to create a travel experience that's perfectly tailored to your interests and preferences. Use the information provided in each chapter to decide what attractions, restaurants, and activities appeal most to you.

3. **Use the Itinerary Planner:** To assist you in organizing your trip, we've included a comprehensive 14-page itinerary planner within the book. This planner is designed to help you document your plans, including daily activities, places to visit, dining options, and more. By filling out the planner as you go through the guide, you'll be able to create a well-structured itinerary that ensures you don't miss out on anything

important. Feel free to print out the planner pages, so you can jot down notes and plans as you read.

4. Explore Each Section at Your Own Pace: Whether you're interested in famous landmarks, hidden gems, dining experiences, or cultural events, this guide covers a wide range of topics. Take your time exploring each section, and don't feel pressured to rush through. The book is designed to be user-friendly, allowing you to navigate between chapters and topics easily.

5. Use the Guide On-the-Go: If you're traveling with a digital version of this book, take advantage of the clickable links and QR codes to access additional resources and maps. This can be especially helpful when you're on the move and need quick access to information.

6. Revisit Key Sections as Needed: Depending on the length of your stay and the time of year you visit, you might find yourself revisiting certain sections for updated information or reminders. The guide is structured to be a resource you can return to throughout your trip, ensuring you have the most relevant information at your fingertips.

7. Adapt the Guide to Your Preferences: New York City offers something for every type of traveler, whether you're a solo adventurer, a family on vacation, or a couple seeking romance. Use the chapters focused on specific types of travelers to find recommendations that align with your travel style.

8. Stay Informed and Flexible: While this guide provides detailed information to help you plan, it's always a good idea to remain flexible and open to spontaneous opportunities. The city is full of surprises, and some of the best experiences may come from unexpected discoveries.

9. Capture Memories Along the Way: The guide includes tips on photography and documenting your journey. Use these tips to capture the memories of your trip, and don't forget to use the planner to note down special moments, favorite spots, and must-try experiences.

By following these steps, you'll be able to use this guide to its fullest potential, ensuring that your trip to New York City is not only well-planned but also filled with unforgettable experiences. Whether you're visiting for the first time or returning for another adventure, this guide is your trusted companion for making the most of your time in the city.

WHY NEW YORK CITY IS A MUST-VISIT DESTINATION

New York City stands as one of the most iconic cities in the world, and there are countless reasons why it is a must-visit destination. The city is not just a place; it's an experience, a world unto itself where culture, history, art, and diversity converge in a way that is unmatched by any other city on the planet. For many, visiting New York is not just about seeing the sights; it's about immersing oneself in the life and energy that make this city so unique.

The sheer scale and diversity of New York City are among the first things that strike visitors. The city is made up of five boroughs—Manhattan, Brooklyn, Queens, The Bronx, and Staten Island—each with its own distinct character and charm. Manhattan is often the first stop for tourists, known for its skyscrapers, bustling streets, and famous landmarks like Times Square, Central Park, and the Empire State Building. But each borough offers something different, from the vibrant arts scene in Brooklyn to the cultural melting pot of Queens, the historic sites in The Bronx, and the scenic beauty of Staten Island.

New York City's history is rich and complex, reflecting its role as a gateway for millions of immigrants who have come to America seeking a new life. This influx of people from all corners of the globe has made New York one of the most diverse cities in the world. Walking through its streets, you can hear dozens of languages, see people from all walks of life, and taste foods from every corner of the globe. This cultural diversity is one of the city's greatest strengths, and it is reflected in everything from its neighborhoods to its restaurants, festivals, and traditions.

The city is also a major center for arts and culture. New York is home to some of the world's most renowned museums, theaters, and galleries. The Metropolitan Museum of Art, the Museum of Modern Art, and the Guggenheim are just a few of the many institutions where visitors can explore vast collections of art and artifacts from around the world. Broadway, with its array of shows, is a symbol of New York's vibrant theater scene, attracting visitors who come to see everything from long-running musicals to cutting-edge plays. For those interested in music, New York offers everything from world-class orchestras to jazz clubs, hip-hop venues, and indie rock scenes.

In addition to its cultural offerings, New York City is also known for its landmarks and attractions that have become symbols of the city itself. The Statue of Liberty, standing in the harbor, is a symbol of freedom and democracy recognized around the world. Central Park, an oasis of green in the midst of the city, offers a place for relaxation and recreation, with its paths, lakes, and open spaces providing a welcome respite from the hustle and bustle of city life. The skyline, dominated by skyscrapers like the Empire State Building and the One World Trade Center, is a testament to the city's status as a global hub of business and finance.

New York City is also a shopper's paradise, offering everything from high-end luxury stores to quirky boutiques and vast department stores. Fifth Avenue is famous for its upscale shopping, while neighborhoods like SoHo and the Lower East Side offer more eclectic and trendy options. For those looking for bargains, the city's many markets and discount stores provide plenty of opportunities to find unique items at great prices.

Food is another area where New York City truly shines. The city's dining scene is as diverse as its population, offering everything from street food to fine dining. Whether you're craving a slice of classic New York pizza, a bagel with lox, or a gourmet meal at a Michelin-starred restaurant, you'll find it here. The city's many food trucks and street vendors also offer a quick and delicious way to sample a wide variety of cuisines without breaking the bank.

But beyond the attractions and experiences, what truly makes New York City a must-visit destination is the energy that permeates every corner of the city. There is a certain feeling you get when you're in New York—an excitement, a sense of possibility, and a vibrancy that is hard to find anywhere else. The city is always on the move, always evolving, and this constant change means that there is always something new to discover, no matter how many times you visit.

For history enthusiasts, New York offers a wealth of sites that tell the story of America itself. From the historic buildings of Lower Manhattan, where the foundations of the country were laid, to Ellis Island and the Statue of Liberty, where millions of immigrants first set foot in the United States, the city is filled with places that bring the past to life. Walking through neighborhoods like Greenwich Village, Harlem, and the

Lower East Side, you can see the layers of history in the architecture, the streets, and the people who live there.

New York City is also a place of innovation and creativity. It's a city where new ideas are born, where trends start, and where people come to push the boundaries of what's possible. Whether it's in the arts, fashion, technology, or business, New York is a place where the future is being shaped every day. This spirit of innovation is evident in everything from the cutting-edge performances on Broadway to the tech startups in Silicon Alley.

For sports fans, New York City is a dream come true. Home to teams in every major sport, the city offers year-round opportunities to catch a game. Whether it's watching the Yankees or Mets play baseball, catching a Knicks or Nets basketball game, or experiencing the intensity of a Rangers or Islanders hockey match, there's something for every sports enthusiast. The city's passion for sports is infectious, and attending a game in New York is an experience like no other.

Lastly, New York City's accessibility is another reason why it's a must-visit destination. With three major airports, an extensive public transportation system, and a wide range of accommodation options, getting to and around the city is relatively easy, no matter where you're coming from or what your budget might be. The city's layout, with its grid system and well-marked streets, makes it easy to navigate, even for first-time visitors. And with so many things to see and do concentrate in a relatively small area, you can pack a lot into even a short visit.

New York City is a destination that offers something for everyone. Whether you're drawn by the history, the culture, the food, the shopping, or simply the chance to be a part of the city's energy, there is no place quite like it. Visiting New York is not just about seeing the sights; it's about experiencing a way of life that is dynamic, diverse, and constantly changing. It's a place where you can make memories that will last a lifetime, and it's a city that will continue to surprise and delight you, no matter how many times you return.

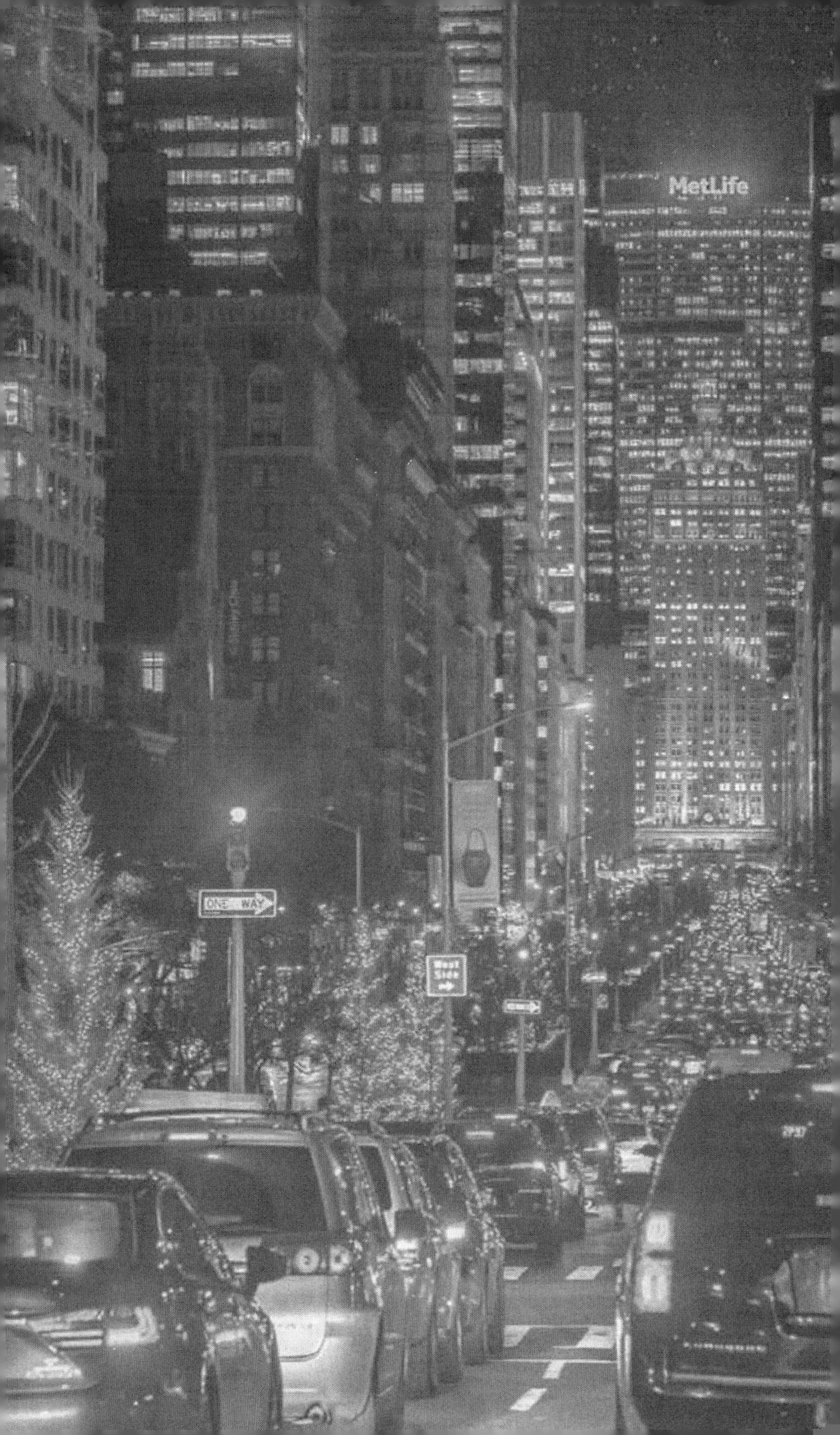
MetLife
ONE WAY
West Side

CHAPTER 1

PREPARING FOR YOUR NEW YORK CITY ADVENTURE

Visa and Entry Requirements

Traveling to New York City is an exciting prospect, but before you can immerse yourself in the energy and attractions of this iconic city, it's essential to understand the visa and entry requirements that you must fulfill. These requirements are critical to ensuring that your journey to the United States is smooth and free of complications. The visa process might seem overwhelming, especially for first-time travelers, but with the right information and preparation, you can navigate it successfully.

The first step in planning your trip to New York City is determining whether you need a visa to enter the United States. The U.S. government offers several types of visas depending on the purpose of your visit. If you're visiting New York as a tourist, you will likely need a B-2 visa, which is specifically for tourism, vacations, and visits to friends or family. This visa allows you to stay in the U.S. for up to six months, giving you plenty of time to explore the city. If your trip involves business activities, such as attending meetings or conferences, you might need a B-1 visa. It's important to apply for the correct type of visa, as entering the U.S. under the wrong visa category can lead to serious complications, including being denied entry.

For citizens of certain countries, there is the option to travel to the U.S. under the Visa Waiver Program (VWP). This program allows citizens of 40 participating countries to visit the U.S. for tourism or business for up to 90 days without needing a visa. However, even if you qualify for the VWP, you must still obtain authorization through the Electronic System for Travel Authorization (ESTA) before your trip. ESTA is an online system that screens travelers for eligibility under the VWP. It's crucial to apply for ESTA well in advance of your trip, as it can take up to 72 hours to receive approval. Without ESTA authorization, you will not be allowed to board your flight to the U.S.

If you determine that you need a visa, the next step is to apply for one. The visa application process involves several steps, so it's important to start early and ensure that you complete each step correctly. The first thing you'll need to do is complete the DS-160 form, which is the online nonimmigrant visa application form. This form requires you to provide detailed information about yourself, your travel plans, and your background. It's important to be thorough and accurate when filling out the DS-160, as any errors or inconsistencies could delay your application or lead to a denial.

After submitting the DS-160 form, you will need to pay the visa application fee. The amount of this fee can vary depending on the type of visa you are applying for, but for most tourist and business visas, the fee is $160. This fee is non-refundable, so even if your visa application is denied, you will not get your money back. Once you've paid the fee, you will need to schedule an appointment at the U.S. embassy or consulate in your country. This appointment is required for all visa applicants and involves an interview with a consular officer.

During your interview, the consular officer will ask you questions about your travel plans, your background, and your ties to your home country. The purpose of the interview is to determine whether you meet the requirements for a U.S. visa and whether you have any intention of overstaying your visa or engaging in activities that are not permitted under your visa category. It's important to be honest and straightforward in your answers. Bring all required documents to your interview, including your passport, the DS-160 confirmation page, the visa application fee receipt, and any additional documents that support your application, such as a letter from your employer or proof of financial support.

If your visa application is approved, the consular officer will inform you at the end of your interview. Your passport will be kept by the embassy or consulate so that the visa can be printed in it, and you will be told when you can expect to receive your passport back. It's important to check your visa carefully once you receive it to ensure that all the information is correct. If there are any errors, contact the embassy or consulate immediately to have them corrected before your trip.

With your visa in hand, you're almost ready to travel to New York City. However, there are still a few important things to keep in mind to ensure a smooth entry at the airport. First, make sure that your passport is valid for at least six months beyond your planned departure date from the U.S. This is a requirement for entering the United States, and if your passport does not meet this requirement, you may be denied entry.

When you arrive at the airport in New York, you will go through U.S. Customs and Border Protection (CBP) inspection. This is where a CBP officer will review your documents and ask you questions about the purpose of your visit, how long you plan to stay, and where you will be staying. It's important to answer these questions clearly and truthfully. The CBP officer has the authority to allow or deny your entry into the U.S., even if you have a valid visa, so it's crucial to cooperate fully with the officer and provide all requested information.

You may also be required to provide biometric information, such as fingerprints and a photograph, as part of the entry process. This is standard procedure for most travelers and helps to ensure the security of the U.S. border. Once the CBP officer is satisfied with your answers and documentation, you will be allowed to enter the U.S. The officer will stamp your passport with the date of entry and the date by which you must leave the country. It's important to keep track of this date and make sure you do not overstay your visa, as overstaying can have serious consequences, including being barred from re-entering the U.S. in the future.

In addition to your visa and passport, it's a good idea to have copies of important documents with you when you travel, such as your flight itinerary, hotel reservations, and proof of funds to cover your stay. These documents can be helpful if the CBP officer asks for additional information or if you encounter any issues during your trip.

Obtaining a visa to travel to New York City involves several important steps, from determining the type of visa you need to ensuring that you have all the necessary documentation for your journey. While the process may seem complex, being well-prepared and informed can help make it smoother and less stressful. By following the guidelines for visa application and entry requirements, you can focus on the exciting part of your trip—exploring everything that New York City has to offer.

Travel Insurance

When planning a trip to New York City, one of the most crucial yet often overlooked aspects of preparation is securing travel insurance. While travel insurance might seem like an unnecessary extra expense, it is, in fact, a vital part of your travel plans. It provides a safety net that protects you from a variety of unforeseen events that could otherwise disrupt your trip or leave you facing significant financial burdens. Whether you are traveling to New York for a short vacation, an extended stay, or business purposes, having travel insurance can make a substantial difference in how you handle unexpected situations.

The importance of travel insurance cannot be overstated. Traveling, even to a well-known destination like New York

City, comes with inherent risks. These risks range from minor inconveniences, such as lost luggage or delayed flights, to more serious issues like medical emergencies or trip cancellations. Travel insurance is designed to cover these risks, giving you peace of mind and allowing you to enjoy your trip without constantly worrying about what might go wrong. For instance, medical care in the United States is known to be extremely expensive, and a sudden illness or injury during your trip could lead to substantial medical bills. With travel insurance, you can be covered for medical expenses, ensuring that you receive the necessary care without the stress of high costs.

Another key reason why travel insurance is important is the protection it offers against trip cancellations or interruptions. Life is unpredictable, and sometimes you may need to cancel or cut short your trip due to unforeseen circumstances such as illness, a family emergency, or natural disasters. Without travel insurance, you could lose the money you've spent on flights, hotels, and other prepaid expenses. However, with the right travel insurance policy, you can be reimbursed for these costs, allowing you to reschedule your trip or recover your losses. This financial protection is particularly important for expensive trips, where the potential loss could be significant.

Travel insurance also covers other common issues that travelers face, such as lost, stolen, or damaged luggage and personal belongings. Imagine arriving in New York City only to find that your suitcase has been misplaced or your personal items have been stolen. Replacing these items can be costly and stressful, especially in an unfamiliar city. Travel insurance can cover the cost of replacing your belongings, helping you get back on track without the added financial burden. In addition, some policies offer assistance services, such as helping you find a local doctor, arranging emergency transportation, or providing translation services, which can be invaluable in a crisis.

When selecting a travel insurance policy, there are several important factors to consider to ensure that you are adequately covered. First, you should assess the types of coverage offered by the policy. The most comprehensive travel insurance policies typically include coverage for medical expenses, trip cancellation and interruption, baggage loss or damage, and emergency evacuation. It's important to review the policy details carefully to understand what is covered and, just as importantly, what is not covered. For example, some policies may exclude coverage for pre-existing medical conditions, or they may have specific limitations on the amount reimbursed for certain expenses.

Another important aspect to consider is the coverage limits of the policy. This refers to the maximum amount the insurance company will pay out for a particular claim. For example, a policy may offer medical coverage up to $100,000 or reimbursement for trip cancellations up to the total cost of the trip. It's crucial to ensure that these limits are sufficient to cover the potential costs you might face during your trip. For instance, if you're planning an expensive trip, you'll want a policy with higher coverage limits to protect your investment fully.

The cost of the travel insurance policy is another key factor to consider. Premiums can vary widely depending on the level of coverage, the length of your trip, and your age and health. While it might be tempting to opt for the cheapest policy available, it's important to balance cost with the level of protection you need. A more expensive policy that offers comprehensive coverage may be a better investment in the long run, especially if it means you are fully protected against a wide range of risks. Remember, the goal of travel insurance is to provide peace of mind, and skimping on coverage could leave you vulnerable when you need protection the most.

When choosing a travel insurance provider, it's advisable to select a reputable company with a strong track record of customer satisfaction and reliable claims processing. Some of the well-known travel insurance providers include Allianz Global Assistance, World Nomads, and Travel Guard. These companies are recognized for their comprehensive coverage options and responsive customer service, which can make a significant difference in how smoothly your claims are handled in the event of an emergency. It's a good idea to read reviews and check ratings from other travelers to ensure that the provider you choose is trustworthy and efficient.

Another factor to consider is the flexibility of the policy. Some travel insurance providers offer policies that can be customized to fit your specific needs. For example, if you're planning a trip that includes adventurous activities like skiing or scuba diving, you may need additional coverage for these activities, as they might not be included in a standard policy. Similarly, if you're traveling with expensive equipment, such as cameras or laptops, you might want to add coverage for these items to protect against loss or damage. Customizable policies allow you to tailor the coverage to your particular travel plans, ensuring that you are fully protected.

It's also important to understand the claims process before purchasing a travel insurance policy. The ease and speed with which claims are processed can vary significantly between providers. Ideally, you should choose a provider with a straightforward claims process that allows you to submit claims online or via a mobile app. Some providers also offer 24/7 assistance, which can be particularly helpful if you need to make a claim while you're still traveling. Familiarizing yourself with the claims process in advance can save you time and stress if you need to file a claim during your trip.

Travel insurance is an essential part of your preparation for visiting New York City. It provides crucial protection against a wide range of risks, from medical emergencies to trip cancellations, lost luggage, and more. By choosing the right policy and provider, you can travel with confidence, knowing that you are covered in case of unexpected events. While travel insurance might seem like an additional expense, the peace of mind it offers is invaluable, allowing you to fully enjoy your trip to New York City without the worry of what might go wrong. Remember to carefully review your policy, understand the coverage it provides, and select a reputable provider that meets your needs. With the right travel insurance in place, you can focus on the excitement and adventure of your trip, knowing that you are well-protected every step of the way.

The Best Time to Visit New York City

Determining the best time to visit New York City is crucial for making the most out of your trip. The city's unique blend of attractions, events, and experiences varies significantly depending on the season, and understanding these seasonal differences can help you plan your visit to match your interests and preferences. Whether you're drawn to the festive atmosphere of winter, the blooming beauty of spring, the vibrant energy of summer, or the crisp charm of autumn, New York City offers something special at every time of the year. To make an informed decision about when to visit, it's important to consider the seasonal weather patterns, the major events and festivals that take place throughout the year, and the pros and cons of traveling during different times.

New York City experiences a full range of seasons, each with its distinct weather patterns. The city's climate is classified as humid subtropical, meaning that it has hot summers and cold winters, with moderate to heavy rainfall spread throughout the year. The seasonal weather plays a significant role in shaping the city's atmosphere and activities, and it's essential to choose a time that aligns with the type of experience you're seeking.

Winter in New York City, from December through February, is characterized by cold temperatures, with average highs ranging from the mid-30s to the low 40s Fahrenheit (around 1 to 6 degrees Celsius). Snowfall is common, especially in January and February, and while snow-covered streets can create a picturesque setting, the cold weather can be challenging for outdoor activities. However, the winter season brings its own unique appeal, particularly during the holiday season. The city comes alive with festive decorations, ice-skating rinks, and holiday markets. The iconic Rockefeller Center Christmas Tree and the New Year's Eve ball drop-in Times Square are major attractions that draw visitors from around the world. If you're a fan of the holiday spirit and don't mind bundling up, winter can be a magical time to visit New York City.

Spring, from March through May, is a favorite time for many to visit New York City. As the city shakes off the chill of winter, temperatures gradually rise, with highs ranging from the upper 40s to the mid-70s Fahrenheit (about 8 to 24 degrees Celsius) by May. Spring is a season of renewal, with flowers blooming in parks and gardens, and the city's outdoor spaces coming back to life. Central Park is particularly stunning in the spring, with cherry blossoms, tulips, and daffodils creating a colorful display. The weather is generally mild and comfortable, making it ideal for walking tours, outdoor dining, and exploring the city's many attractions. Spring is also the season for major cultural events, such as the Tribeca Film Festival and the Easter Parade and Bonnet Festival, which showcase the city's creative and celebratory spirit.

Summer in New York City, from June through August, brings hot and humid weather, with temperatures often reaching the mid-80s to 90s Fahrenheit (around 29 to 35 degrees Celsius). The city's streets can feel sweltering during peak summer, but this season is also when New York truly comes alive with a plethora of outdoor activities, festivals, and events. The long days and warm evenings make it the perfect time for enjoying outdoor concerts, food festivals, and rooftop bars. Summer is also the season for iconic events like the Fourth of July fireworks, the New York City Pride March, and the US Open tennis tournament. The city's beaches, such as those in Coney Island and the Rockaways, provide a refreshing escape from the urban heat. However, the summer months are also the peak tourist season, meaning that popular attractions can be crowded, and hotel rates are often higher. If you thrive in warm weather and enjoy lively atmospheres, summer can be an exciting time to visit.

Autumn, from September through November, is another popular time to visit New York City, as the weather cools down and the city takes on a different kind of charm. Temperatures in the fall range from the mid-60s to the mid-50s Fahrenheit (about 15 to 12 degrees Celsius), creating a comfortable and crisp environment perfect for exploring the city on foot. Autumn is known for its beautiful foliage, with trees in Central Park and other green spaces turning vibrant shades of red, orange, and yellow. The fall season also brings a sense of cultural richness, with events like the New York Film Festival, the Village Halloween Parade, and the Macy's Thanksgiving Day Parade attracting large crowds. The combination of pleasant weather and fewer tourists compared to the summer makes autumn an ideal time for those who prefer a more relaxed and scenic visit.

When considering the best time to visit New York City, it's important to weigh the pros and cons of each season. Winter, while festive and filled with holiday cheer, can be challenging due to the cold weather and potential for snowstorms. However, if you enjoy winter activities and holiday events, the city offers a unique and unforgettable experience during this time. On the other hand, if you prefer milder weather and blossoming landscapes, spring is an excellent choice, with plenty of cultural events and outdoor activities to enjoy.

Summer is perfect for those who thrive in warm weather and want to experience the city at its most vibrant. The long days allow for extended sightseeing, and the city's outdoor events and festivals are in full swing. However, the heat and humidity, along with the large crowds, may be a downside for some travelers. Autumn offers a balance between pleasant weather and cultural richness, with the added bonus of stunning fall foliage. It's a great time for walking tours, photography, and attending seasonal events without the summer crowds.

The best time to visit New York City depends on your personal preferences and what you hope to experience during your trip. Each season brings its own unique flavor to the city, and by understanding the seasonal weather patterns, major events, and the advantages and disadvantages of each time of year, you can plan a trip that aligns with your interests and ensures a memorable visit to the city that never sleeps.

Packing Guide

When preparing for a trip to New York City, packing effectively is crucial to ensure that you have everything you need for a comfortable and enjoyable experience. New York is a city of endless possibilities, with diverse activities, varying weather conditions, and a fast-paced lifestyle. Packing the right items will help you navigate the city with ease, whether you're exploring famous landmarks, dining in world-class restaurants, or simply strolling through its vibrant neighborhoods.

First and foremost, there are essential items that every traveler should include in their luggage, regardless of the time of year or the length of their stay. These items serve as the foundation of your packing list and ensure that you're well-prepared for your trip. A reliable and comfortable pair of walking shoes is perhaps the most important item to bring. New York City is best explored on foot, and you'll likely be walking several miles each day. Choose shoes that provide good support and are suitable for a variety of surfaces, from city streets to parks. Another must-have item is a portable phone charger. With so many places to visit and things to do, you'll be relying heavily on your smartphone for navigation, taking photos, and staying connected. A portable charger ensures that your phone stays powered throughout the day, even when you're on the go.

In addition to these essentials, it's important to pack clothing that is versatile and can be easily layered. New York City's weather can be unpredictable, and temperatures can vary widely throughout the day. Layering allows you to adjust to changing conditions, whether you're braving the winter chill or enjoying a warm summer day. Lightweight, breathable fabrics are ideal for layering, as they can be worn comfortably under jackets or sweaters. A good rule of thumb is to pack a mix of short-sleeve and long-sleeve tops, along with a few sweaters or cardigans that can be added or removed as needed.

When it comes to weather-specific packing, your choices will depend largely on the time of year you plan to visit. New York experiences four distinct seasons, each with its own climate and weather patterns. Packing appropriately for the season will help you stay comfortable and make the most of your trip, regardless of the weather.

If you're visiting New York City in the winter, from December through February, you'll need to be prepared for cold temperatures, snow, and wind. A warm, insulated coat is essential, preferably one that is waterproof to protect against snow and rain. Hats, gloves, and scarves are also important to keep you warm, especially when spending time outdoors. Layering is key during the winter months, so pack thermal underwear, sweaters, and thick socks. Boots that are both warm and waterproof are a good choice, as they will keep your feet dry and comfortable in the snow and slush.

For those planning a spring visit, from March through May, the weather can be unpredictable, with temperatures ranging from cool to mild. It's a good idea to pack a light jacket or a trench coat, as well as a few sweaters for layering. An umbrella or a raincoat is also recommended, as spring showers are common. Comfortable walking shoes are still a must, but you can opt for lighter footwear than you would in the winter. Spring in New York is often breezy, so consider packing a scarf or a shawl that you can wrap around your shoulders if needed.

Summer in New York, from June through August, can be hot and humid, with temperatures often reaching the 80s and 90s Fahrenheit. Lightweight, breathable clothing is essential to stay cool and comfortable in the heat. Cotton and linen fabrics are ideal, as they allow air to circulate and help wick away moisture. Sunglasses, a wide-brimmed hat, and sunscreen are also important to protect yourself from the sun. While sandals or open-toed shoes may be tempting, it's still a good idea to bring a pair of supportive walking shoes, as you'll be doing a lot of walking. A refillable water bottle is another useful item to have, as it will help you stay hydrated in the summer heat.

Autumn, from September through November, is a beautiful time to visit New York, with cooler temperatures and colorful fall foliage. During this season, you'll want to pack layers, as the weather can be quite variable. A light jacket or a sweater is usually sufficient during the day, but you may need a warmer coat in the evenings as temperatures drop. Comfortable shoes are, once again, essential, as fall is an ideal time for exploring the city's parks and outdoor spaces. A scarf or a shawl can add an extra layer of warmth, and it's a good idea to have an umbrella on hand, as rain is common in the fall.

In addition to seasonal clothing, there are a few other items that you may want to include in your packing list, depending on your planned activities. For example, if you plan to visit New York's many museums, galleries, and theaters, consider bringing a few dressier outfits for evenings out. While the city is known for its casual style, some venues may have dress codes, and you'll feel more comfortable if you're appropriately dressed. If you're planning outdoor activities, such as a day trip to the beach or a hike in the nearby mountains, be sure to pack swimwear, athletic wear, or hiking boots as needed.

While packing for your trip to New York City, it's also important to consider what not to bring. Overpacking is a common mistake, especially when visiting a city like New York, where space can be limited. Most hotels and accommodations in the city have limited closet space, so try to pack only what you truly need. Avoid bringing bulky or heavy items that will be difficult to carry around, especially if you plan to use public transportation or walk long distances. Another thing to avoid is packing expensive or valuable items that could be lost or stolen. While New York is generally safe, it's always better to leave items like expensive jewelry or electronics at home unless they are absolutely necessary for your trip.

In terms of prohibited items, it's important to remember that New York City, like all major cities, has strict security regulations, especially in public places and at major attractions. Avoid bringing large bags or backpacks to certain venues, as they may not be allowed, or you may be required to check them at the entrance. It's also a good idea to leave any items that could be considered weapons, such as pocket knives or sharp tools, at home, as these are not permitted in many public spaces and could result in delays or security issues.

Packing for a trip to New York City requires careful consideration of the essentials, the weather, and the activities you plan to do. By packing thoughtfully and focusing on versatility and comfort, you'll be well-prepared for your adventure in the city that never sleeps. Remember to tailor your packing list to the specific season and your planned itinerary, and avoid overpacking or bringing unnecessary items. With the right preparation, you'll be ready to explore all that New York City has to offer, from its iconic landmarks to its hidden gems, with confidence and ease.

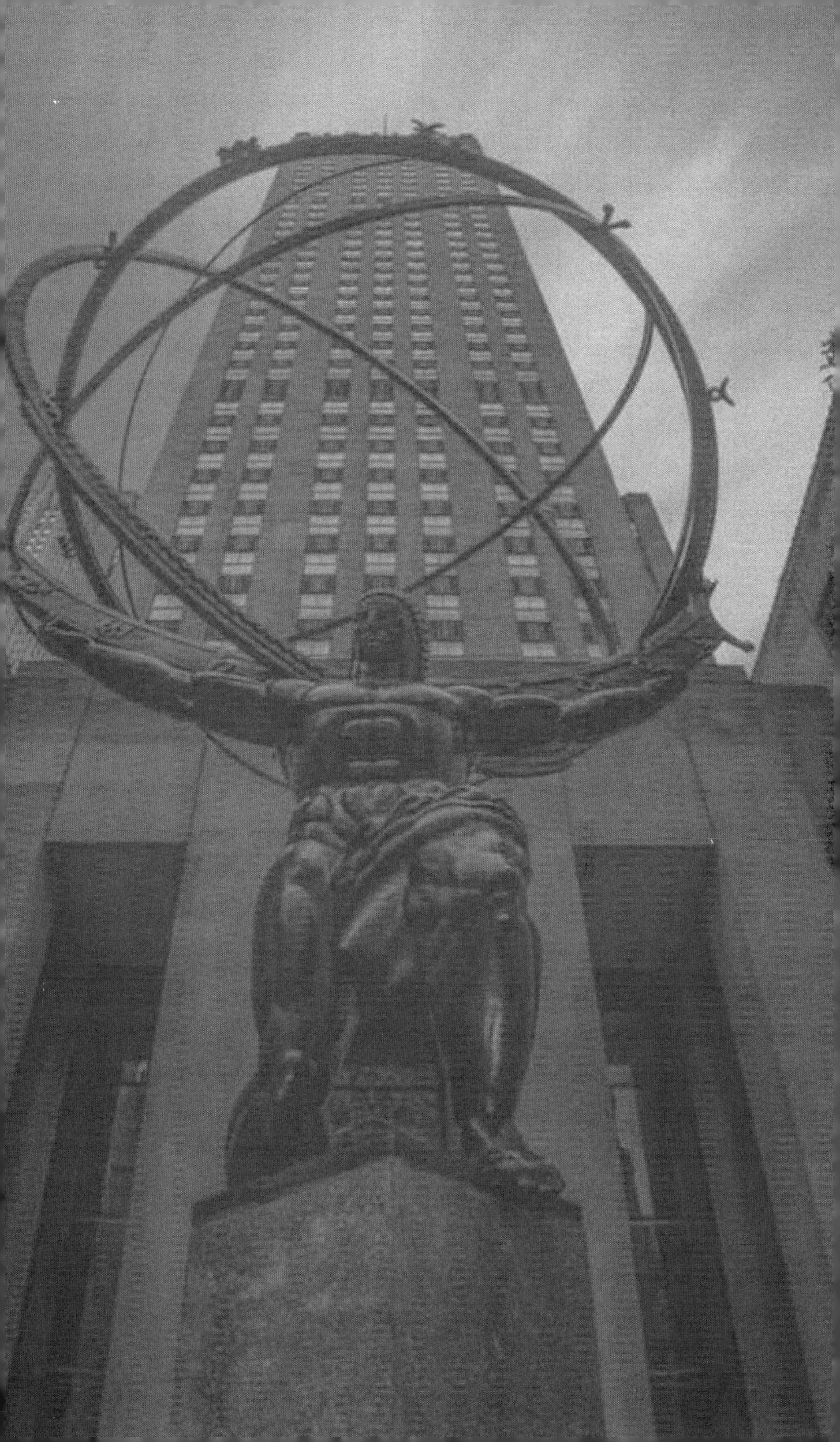

CHAPTER 2

GETTING TO NEW YORK CITY

How to Get There

Getting to New York City is a straightforward process thanks to the city's status as a major global hub. Whether you're flying in from an international destination, taking a train or bus from a nearby city, or driving yourself, there are multiple options available to ensure you arrive in the heart of the city smoothly. Understanding these options and planning your journey carefully will help you begin your New York adventure without unnecessary stress.

New York City is served by three major airports: John F. Kennedy International Airport (JFK), LaGuardia Airport (LGA), and Newark Liberty International Airport (EWR). These airports are some of the busiest in the United States, offering a wide range of domestic and international flights. Each airport has its unique characteristics, and the choice of which one to fly into can depend on various factors, including your departure city, airline preference, and final destination within New York City.

John F. Kennedy International Airport, commonly referred to as JFK, is the largest and busiest of the three airports, handling most of the city's international air traffic. Located in the Queens borough, about 15 miles southeast of Midtown Manhattan, JFK is a primary gateway for travelers coming from Europe, Asia, and other parts of the world. The airport has several terminals, each serving different airlines, and it offers a wide array of amenities, including shops, restaurants, and lounges. Getting from JFK to Manhattan is relatively easy, with multiple transportation options available. The AirTrain JFK connects the airport to the city's subway system and Long Island Rail Road (LIRR), providing a quick and affordable way to reach your destination. Taxis and ride-sharing services are also readily available at JFK, although they can be more expensive, especially during peak travel times.

LaGuardia Airport, or LGA, is also located in Queens, closer to Manhattan than JFK. LGA primarily handles domestic flights and a smaller number of international flights. The airport is undergoing significant renovations to modernize its facilities and improve the passenger experience. Due to its proximity to Manhattan, LGA is often the preferred choice for travelers flying in from other parts of the United States, especially for those on short trips or business travelers. Transportation options from LGA to Manhattan include taxis, ride-sharing services, and public buses that connect to the subway system. While LaGuardia is closer to the city center, it is important to note that traffic can be heavy, particularly during rush hours, so allowing extra time for your journey is advisable.

Newark Liberty International Airport, or EWR, is located in New Jersey, just across the Hudson River from Manhattan. Despite being in a different state, Newark is a convenient option for travelers heading to New York City, particularly those coming from the western United States or Latin America. Newark is a major hub for United Airlines and offers extensive domestic and international connections. The airport is well-connected to Manhattan by the AirTrain Newark, which links the airport to New Jersey Transit and Amtrak trains. These trains can take you directly to Penn Station in Midtown Manhattan, making Newark a practical choice for travelers who prefer rail transportation into the city. As with JFK and LGA, taxis and ride-sharing services are also available at Newark, though they tend to be more expensive due to the longer distance.

For travelers coming from nearby cities, taking a train or bus to New York City is an excellent option. The city's central location on the northeastern corridor makes it easily accessible by rail or road. Amtrak, the national rail operator, provides frequent service to Penn Station in Manhattan from major cities such as Boston, Philadelphia, Washington, D.C., and beyond. The train is often the preferred mode of transportation for those who value comfort, convenience, and the ability to avoid the hassles of air travel. Amtrak offers a variety of service levels, from standard coach seating to more luxurious options like business class and the Acela Express, which is the fastest train on the route. Traveling by train allows you to arrive directly in the heart of Manhattan, avoiding the need for additional transportation from the airport.

Buses are another popular and cost-effective way to reach New York City from nearby cities. Several bus companies operate routes to New York, including Greyhound, Megabus, and BoltBus. These buses typically arrive at the Port Authority Bus Terminal in Midtown Manhattan, which is conveniently located near many hotels, restaurants, and attractions. Bus travel is generally cheaper than train travel, making it a good option for budget-conscious travelers. However, it is important to note that buses are subject to traffic delays, particularly when entering Manhattan during peak hours. If you choose to travel by bus, it is wise to plan for potential delays and allow extra time in your schedule.

For those who prefer the flexibility and independence of driving, getting to New York City by car is also an option. The city is well-connected by a network of highways and interstates, making it accessible from all directions. However, driving in New York City comes with its own set of challenges, particularly due to the heavy traffic, complex roadways, and limited parking options. If you decide to drive, it is essential to familiarize yourself with the main routes into the city and plan your trip carefully.

From the north, travelers can take Interstate 87 (I-87), also known as the New York State Thruway, which connects New York City to Albany and the Canadian border. The I-95 corridor, also known as the New England Thruway, is another major route that runs along the eastern seaboard, providing access to the city from New England states like Connecticut and Massachusetts. From the south, Interstate 95 (I-95) is the primary route, connecting New York City to cities such as Philadelphia, Baltimore, and Washington, D.C. If you're coming from the west, you'll likely take Interstate 80 (I-80), which runs from San Francisco to New York City, passing through states like Pennsylvania and Ohio.

When driving to New York City, it's important to plan for tolls, as many of the bridges and tunnels leading into

Manhattan require payment. The George Washington Bridge, Lincoln Tunnel, and Holland Tunnel are the main entry points into the city from New Jersey, while the Queensboro Bridge, Brooklyn Bridge, and Williamsburg Bridge connect Manhattan to other boroughs. Tolls can be paid using electronic systems like E-ZPass, which can save time at toll booths. It's also crucial to consider parking options in advance, as parking in Manhattan can be both expensive and difficult to find. Many hotels offer valet parking, but this can be costly. Alternatively, there are several parking garages and lots throughout the city where you can leave your car, though rates vary depending on location and demand.

Getting to New York City is made easy by the variety of transportation options available. Whether you choose to fly, take a train or bus, or drive, understanding the logistics of each method will help you plan a smooth and stress-free arrival. Each mode of transportation offers its own set of advantages, so consider your preferences, budget, and schedule when deciding how to get to the city. By preparing in advance and choosing the option that best suits your needs, you can start your New York City adventure on the right foot, ready to explore all that this incredible city has to offer.

How to Get Around

When you arrive in New York City, one of the first things you'll need to figure out is how to get around this vast, bustling metropolis. The city's transportation network is extensive and varied, offering multiple options to suit different preferences, budgets, and itineraries. Whether you're planning to visit iconic landmarks, explore different neighborhoods, or simply experience the daily rhythm of life in the city, knowing how to navigate New York efficiently is essential. With a bit of planning and a basic understanding of the available transportation options, you'll be able to move around the city with ease, making the most of your visit.

New York City is known for its efficient and comprehensive public transportation system, which is operated by the Metropolitan Transportation Authority (MTA). The MTA oversees the city's subways, buses, and commuter trains, all of which are integrated to provide seamless travel across the five boroughs—Manhattan, Brooklyn, Queens, The Bronx, and Staten Island. The subway is the backbone of the system, with an extensive network of lines that crisscross the city, making it possible to travel quickly between neighborhoods and boroughs. For many visitors, the subway is the most convenient and cost-effective way to get around, especially in Manhattan, where traffic congestion can make other modes of transport slower.

Using the subway for the first time can be a bit daunting, but with a few tips and some basic knowledge, you'll find it to be a reliable and efficient way to explore the city. The New York City subway operates 24 hours a day, seven days a week, which means you can travel whenever you need to, whether it's early in the morning or late at night. The subway system is organized into different lines, each identified by a letter or number, and color-coded on the subway map. These lines run through various parts of the city, often intersecting at key stations, allowing for easy transfers between lines. When using the subway, it's important to pay attention to the direction of the trains—Uptown, Downtown, or Brooklyn-bound—to ensure you're heading in the right direction.

Before boarding the subway, you'll need to purchase a MetroCard, which is used to pay for rides on the subway and buses. MetroCards can be purchased at vending machines located in subway stations, as well as at some newsstands and convenience stores. You can choose between a pay-per-ride card, where you load a specific amount of money, or an unlimited ride card, which allows you unlimited travel for a set period (e.g., 7 days or 30 days). For most tourists, the unlimited ride card is a great value, as it allows you to hop on and off the subway as often as you like without worrying about running out of funds.

Navigating the subway system is made easier with the use of maps and apps. Subway maps are available at most stations and can also be downloaded online. Additionally, smartphone apps like Google Maps or the official MTA app can help you plan your route, providing real-time updates on train schedules and service changes. It's worth noting that some subway stations, especially older ones, may not have elevators or escalators, so if you have mobility issues, you may want to check for accessible stations before planning your journey.

While the subway is the most popular mode of transportation for many, New York City's bus system offers another convenient option, especially for short trips within a specific neighborhood or when you want to travel along major avenues. Buses cover the entire city, with routes that complement the subway system, providing access to areas that the subway doesn't reach. Bus stops are marked by signs with the bus route number, and buses typically arrive every 5 to 15 minutes, depending on the time of day and the route.

To ride the bus, you can use the same MetroCard that you use for the subway, or you can pay with exact change in coins. If you're transferring from the subway to the bus, or vice versa, within two hours of your initial fare, the transfer is free. Riding the bus has the added advantage of allowing you to see the city as you travel, which can be a more scenic and leisurely way to get around, especially if you're not in a rush. However, it's important to keep in mind that traffic in New York can be heavy, particularly during rush hours, so buses may be slower than the subway at certain times.

For those who prefer private transportation, taxis and ride-sharing services are readily available throughout New York City. The iconic yellow cabs are a familiar sight on the city's streets, and hailing one is as simple as raising your hand at the curb. Taxis are metered, with fares based on the time and distance traveled, plus any applicable surcharges. Tipping the driver (around 15-20% of the fare) is customary. Taxis are a convenient option, particularly if you're traveling with luggage, in a group, or during late hours when subway service may be less frequent.

In addition to traditional taxis, ride-sharing services like Uber and Lyft are widely used in New York City. These services allow you to request a ride through a smartphone app, with the option to choose different types of vehicles, from budget-friendly shared rides to luxury cars. Ride-sharing can be a more comfortable and sometimes more affordable option than taxis, especially for longer trips or when traveling to areas with less frequent public transportation. However, as with buses, ride-sharing vehicles are subject to the city's traffic conditions, which can affect travel time.

Walking is one of the most enjoyable ways to experience New York City. The city is designed with pedestrians in mind, and many of its most famous attractions are within walking distance of each other, particularly in Manhattan. Walking allows you to take in the sights, sounds, and energy of the city up close, from the bustling streets of Times Square to the serene paths of Central Park. Sidewalks are wide, and crosswalks are well-marked, making it easy to navigate even the busiest areas. Additionally, New York's grid system, where streets are numbered and avenues run north-south, makes it straightforward to find your way around.

If you prefer a faster pace, biking is another excellent option for getting around the city. New York has become increasingly bike-friendly in recent years, with an expanding network of bike lanes and the introduction of the Citi Bike program. Citi Bike is a bike-sharing system that allows you to rent a bike from one of hundreds of docking stations located throughout the city. You can rent a bike for a single ride or purchase a day pass or multi-day pass if you plan to use the service frequently during your stay. Biking is a great way to explore areas like Brooklyn or the waterfront, and it allows you to cover more ground than walking while still enjoying the outdoors.

However, it's important to be aware of safety considerations when biking in New York City. Always wear a helmet, follow traffic signals, and use bike lanes where available. Be mindful of pedestrians, especially in crowded areas, and avoid biking during peak traffic hours if possible. If you're new to biking in the city, consider starting with quieter routes, such as the Hudson River Greenway, which offers a scenic and relatively stress-free ride along the west side of Manhattan.

Getting around New York City is made easy by a variety of transportation options, each offering different advantages depending on your needs and preferences. The subway is the fastest and most efficient way to travel long distances, while buses provide a more scenic route for shorter trips. Taxis and ride-sharing services offer convenience and comfort, particularly for late-night travel or when carrying luggage.

Walking and biking allow you to experience the city at a more leisurely pace, giving you the freedom to explore at your own speed. By understanding these options and planning your routes in advance, you can navigate New York City with confidence, making the most of your time in this dynamic and exciting city.

Public Transportation

Navigating New York City through its public transportation system is one of the most efficient and practical ways to explore the city. As a visitor, understanding how to use the city's subways and buses will not only save you time but also give you the flexibility to experience everything from the iconic landmarks to the hidden gems scattered throughout the five boroughs. The city's public transportation network is vast and comprehensive, designed to connect nearly every corner of the city, making it accessible to both locals and tourists alike. With a bit of preparation and knowledge, you can easily move through the city, maximizing your time and minimizing the stress that can come with navigating a new environment.

The New York City subway system is the backbone of the city's public transportation network. It is one of the largest and most complex subway systems in the world, with 472 stations spread across four of the five boroughs—Manhattan, Brooklyn, Queens, and The Bronx. The subway operates 24 hours a day, seven days a week, making it one of the most reliable ways to get around the city at any time, day or night. The subway is organized into different lines, each identified by a letter or number and color-coded on the subway map. These lines serve various routes, often intersecting at key stations, allowing for easy transfers between lines.

When you first arrive in New York City, one of the most important steps is to familiarize yourself with the subway routes and how they correspond to the areas you want to visit. The subway map, which is available at most stations and online, will be your primary guide. Each line runs in two directions—Uptown (northbound) or Downtown (southbound)—and it's essential to know which direction you need to travel in based on your location and destination. For example, if you're staying in Midtown Manhattan and want to visit the American Museum of Natural History, you'll need to take an Uptown train on the C line, heading toward 81st Street-Museum of Natural History.

To use the subway, you'll need a MetroCard, which serves as your ticket for the subway and bus systems. MetroCards can be purchased at vending machines located in every subway station, as well as at some convenience stores. You can choose between a pay-per-ride card, where you load a specific amount of money, or an unlimited ride card, which allows unlimited travel for a set period, such as 7 or 30 days. For tourists planning to use public transportation frequently, the unlimited ride card is often the best value, as it gives you the freedom to explore the city without worrying about running out of fare.

There are also mobile apps available that make navigating the subway system much easier. Apps like Google Maps, Citymapper, and the official MTA app provide real-time updates on train arrivals, service changes, and the fastest routes to your destination. These apps can be particularly helpful during peak hours or when there are unexpected delays or construction work on certain lines. By entering your starting point and destination, the app will guide you step by step, indicating which lines to take, where to transfer, and how long your journey will take.

While the subway is the most efficient way to travel long distances in New York City, the bus system offers a more scenic and often more direct route for shorter trips or for reaching areas that the subway doesn't serve. The MTA operates a comprehensive network of buses that cover all five boroughs, with routes that often complement the subway system. Buses are particularly useful for traveling along major avenues or crossing from east to west in Manhattan, where subway options are more limited. For example, if you're visiting the Metropolitan Museum of Art on the Upper East Side and want to head to the Museum of Natural History on the Upper West Side, the M79 crosstown bus provides a direct route through Central Park.

To ride the bus, you can use the same MetroCard that you use for the subway. If you're transferring from the subway to the bus, or vice versa, within two hours of your initial fare, the transfer is free. Buses typically run every 5 to 15 minutes during peak hours and less frequently during late nights and weekends. Each bus stop is marked with a sign indicating the route number and destination, and many stops feature digital displays showing the estimated arrival times for the next buses.

One of the advantages of taking the bus is the opportunity to see more of the city as you travel. Unlike the subway, where much of the journey is underground, buses offer views of the city's streets, architecture, and daily life. This makes bus travel a more leisurely option for those who want to experience the city at a slower pace. However, it's important to keep in mind that traffic in New York can be heavy, particularly during rush hours, so buses may take longer than the subway to reach their destination.

Navigating the city's public transportation system is made easier with the use of maps and apps that provide detailed information on routes, stops, and schedules. The official MTA subway map is a must-have tool, offering a visual representation of all the subway lines and stations. It's a good idea to study the map before your trip to get a sense of where the major attractions are located in relation to the subway lines. Many stations also have large, wall-mounted maps that you can reference while waiting for your train.

In addition to the subway map, the MTA provides bus maps that show the routes and stops for each bus line. These maps are available at major transit hubs, such as the Port Authority Bus Terminal, and can also be accessed online. Using these maps in conjunction with a navigation app will help you plan your routes efficiently, whether you're traveling by subway, bus, or a combination of both.

Accessibility is an important consideration when using public transportation in New York City. The MTA has made significant efforts to improve accessibility across its subway and bus systems, although challenges remain, particularly in older subway stations. Currently, not all subway stations are equipped with elevators or ramps, which can make travel difficult for those with mobility issues. However, the MTA has identified accessible stations on its maps, marked with a wheelchair symbol, indicating that these stations have elevators, ramps, or other accommodations for passengers with disabilities.

For those who require accessible transportation, the bus system is often a more reliable option, as all MTA buses are equipped with ramps and are fully accessible to passengers with wheelchairs or mobility aids. Additionally, the MTA offers a paratransit service called Access-A-Ride, which provides door-to-door transportation for individuals who cannot use the subway or bus due to a disability. Access-A-Ride can be scheduled in advance and is available throughout the city, offering a flexible and accessible transportation option for those who need it.

New York City's public transportation system is a vital resource for tourists, providing a convenient and affordable way to explore the city. Whether you choose to navigate the city by subway, bus, or a combination of both, understanding the routes, passes, and tools available to you will ensure a smooth and enjoyable experience. With the right preparation, you'll be able to move around the city with confidence, making the most of your time in this dynamic and diverse metropolis. By familiarizing yourself with the public transportation options and planning your routes in advance, you can focus on what really matters—immersing yourself in the incredible sights, sounds, and experiences that New York City has to offer.

Local Transportation Apps

Navigating New York City as a tourist can be overwhelming due to the city's size, complexity, and constant activity. Fortunately, technology has made it much easier to find your way around and access transportation services efficiently. Local transportation apps have become essential tools for both residents and visitors, offering real-time information, navigation assistance, and seamless access to various transportation options. These apps help you move through the city with ease, whether you're taking the subway, hailing a ride, or simply walking through the streets.

One of the most valuable tools for navigating New York City is a reliable navigation app. These apps are designed to provide you with step-by-step directions, helping you get from point A to point B with minimal stress. Google Maps is widely regarded as one of the best apps for navigating the city, offering comprehensive coverage of public transportation, walking routes, and driving directions. When you enter your destination into Google Maps, the app will provide you with several options, including subway routes, bus routes, walking paths, and even cycling routes if you prefer to bike. The app also offers estimated travel times for each option, allowing you to choose the quickest or most convenient route based on your preferences.

Google Maps goes beyond basic navigation by offering real-time updates on traffic conditions and public transportation schedules. If there are delays on a particular subway line or heavy traffic on the streets, Google Maps will adjust its recommendations accordingly, helping you avoid potential disruptions. This feature is particularly useful in a city like New York, where transportation conditions can change rapidly due to weather, construction, or special events. Additionally, Google Maps includes information about nearby points of interest, such as restaurants, shops, and attractions, making it easier to plan your day and discover new places as you explore the city.

Another popular app for navigating New York City is Citymapper. Like Google Maps, Citymapper provides detailed directions for getting around the city using public transportation, walking, biking, or driving. However, Citymapper is specifically designed for urban environments and offers some unique features that are particularly useful in a city like New York. For example, Citymapper provides step-by-step instructions for navigating complex subway stations, including which train car to board to be closest to the exit at your destination. This can save you time and reduce the hassle of navigating crowded stations during rush hours.

Citymapper also integrates with ride-sharing services like Uber and Lyft, allowing you to compare the cost and travel time of different transportation options within a single app. This feature is especially helpful if you're deciding between taking a subway, bus, or ride-sharing service based on factors like convenience, cost, and timing. Citymapper's real-time updates and alerts ensure that you're always aware of any changes or disruptions to your planned route, helping you stay one step ahead as you move through the city.

Ride-sharing apps like Uber and Lyft have revolutionized how people get around in New York City, offering a convenient and often cost-effective alternative to traditional taxis. These apps allow you to request a ride directly from your smartphone, and within minutes, a driver will arrive to take you to your destination. Using ride-sharing apps is straightforward, and they offer several benefits, particularly for tourists who may be unfamiliar with the city.

To use Uber or Lyft, you'll need to download the app and create an account. Once you've done this, you can enter your destination, and the app will show you the estimated fare and travel time for the ride. Both Uber and Lyft offer different types of rides to suit various needs and budgets. For example, you can choose a standard ride for one or two passengers, a larger vehicle for groups, or even a luxury car if you want to travel in style. If you're looking to save money, you can opt for a shared ride, where you'll be matched with other passengers heading in the same direction. This option typically costs less than a private ride but may take a bit longer due to additional stops.

One of the advantages of using ride-sharing apps is the transparency they offer. You'll see the estimated fare upfront, so there are no surprises when you reach your destination. Additionally, the apps provide real-time tracking of your driver's location, so you'll know exactly when they will arrive. Once your ride is complete, you can pay through the app using your credit card, and you'll receive a receipt via email. This cashless system is convenient and secure, reducing the need to carry large amounts of cash or worry about exact change.

Ride-sharing apps also offer a ratings system, where both passengers and drivers can rate their experience. This ensures a certain level of quality and accountability, as drivers with consistently low ratings may be removed from the platform. As a tourist, this feature can give you added peace of mind, knowing that your driver has been vetted and rated by other users.

In addition to navigation and ride-sharing, there are several apps available that provide real-time updates on traffic and public transportation conditions in New York City. One such app is the MTA's official app, MYmta, which offers comprehensive information on subway and bus schedules, service changes, and real-time train arrivals. MYmta allows you to check the status of your subway line before heading to the station, ensuring that you're aware of any delays or service interruptions. The app also provides information on bus routes and real-time bus locations, helping you plan your journey more efficiently.

Another useful app for real-time updates is Waze, which is particularly helpful if you're driving or using a ride-sharing service. Waze relies on crowd-sourced data from other drivers to provide real-time information on traffic conditions, road closures, and accidents. The app will suggest alternate routes to help you avoid traffic jams and get to your destination more quickly. Waze also includes features like alerts for speed traps and hazards on the road, making it a valuable tool for anyone navigating New York City's busy streets.

For subway riders, an app like Transit is also worth considering. Transit provides real-time tracking of subway trains, buses, and even Citi Bikes, making it easy to see when the next train or bus is arriving. The app also includes service alerts and notifications for planned subway maintenance, which is especially useful during weekends when service changes are more common. With Transit, you can plan your route, check for any delays, and receive notifications if there are any changes to your usual route.

Using these apps together will give you a comprehensive view of New York City's transportation landscape, allowing you to navigate the city with confidence and efficiency. Whether you're relying on public transportation, ride-sharing services, or your own two feet, these apps provide the tools and information you need to make the most of your time in the city.

local transportation apps are invaluable resources for anyone visiting New York City. They offer a wide range of services, from navigation assistance and real-time updates to ride-sharing options and traffic alerts. By downloading and familiarizing yourself with these apps, you can simplify your travel experience, avoid unnecessary delays, and focus on enjoying all that the city has to offer. Whether you're planning a visit to a famous landmark, exploring a new neighborhood, or simply trying to get across town, these apps will help you reach your destination quickly and easily, ensuring that your time in New York City is as smooth and enjoyable as possible.

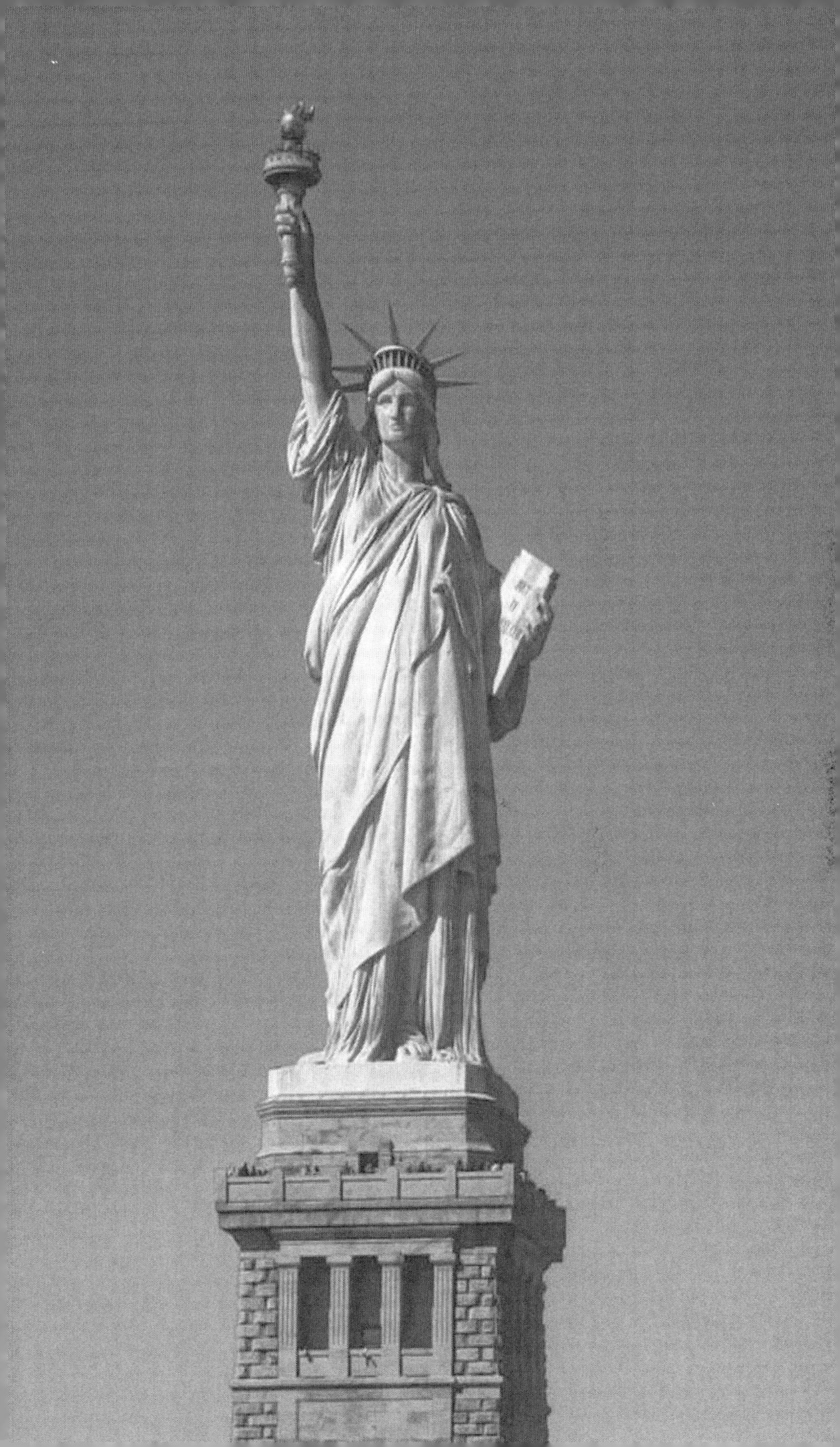

CHAPTER 3

MANAGING YOUR MONEY IN NEW YORK CITY

Currency Exchange Locations

When visiting New York City, having access to local currency is essential for making everyday purchases, especially in situations where cash is more convenient or where credit cards might not be accepted. Whether you're planning to use U.S. dollars primarily or rely on a combination of cash and credit cards, understanding the best ways to exchange your foreign currency, and where to do so, can save you both time and money during your stay.

New York City, as a global financial hub, offers numerous locations for currency exchange. These include currency exchange bureaus, banks, and even hotels. One of the most convenient places to exchange currency is at the airport. John F. Kennedy International Airport (JFK), LaGuardia Airport (LGA), and Newark Liberty International Airport (EWR) all have currency exchange counters where you can exchange your money as soon as you arrive. However, while airport exchanges are convenient, they often offer less favorable exchange rates and may charge higher fees compared to other options in the city. If you choose to exchange money at the airport, it may be best to only exchange a small amount to cover immediate expenses like transportation to your hotel, and then seek better rates elsewhere.

Once you're in the city, you'll find numerous currency exchange bureaus, particularly in areas popular with tourists, such as Times Square, Midtown Manhattan, and near major attractions. These bureaus specialize in foreign exchange and can offer competitive rates, especially if you shop around and compare a few different places. Some well-known currency exchange companies in New York include Travelex, Currency Exchange International, and Thomas Cook. These companies have multiple locations throughout the city and often provide better rates than airports or hotels. It's a good idea to check their websites or call ahead to inquire about their rates and fees before visiting.

Another option for currency exchange is visiting a bank. Major banks in New York City, such as Chase, Bank of America, Citibank, and Wells Fargo, often provide currency exchange services to their customers. If you have an account with an international bank that has a presence in New York, such as HSBC, you might be able to exchange currency at more favorable rates, especially if you're exchanging a large amount of money. However, keep in mind that not all bank branches offer currency exchange services, and some may require that you be an account holder. It's also worth noting that banks typically have set business hours, which may not be as convenient as currency exchange bureaus that stay open late or operate on weekends.

Hotels in New York City may also offer currency exchange services, particularly at higher-end establishments that cater to international guests. While this can be convenient, hotel exchange rates are usually less favorable than those at dedicated currency exchange bureaus or banks, and the fees may be higher. If you're staying at a hotel and prefer the convenience of exchanging currency on-site, it's still a good idea to check the rates and fees in advance.

To get the best exchange rates, there are a few tips you can follow. First, it's important to compare rates at different locations before making a transaction. Even a small difference in the exchange rate can have a significant impact if you're exchanging a large amount of money. Many currency exchange bureaus display their rates on digital boards or posters outside their locations, making it easy to compare rates as you walk around. Some bureaus also offer online rate calculators where you can check the current rate and lock it in before you visit. This can be particularly useful if you want to avoid fluctuations in exchange rates throughout the day.

Another tip is to be mindful of hidden fees and charges. Some currency exchange locations may advertise attractive rates but then add on hefty fees or commissions. Always ask if there are any additional fees before completing your transaction. Some bureaus may offer "no fee" exchanges but compensate for this by offering a less favorable rate, so it's important to consider the overall cost of the transaction, not just the rate. Additionally, you might find that larger transactions often result in better rates, so if you need to exchange a substantial amount of money, it may be beneficial to do it all at once rather than in smaller increments.

While exchanging currency at a bureau or bank is a straightforward option, another efficient way to access local currency is by using ATMs. ATMs are widely available throughout New York City, and many allow you to withdraw cash directly from your home bank account in U.S. dollars. The advantage of using ATMs is that they typically offer better exchange rates than currency exchange bureaus or hotels, as the rates are closer to the official interbank rates used by financial institutions. However, it's important to be aware of the fees that may be associated with ATM withdrawals. These fees can include a flat fee charged by the ATM operator, as well as foreign transaction fees imposed by your home bank.

To minimize ATM fees, consider withdrawing larger amounts of cash at once rather than making multiple smaller withdrawals. This reduces the number of times you're charged a fee. Additionally, check with your home bank before traveling to see if they have any partnerships with U.S. banks that might allow you to use certain ATMs without incurring additional fees. For example, some international banks have agreements with U.S. banks to waive fees for their customers when using specific ATMs.

Credit cards are another convenient and widely accepted method of payment in New York City. Using a credit card for purchases can often provide you with a competitive exchange rate, especially if your card doesn't charge foreign transaction fees. Many credit card companies use the interbank exchange rate, which is generally more favorable than the rates offered by currency exchange bureaus. However, it's essential to check with your credit card issuer before you travel to understand any fees that may apply when using your card abroad. Some credit cards, particularly travel-focused cards, offer zero foreign transaction fees, making them an excellent option for international travelers.

When using a credit card in New York, be mindful of dynamic currency conversion (DCC). This is a service offered by some merchants that allows you to pay in your home currency rather than U.S. dollars. While this might seem convenient, it's generally best to decline this option and pay in the local currency. DCC transactions often come with unfavorable exchange rates and additional fees, resulting in a higher overall cost. Always choose to pay in U.S. dollars to ensure you get the best exchange rate offered by your credit card company.

Exchanging currency and managing your finances in New York City is made easier by the numerous options available, including currency exchange bureaus, banks, ATMs, and credit cards. By understanding where to exchange your money, how to get the best rates, and the potential fees involved, you can make informed decisions that help you maximize your spending power while minimizing unnecessary costs. Whether you prefer to carry cash, use your credit card, or withdraw money as needed, careful planning and a bit of research can ensure that your financial transactions in New York City are smooth, secure, and cost-effective.

Money Matters

Planning a trip to New York City requires careful consideration of your financial arrangements to ensure that you can fully enjoy all the city has to offer without worrying about running out of funds. New York is one of the most expensive cities in the world, so having a clear budget, understanding local tipping practices, and being prepared for unexpected expenses are crucial to making the most of your visit. Additionally, knowing how to manage your banking and credit card usage while in the city can help you avoid unnecessary fees and complications.

Budgeting for your trip to New York City is an essential first step in your planning process. The city offers a wide range of experiences, from free attractions to high-end dining and entertainment, so your budget will depend largely on your preferences and the type of experiences you wish to have. It's important to start by outlining your expected costs in several key areas: accommodation, transportation, food, attractions, and shopping. By estimating these expenses in advance, you can determine how much you'll need to allocate for each category and make adjustments if necessary.

Accommodation is likely to be one of the most significant expenses of your trip. New York City has a wide variety of lodging options, from budget-friendly hostels and Airbnb rentals to luxury hotels. Prices can vary significantly depending on the time of year, location, and the level of comfort you desire. For example, staying in a hotel in Midtown Manhattan will generally be more expensive than staying in a hotel in Queens or Brooklyn. It's also important to consider the proximity of your accommodation to the attractions you plan to visit, as this can impact your transportation costs. Booking your accommodation well in advance can often result in better rates, especially during peak travel seasons.

Transportation costs in New York City can also add up quickly, especially if you plan to use taxis or ride-sharing services frequently. The city's public transportation system, including the subway and buses, is a more budget-friendly option and provides extensive coverage of the city. If you plan to use public transportation often, consider purchasing an unlimited MetroCard, which allows you to ride the subway and buses as many times as you like for a set period (e.g., 7 days). This can be a cost-effective way to get around, especially if you're staying for several days. Walking and biking are also excellent ways to explore the city while saving money on transportation.

Food is another area where costs can vary widely. New York City is known for its diverse culinary scene, offering everything from affordable street food to Michelin-starred restaurants. To manage your food budget, consider mixing high-end dining experiences with more budget-friendly options. For example, you might choose to have lunch at a food truck or a casual eatery and save your money for a special dinner at a renowned restaurant. Many restaurants in New York also offer prix fixe menus, which can provide a multi-course meal at a fixed price, allowing you to enjoy fine dining without overspending.

When it comes to attractions, New York City has something for everyone, from world-famous museums and Broadway shows to free parks and historic sites. Some attractions, like the Metropolitan Museum of Art or the Statue of Liberty, charge admission fees, while others, like Central Park or the Brooklyn Bridge, are free to visit. If you plan to visit several paid attractions, consider purchasing a CityPASS or New

York Pass, which offer discounted admission to multiple attractions and can save you money in the long run. Additionally, many museums offer free or pay-what-you-wish admission on certain days of the week, so it's worth checking the schedules in advance.

Tipping is an important aspect of the service industry in New York City, and understanding the local tipping etiquette is essential for budgeting and ensuring you don't inadvertently offend anyone. In the United States, tipping is customary in many situations, particularly in restaurants, bars, taxis, and hotels. In restaurants, it's standard to tip 15-20% of the total bill, depending on the quality of service. Some restaurants may automatically add a gratuity to the bill for larger groups, so be sure to check your receipt before adding an additional tip. If you're dining at a bar, it's customary to tip $1-$2 per drink.

Tipping is also expected in other service-related situations, such as when taking a taxi or using a ride-sharing service. For taxi drivers, a tip of 10-15% of the fare is standard. For ride-sharing services like Uber or Lyft, the app will often suggest a tip amount based on the fare, and you can choose to tip accordingly. If you're staying at a hotel, it's customary to tip the bellhop $1-$2 per bag for assistance with your luggage and to leave a small tip (usually $1-$5 per day) for the housekeeping staff. Tipping is also appropriate for other services, such as valet parking attendants and doormen, particularly if they provide assistance beyond opening the door, such as hailing a cab for you.

Unexpected expenses are an inevitable part of any trip, and it's important to budget for them to avoid being caught off guard. These expenses can range from minor costs, such as a forgotten toiletry item or a souvenir you didn't plan to buy, to more significant expenses, such as medical care or a last-minute change in travel plans. One way to prepare for unexpected expenses is to set aside a contingency fund within your overall travel budget. This fund can be used to cover any unplanned costs that arise during your trip, providing peace of mind and ensuring that you don't have to dip into your savings or credit cards unexpectedly.

If you do encounter unexpected expenses, it's important to have a plan for how to handle them. For example, if you experience a medical emergency, having travel insurance can help cover the costs of treatment and hospitalization, which can be prohibitively expensive in the United States. Similarly, if you need to change your travel plans due to unforeseen circumstances, such as a flight cancellation or a personal emergency, having travel insurance with trip cancellation coverage can help you recover some or all of the costs associated with rebooking or canceling your trip.

When it comes to banking and credit card use, there are several tips that can help you manage your finances effectively while in New York City. First, it's important to inform your bank and credit card company of your travel plans before you leave. This helps prevent any issues with your cards being declined due to suspected fraud, as international transactions may trigger alerts. Many banks and credit card companies allow you to set up travel notifications online or through their mobile apps, making the process quick and easy.

Using credit cards in New York City is generally safe and convenient, and they are widely accepted at most businesses. However, it's important to be aware of potential foreign transaction fees, which some credit card companies charge for purchases made in a foreign currency or processed through a foreign bank. These fees typically range from 1-3% of the transaction amount and can add up quickly if you're using your card frequently. To avoid these fees, consider using a credit card that offers no foreign transaction fees. Many travel-focused credit cards offer this benefit, along with other perks such as travel rewards and insurance coverage.

ATMs are readily available throughout New York City, making it easy to withdraw cash as needed. However, it's important to be mindful of ATM fees, which can include both a fee charged by the ATM operator and a fee imposed by your home bank. To minimize these fees, try to withdraw larger amounts of cash at once rather than making multiple smaller withdrawals. Additionally, some international banks have partnerships with U.S. banks that allow their customers to use certain ATMs without incurring additional fees. Check with your bank before your trip to see if any such partnerships exist and which ATMs you can use fee-free.

Managing your money effectively during your trip to New York City requires careful planning, an understanding of local practices, and a readiness to handle unexpected expenses. By budgeting for your trip, following local tipping etiquette, preparing for unforeseen costs, and using your banking and credit cards wisely, you can ensure that your financial arrangements support a smooth and enjoyable experience in one of the world's most dynamic cities. Whether you're dining at a famous restaurant, taking in a Broadway show, or simply exploring the city's many neighborhoods, being financially prepared will help you focus on making the most of your time in New York City.

Currency Symbols and Denominations

When visiting New York City, understanding the local currency is essential for making transactions smoothly and confidently. The currency used in the United States is the U.S. dollar, which is abbreviated as USD and symbolized by the dollar sign ($). Familiarizing yourself with U.S. currency symbols, denominations, and the physical appearance of bills and coins will help you navigate your spending more effectively during your stay. Additionally, being aware of how to avoid counterfeit money and understanding basic banking and credit card tips will further enhance your experience as a tourist in the city.

The U.S. dollar is divided into 100 smaller units called cents, symbolized by ¢. U.S. currency is available in both paper bills (often referred to as "notes") and coins, each with specific denominations. The most commonly used paper bills in the U.S. are $1, $5, $10, $20, $50, and $100. These bills are all the same size and are made of a blend of cotton and linen, giving them a distinct feel. Each denomination features the portrait of a notable American figure on the front and an iconic American symbol or landmark on the back.

The $1 bill is the most frequently used and features the portrait of George Washington, the first president of the United States, on the front. The reverse side of the $1 bill displays the Great Seal of the United States. The $5 bill bears the portrait of Abraham Lincoln, the 16th president, with an image of the Lincoln Memorial on the reverse. The $10 bill features Alexander Hamilton, the first Secretary of the Treasury, on the front, and the U.S. Treasury building on the back. The $20 bill has a portrait of Andrew Jackson, the seventh president, with an image of the White House on the reverse. The $50 bill features Ulysses S. Grant, the 18th president, on the front, and the U.S. Capitol on the back. Lastly, the $100 bill, often referred to as a "Benjamin" in reference to Benjamin Franklin, whose portrait it bears, shows an image of Independence Hall on the reverse.

In addition to paper bills, U.S. currency includes several denominations of coins: 1¢ (penny), 5¢ (nickel), 10¢ (dime), 25¢ (quarter), 50¢ (half dollar), and $1 coins. The penny, which is copper-colored, features the portrait of Abraham Lincoln on the front and the Lincoln Memorial on the reverse. The nickel is larger and thicker than the penny and features Thomas Jefferson on the front and Monticello, his Virginia estate, on the reverse. The dime, the smallest U.S. coin in both size and value, features Franklin D. Roosevelt on the front and a torch, olive branch, and oak branch on the reverse. The quarter, a popular coin in everyday transactions, bears the portrait of George Washington on the front, while the reverse varies depending on the design, often featuring a state or national landmark as part of the U.S. Mint's commemorative series.

While half-dollar coins and $1 coins are less commonly encountered in everyday transactions, they are still in circulation. The half-dollar coin features John F. Kennedy, the 35th president, on the front, and the presidential seal on the reverse. The $1 coin has been issued in various designs, with more recent versions featuring Sacagawea, a Native American woman who assisted the Lewis and Clark expedition, and a series honoring U.S. presidents.

When handling U.S. currency, it's important to be aware of the potential for counterfeit money, although it is relatively uncommon. Counterfeiters tend to target higher denominations, such as $20, $50, and $100 bills. To avoid accepting counterfeit money, familiarize yourself with the security features of U.S. bills. Modern U.S. bills have several built-in security features designed to make counterfeiting difficult. These include watermarks, security threads, color-shifting ink, and microprinting. The watermark is visible when the bill is held up to light and should match the portrait on the bill. The security thread is embedded in the paper and can be seen when held up to light, with the denomination of the bill printed on it. Color-shifting ink, used in the numeral at the bottom right corner of the bill, changes color when the bill is tilted. Microprinting consists of tiny text that is difficult to reproduce and can be found in various locations on the bill.

If you suspect that a bill is counterfeit, do not accept it. Instead, ask for another bill and politely inform the person that you believe the bill may not be genuine. If you find yourself in possession of a counterfeit bill, take it to a bank or contact the local police to report it. Never attempt to pass a counterfeit bill, as this is illegal and can lead to serious consequences.

Using your credit or debit card in New York City is generally safe and convenient, with most businesses accepting major cards like Visa, MasterCard, American Express, and Discover. However, it's important to take a few precautions to ensure that you manage your finances effectively while avoiding unnecessary fees and potential security issues. Before your trip, inform your bank and credit card companies of your travel plans. This prevents your cards from being flagged for suspicious activity when you make purchases in the U.S. Many financial institutions allow you to set up travel notifications online or through their mobile apps, making the process quick and easy.

Be aware of potential foreign transaction fees when using your credit or debit card in New York City. Some banks and credit card companies charge a fee, typically around 1-3% of the transaction amount, for purchases made in a foreign currency or processed through a foreign bank. To avoid these fees, consider using a credit card that offers no foreign transaction fees. Travel-focused credit cards often come with this benefit, as well as other perks like travel rewards, insurance coverage, and access to airport lounges.

When using an ATM in New York City, it's important to be mindful of the fees that may apply. These can include both a fee charged by the ATM operator and a foreign transaction fee imposed by your home bank. To minimize these fees, try to withdraw larger amounts of cash at once rather than making multiple smaller withdrawals. Additionally, some international banks have partnerships with U.S. banks that allow their customers to use specific ATMs without incurring additional fees. Check with your bank before your trip to find out if any such partnerships exist and which ATMs you can use for free or at a reduced cost.

Lastly, when using your credit card in New York City, be cautious of dynamic currency conversion (DCC). DCC is a service offered by some merchants that allows you to pay in your home currency rather than U.S. dollars. While this may seem convenient, it often comes with unfavorable exchange rates and additional fees, resulting in a higher overall cost. It's best to decline DCC and choose to pay in U.S. dollars, ensuring that you get the best exchange rate offered by your credit card company.

Understanding U.S. currency symbols, denominations, and security features is crucial for managing your money effectively during your visit to New York City. By familiarizing yourself with the appearance and value of U.S. bills and coins, taking steps to avoid counterfeit money, and using your credit and debit cards wisely, you can ensure that your financial transactions in the city are smooth, secure, and cost-effective. Whether you're paying for a meal at a restaurant, buying souvenirs, or withdrawing cash from an ATM, being well-informed about U.S. currency and banking practices will help you navigate your financial needs with confidence, allowing you to focus on enjoying all that New York City has to offer.

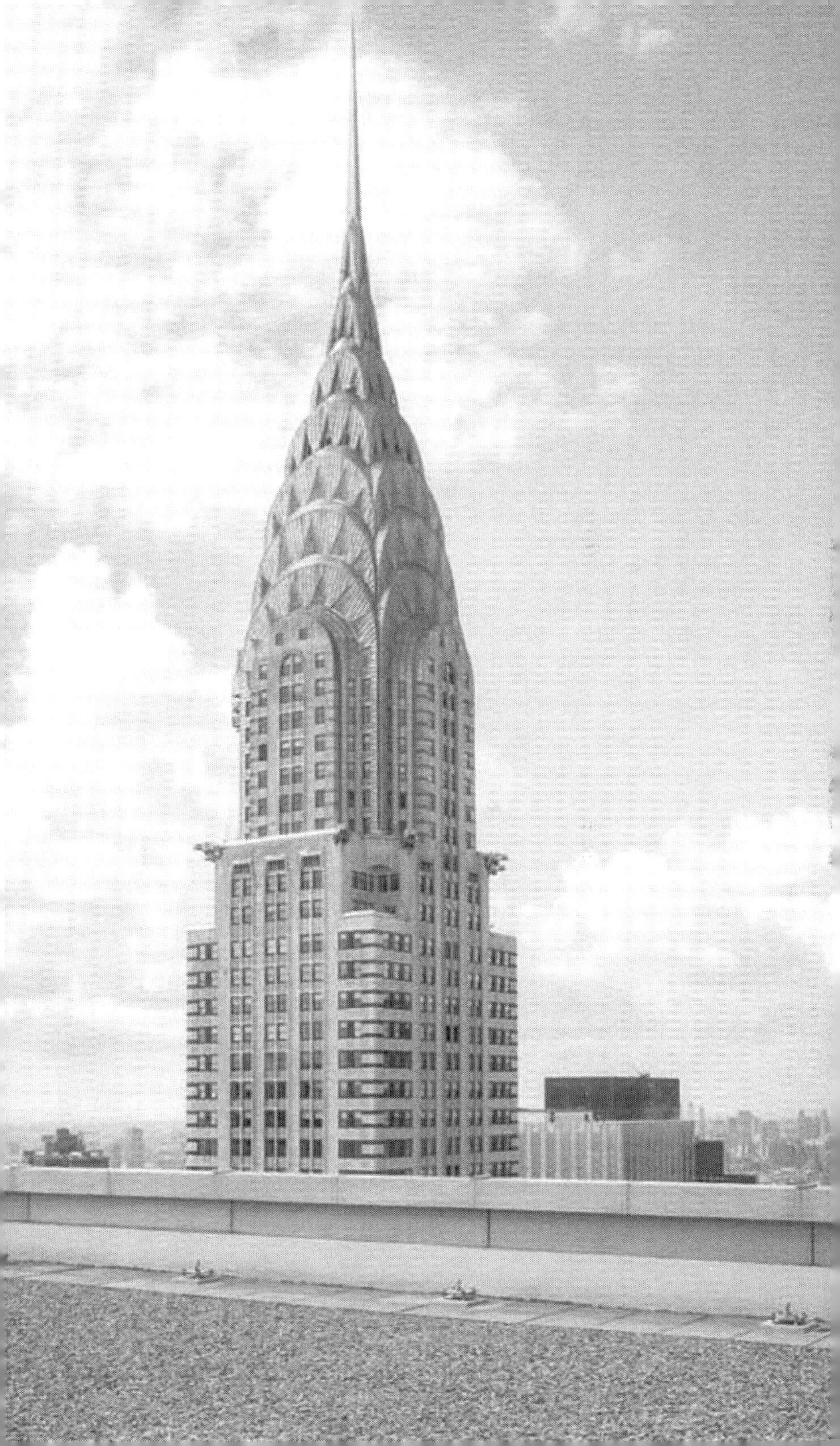

CHAPTER 4

STAYING CONNECTED AND POWERED UP

Electricity and Plug Adapters

When traveling to New York City, understanding the local electrical system and ensuring that you have the right plug adapters for your devices is essential for a smooth and hassle-free experience. The United States operates on a specific electrical voltage and uses distinct plug types that may differ from what is used in other parts of the world. For international travelers, this means taking steps to ensure that your electronic devices can be safely charged and used during your stay.

In the United States, including New York City, the standard electrical voltage is 120 volts at a frequency of 60 hertz. This voltage is lower than what is used in many other countries, particularly in Europe and parts of Asia, where the standard voltage is often 220-240 volts at 50 hertz. The difference in voltage means that if you bring electronic devices from a country with a higher voltage, you will need to ensure that your devices are compatible with the lower voltage in the U.S., or use a voltage converter to safely use them.

The plug types used in the United States are also specific and may differ from those used in your home country. The U.S. primarily uses two plug types: Type A and Type B. Type A plugs have two flat parallel pins and are ungrounded, while Type B plugs have two flat parallel pins and a round grounding pin, making them grounded. Type B outlets can accept both Type A and Type B plugs, but devices with Type A plugs cannot be used in outlets designed exclusively for Type B plugs without an adapter.

Before traveling to New York City, it's important to check the power specifications of your electronic devices to determine whether they are compatible with the 120-volt system used in the U.S. Many modern electronic devices, such as smartphones, laptops, and cameras, are designed to be dual voltage, meaning they can operate on both 110-120 volts and 220-240 volts. If your device is dual voltage, it will typically be labeled with a voltage range, such as "100-240V" or "110-220V." In this case, you will only need a plug adapter to convert the plug type to match the U.S. outlet, without the need for a voltage converter.

If your device is not dual voltage and is designed to operate only on a higher voltage, such as 220-240 volts, you will need to use a voltage converter in addition to a plug adapter. A voltage converter steps down the voltage from 220-240 volts to 120 volts, allowing you to safely use your device in the U.S. It's important to note that voltage converters are typically used for simpler devices, such as hair dryers or electric razors, and may not be suitable for more sensitive electronics like laptops or smartphones, which could be damaged by incorrect voltage.

For international travelers, investing in a reliable plug adapter is crucial to ensure that your devices can be connected to U.S. outlets. Universal plug adapters are a convenient option, as they are designed to work with multiple plug types and can be used in various countries. These adapters typically come with interchangeable plugs that can be easily switched out to match the outlet configuration of the country you are visiting. When choosing a universal plug adapter, look for one that is compact, durable, and easy to use, with clearly labeled plug types and a secure fit in the outlet.

Another option is to purchase a dedicated U.S. plug adapter that is specifically designed for use with Type A and Type B outlets. These adapters are generally smaller and more lightweight than universal adapters, making them a good choice if you plan to travel primarily to the U.S. and do not need the flexibility of a universal adapter. U.S. plug adapters are widely available and can be purchased online before your trip or at various locations once you arrive in New York City.

If you arrive in New York City without a plug adapter, there are several places where you can purchase one. Many electronics stores, such as Best Buy, carry a range of plug adapters, voltage converters, and travel accessories. These stores are conveniently located throughout the city, including popular shopping areas like Times Square and Herald Square. Additionally, large department stores like Macy's and Target often have a travel section where you can find plug adapters and other essential items for international travelers.

Pharmacies and convenience stores, such as Walgreens, CVS, and Duane Reade, also commonly stock plug adapters, particularly in neighborhoods frequented by tourists. These stores are open late or 24 hours a day, making them a convenient option if you need to purchase an adapter after regular business hours. For travelers staying in hotels, the hotel gift shop may also carry plug adapters, though the selection may be more limited, and prices may be higher compared to other retail locations.

In addition to ensuring that you have the right plug adapter, it's also important to be mindful of the potential risks associated with using electrical devices in a foreign country. Overloading an outlet by plugging in too many devices at once can create a fire hazard, particularly if the devices draw more power than the outlet is designed to handle. To avoid this, consider using a power strip with surge protection, which allows you to safely connect multiple devices to a single outlet while protecting them from power surges.

When traveling with expensive electronics, such as laptops or cameras, it's a good idea to carry them in a protective case and use a surge protector to guard against electrical surges that could damage your devices. Some universal plug adapters come with built-in surge protection, providing an added layer of security for your electronics. If you're using a voltage converter, ensure that it is compatible with the wattage of your device to prevent overheating or damage.

Understanding the electrical system and plug types used in the United States, and ensuring that you have the appropriate plug adapters and voltage converters, is essential for international travelers visiting New York City. By taking the time to check your devices' power specifications, investing in a reliable plug adapter, and following safety precautions, you can ensure that your electronic devices function smoothly and safely during your stay. Whether you're charging your smartphone, using your laptop, or operating other electronic devices, being well-prepared will allow you to focus on enjoying all that New York City has to offer, without worrying about power compatibility issues

Internet and Communication

Staying connected while traveling in New York City is crucial for navigating the city, staying in touch with family and friends, and accessing essential information on the go. Whether you need reliable internet access, a local SIM card, or guidance on using your phone in the U.S., understanding the options available for internet and communication will help ensure that your trip is both seamless and enjoyable.

For international travelers, one of the most practical ways to stay connected in New York City is by purchasing a local SIM card. Using a U.S. SIM card with a mobile plan designed for domestic use can significantly reduce the cost of making calls, sending texts, and using data compared to relying on international roaming from your home carrier. Several major mobile network operators in the U.S. offer prepaid SIM cards that are ideal for tourists, including AT&T, T-Mobile, and Verizon.

AT&T is one of the largest mobile network providers in the U.S., and they offer a range of prepaid SIM card options that cater to tourists. AT&T's prepaid plans typically include unlimited talk and text within the U.S. and a set amount of high-speed data, which can vary depending on the plan you choose. After you reach the data limit, you can still use the internet, but at reduced speeds. AT&T's network is extensive, providing reliable coverage throughout New York City, including in most subway stations and inside many buildings. You can purchase an AT&T SIM card at their retail stores, which are conveniently located throughout the city, or at major electronics stores and airports.

T-Mobile is another popular choice for tourists visiting New York City. Known for its strong coverage in urban areas, T-Mobile offers prepaid plans that include unlimited talk, text, and data within the U.S., along with additional features such as international texting and data usage in other countries. T-Mobile's prepaid SIM cards are available at T-Mobile stores, which are easily found in most neighborhoods, as well as at major airports and electronics retailers. T-Mobile is also known for its customer-friendly policies, such as no contracts and the ability to easily top up your plan online or through their app.

Verizon is the third major carrier, offering extensive coverage across the U.S., including New York City. Verizon's prepaid plans provide options for varying levels of data, from basic plans with limited data to unlimited plans. While Verizon's prepaid options might be slightly more expensive than those of AT&T or T-Mobile, the network is known for its reliability, particularly in areas where other networks may struggle with signal strength. Verizon SIM cards can be purchased at Verizon stores, as well as at airports and major retail outlets.

If you have an unlocked phone, using a local SIM card is straightforward. Simply insert the SIM card into your phone, follow the activation instructions provided by the carrier, and you'll be ready to use your phone with a U.S. number. If your phone is locked to your home carrier, you'll need to either unlock it before your trip or use an international roaming plan from your home carrier, which can be more expensive.

For travelers who prefer not to change their SIM card, international roaming is another option, though it tends to be more costly. Most international carriers offer roaming plans that allow you to use your phone in the U.S., often with a daily or weekly fee that covers calls, texts, and a limited amount of data. It's important to check with your home carrier before your trip to understand the costs and limitations of international roaming. Some carriers may also offer special travel plans or add-ons that provide discounted rates for roaming in the U.S.

In addition to mobile plans, Wi-Fi is widely available throughout New York City, making it easy to stay connected without relying solely on cellular data. Many hotels, cafes, restaurants, and public spaces offer free Wi-Fi to customers and visitors. For example, most major coffee chains, such as Starbucks, provide free Wi-Fi to patrons, making it a convenient place to catch up on emails, check maps, or browse the internet. Many hotels also offer complimentary Wi-Fi as part of your stay, though some may charge for higher-speed access or premium services.

New York City has also implemented free public Wi-Fi in many parts of the city through the LinkNYC initiative.

LinkNYC kiosks are located on streets throughout the five boroughs, providing free, high-speed Wi-Fi to anyone nearby. These kiosks also offer USB charging ports, access to city services, and the ability to make free phone calls within the U.S. LinkNYC kiosks are particularly useful for tourists who may need to quickly access the internet while exploring the city without using their mobile data. The service is fast, reliable, and available in many popular tourist areas, including Times Square, Central Park, and major transportation hubs.

For travelers who need more consistent or high-speed internet access, internet cafes are another option, though they have become less common in recent years due to the widespread availability of Wi-Fi. However, a few internet cafes and business centers still exist in New York City, particularly in neighborhoods with a high concentration of tourists or business travelers. These establishments typically offer computer stations with internet access, printing, and scanning services, making them a good choice for travelers who need to work or handle other tasks that require a stable internet connection.

When using Wi-Fi in public places, it's important to be mindful of security. Public Wi-Fi networks are often unsecured, meaning that your data could potentially be intercepted by others on the same network. To protect your personal information, avoid accessing sensitive accounts, such as online banking or email, when using public Wi-Fi. If you need to access these accounts, consider using a virtual private network (VPN), which encrypts your internet connection and adds an extra layer of security.

For travelers who plan to use their phones extensively in New York City, understanding how to manage roaming charges and optimize mobile usage is essential. Roaming charges can quickly add up if you're not careful, especially if you're using data-intensive services like streaming video or using GPS for navigation. To avoid unexpected charges, consider turning off data roaming in your phone's settings when you're not actively using your phone or when Wi-Fi is available. Many smartphones also allow you to set data usage limits or alerts, which can help you monitor your data consumption and avoid exceeding your plan's allowance.

Using messaging apps like WhatsApp, Viber, or Skype can also help you stay connected with family and friends back home without incurring high international calling or texting fees. These apps use internet data rather than cellular service to send messages and make calls, which can be more cost-effective if you're connected to Wi-Fi. Many of these apps also offer end-to-end encryption, ensuring that your communications remain private and secure.

When it comes to banking and credit card use, it's important to inform your bank and credit card companies of your travel plans before you arrive in New York City. This helps prevent your cards from being flagged for suspicious activity when you make transactions in the U.S. Many banks allow you to set up travel notifications online or through their mobile apps, making the process quick and easy. Additionally, be aware of potential foreign transaction fees that may apply when using your credit or debit card in the U.S. Some credit card companies charge a fee, typically around 1-3% of the transaction amount, for purchases made in a foreign currency or processed through a foreign bank. To avoid these fees, consider using a credit card that offers no foreign transaction fees, which is often the case with travel-focused credit cards.

Staying connected in New York City is made easy by a variety of options, from purchasing a local SIM card to utilizing free Wi-Fi hotspots throughout the city. By choosing the right mobile plan, managing your data usage, and taking advantage of available internet services, you can ensure that your communication needs are met without incurring unnecessary costs. Whether you're navigating the city, keeping in touch with loved ones, or handling important tasks online, being well-prepared and informed about your internet and communication options will allow you to focus on enjoying your time in New York City.

Public Wi-Fi Availability

Staying connected while exploring New York City is essential, whether you're navigating the city, keeping in touch with loved ones, or simply browsing the web. Fortunately, New York City offers an extensive network of public Wi-Fi hotspots, providing free internet access across various locations throughout the city. This widespread availability of free Wi-Fi makes it easier for tourists to stay connected without incurring hefty data charges. However, using public Wi-Fi also comes with potential security risks, so it's important to be aware of best practices to protect your personal information.

One of the most comprehensive public Wi-Fi initiatives in New York City is the LinkNYC program. LinkNYC has transformed old payphone booths into modern kiosks that provide free, high-speed Wi-Fi across the five boroughs. These kiosks, known as Links, are equipped with fast internet connections, USB charging ports, and touchscreens for accessing city services and maps. You can find LinkNYC kiosks on major streets, in busy commercial areas, and near popular attractions. The network is designed to be fast and reliable, making it a convenient option for tourists who need quick access to the internet while on the go. Connecting to LinkNYC Wi-Fi is simple: just look for the "LinkNYC Free Wi-Fi" network on your device, select it, and you're online.

Beyond LinkNYC, many public parks and open spaces in New York City offer free Wi-Fi, allowing you to stay connected while enjoying the city's outdoor areas. Central Park, one of the most famous parks in the world, has several Wi-Fi hotspots scattered throughout its 843 acres. Whether you're relaxing by the Bethesda Terrace, visiting the Great Lawn, or strolling through the Ramble, you'll find free Wi-Fi access available. Bryant Park, located in Midtown Manhattan, also offers free Wi-Fi, making it a great spot to take a break, enjoy a coffee, and catch up on emails. Washington Square Park in Greenwich Village and Union Square Park are other popular green spaces where free Wi-Fi is readily available, providing a convenient way to stay connected while experiencing the city's vibrant outdoor culture.

New York City's public libraries are another excellent resource for free Wi-Fi. The New York Public Library (NYPL) system operates numerous branches across

Manhattan, the Bronx, and Staten Island, all of which offer free Wi-Fi access to visitors. The iconic Stephen A. Schwarzman Building on Fifth Avenue, with its grand architecture and historic reading rooms, is a popular destination for both tourists and locals. Visitors can take advantage of the free Wi-Fi to research their next destination, check social media, or simply relax in a quiet environment. In addition to Wi-Fi, many NYPL branches provide public computers and printing services, making them a useful stop if you need to print tickets, maps, or other important documents during your trip.

Cafes and coffee shops are another common source of free Wi-Fi in New York City. Major chains like Starbucks and Dunkin' offer free Wi-Fi to customers at all their locations, making it easy to find a place to connect, whether you're in Midtown Manhattan, Brooklyn, or Queens. Independent cafes often provide free Wi-Fi as well, though some may require you to make a purchase or ask for the password. Spending time in a cafe not only gives you access to the internet but also provides a chance to rest, enjoy a snack or drink, and experience the local coffee culture. Many cafes in New York have a cozy, welcoming atmosphere, making them ideal spots to recharge both your devices and yourself.

Shopping centers and department stores in New York City also frequently offer free Wi-Fi to customers. Iconic locations like Macy's Herald Square, the largest department store in the world, provide free Wi-Fi throughout the store, allowing you to browse the internet while you shop. Other shopping destinations, such as the Westfield World Trade Center, the Shops at Columbus Circle, and the upscale boutiques along

Fifth Avenue, also offer complimentary Wi-Fi. This can be particularly useful if you're comparison shopping, looking for reviews, or coordinating plans with friends while you explore the city's retail offerings.

In addition to these specific locations, many restaurants, bars, and even some museums and cultural institutions provide free Wi-Fi to visitors. It's always worth asking if Wi-Fi is available when you visit these places, especially if you plan to spend some time there.

While free public Wi-Fi is incredibly convenient, it's important to be mindful of the potential security risks associated with using unsecured networks. Public Wi-Fi networks are typically less secure than private networks, making them more vulnerable to cyber threats like hacking, phishing, and data interception. To protect your personal information while using public Wi-Fi in New York City, there are several best practices you should follow.

First, avoid accessing sensitive accounts, such as online banking or email, when connected to public Wi-Fi. If you need to log into these accounts, consider using a virtual private network (VPN), which encrypts your internet connection and makes it more difficult for others to intercept your data. VPN services are available as apps or software that you can install on your device, and they provide an additional layer of security when using public Wi-Fi.

Second, make sure that any website you visit while on public Wi-Fi uses HTTPS, which indicates that the site is encrypted and secure. You can tell if a website is using HTTPS by looking for the padlock icon in the address bar of your browser. Avoid entering personal information, such as passwords or credit card details, on websites that do not use HTTPS.

Third, disable file sharing and AirDrop (on Apple devices) on your device before connecting to public Wi-Fi. These features can be exploited by hackers to access your files or send malicious content to your device. You can usually disable file sharing in your device's settings under the network or sharing options.

Fourth, consider turning off automatic Wi-Fi connections on your device. Many smartphones and laptops are set to automatically connect to known Wi-Fi networks, but this can make you more vulnerable to connecting to a fake or malicious network that is designed to look legitimate. By disabling automatic connections, you can manually select the Wi-Fi networks you want to join, ensuring that you only connect to trusted networks.

Lastly, keep your device's operating system and security software up to date. Software updates often include important security patches that protect your device from the latest threats. Keeping your device updated ensures that you have the best possible protection when using public Wi-Fi.

When it comes to banking and credit card use, it's essential to be cautious, especially when using public Wi-Fi networks. Avoid accessing your bank accounts or making online purchases while connected to public Wi-Fi, as this can expose your financial information to potential threats. If you need to make a transaction or check your bank account, use your mobile data connection instead, as it is generally more secure than public Wi-Fi. Additionally, consider using contactless payment methods, such as Apple Pay or Google Pay, which offer a more secure way to make purchases without exposing your credit card details.

Public Wi-Fi is widely available in New York City, making it easy for tourists to stay connected throughout their visit. From LinkNYC kiosks and public parks to cafes, libraries, and shopping centers, there are numerous locations where you can access free internet. However, it's important to use public Wi-Fi safely by following security best practices, such as avoiding sensitive transactions, using a VPN, and keeping your device updated. By staying informed and taking precautions, you can enjoy the convenience of public Wi-Fi while protecting your personal information, allowing you to focus on making the most of your time in New York City.

Important Applications and Tool

When planning a trip to New York City, equipping yourself with the right applications and tools can significantly enhance your experience, helping you navigate the city more easily, communicate effectively, and make the most of your visit. The vastness and complexity of New York can be overwhelming for first-time visitors, but with the right digital tools, you can streamline your travel experience, avoid common pitfalls, and focus on enjoying all the city has to offer.

One of the first things you'll want to do before arriving in New York is to download some must-have apps that cater specifically to tourists. These apps cover a wide range of needs, from transportation and navigation to dining and sightseeing, ensuring that you're well-prepared for whatever the city throws your way.

Google Maps is one of the most essential apps for any traveler, especially in a sprawling metropolis like New York City. With its comprehensive coverage, Google Maps provides detailed navigation for walking, driving, biking, and using public transportation. The app offers real-time updates on traffic conditions, subway schedules, and route changes, helping you avoid delays and find the fastest way to your destination. Additionally, Google Maps allows you to search for nearby attractions, restaurants, and services, complete with user reviews and ratings, making it easier to discover hidden gems and make informed decisions on where to go and what to do.

For those relying on public transportation, the MYmta app is an indispensable tool. Created by the Metropolitan Transportation Authority (MTA), this app provides real-time information on subway, bus, and commuter rail services across New York City. You can use the app to check train arrival times, view service alerts, and plan your route based on current conditions. The MYmta app also includes accessibility information, such as elevator and escalator statuses, making it a valuable resource for travelers with mobility needs. The app's user-friendly interface and accurate data make it a must-have for navigating the city's extensive public transportation network.

Citymapper is another excellent app for navigating New York City, particularly for those who prefer a more detailed and customizable experience. Citymapper offers step-by-step directions for getting around the city, including walking, biking, and public transportation options. The app is known for its innovative features, such as providing recommendations on which subway car to board for the quickest exit or transfer, and it integrates with ride-sharing services like Uber and Lyft. Citymapper also offers a "rain safe" option, which helps you find routes that minimize exposure to the elements on rainy days, a feature particularly useful in New York's unpredictable weather.

For dining, Yelp is a popular app that helps you find restaurants, cafes, and bars that suit your tastes and budget. Yelp offers a vast database of user-generated reviews, photos, and ratings, making it easier to choose where to eat in a city with seemingly endless dining options. The app also allows you to search for specific types of cuisine, price ranges, and even specific dishes, ensuring that you find exactly what you're craving. Many restaurants listed on Yelp offer online reservations or delivery options, which can be especially convenient if you're looking to secure a table at a busy spot or prefer to enjoy a meal in the comfort of your hotel.

Another app that can greatly enhance your dining experience is OpenTable, which focuses specifically on making restaurant reservations. OpenTable allows you to browse available tables at a wide range of restaurants, read reviews, and make instant reservations. The app also offers suggestions for nearby restaurants based on your current location and dining preferences. OpenTable's seamless reservation system helps you avoid long waits at popular restaurants, giving you more time to explore the city.

When it comes to sightseeing, the NYCgo app is a valuable resource for tourists. Developed by NYC & Company, the city's official tourism organization, the NYCgo app offers curated guides to New York's top attractions, events, and neighborhoods. The app provides detailed information on everything from iconic landmarks like the Statue of Liberty and the Empire State Building to lesser-known attractions like local markets and art galleries. NYCgo also includes maps and directions, making it easy to plan your itinerary and navigate the city's many sights.

Language barriers can be a concern for some travelers, particularly those who do not speak English fluently. Fortunately, several language translation apps can help bridge this gap, allowing you to communicate more effectively and navigate the city with confidence. Google Translate is one of the most popular and versatile translation apps available. It supports translation between dozens of languages, including real-time voice translation and the ability to translate text by simply pointing your camera at signs or menus. Google Translate also offers an offline mode, allowing you to download language packs and use the app even when you don't have internet access. This can be particularly helpful when navigating areas with limited connectivity or when using public transportation.

iTranslate is another excellent language translation app that offers similar features to Google Translate, with a focus on ease of use and a clean, intuitive interface. iTranslate supports text, voice, and camera translation, and it offers a "Pro" version that includes additional features like offline translation and verb conjugation. The app also includes a phrasebook feature, which provides commonly used phrases in various languages, making it easier to communicate basic needs like ordering food or asking for directions.

For those who prefer a more immersive language experience, Duolingo is a fun and engaging app that helps you learn a new language before or during your trip. While not a translation app, Duolingo offers lessons in a wide range of languages, allowing you to build your vocabulary and improve your understanding of basic grammar. The app's bite-sized lessons and gamified approach make language learning enjoyable and accessible, even for beginners. While you won't become fluent overnight, using Duolingo can give you the confidence to navigate basic conversations and understand common phrases during your visit to New York.

Navigating New York City's vast and busy streets can be challenging, especially if you find yourself without a reliable internet connection. This is where offline maps and navigation tools come in handy. Google Maps, as mentioned earlier, offers the ability to download maps for offline use, allowing you to access directions and location information even when you're not connected to the internet. Simply select the area of the city you'll be exploring and download the map to your device. Once the map is downloaded, you can use it to find your way around, search for points of interest, and access saved locations without using data.

Maps.me is another highly recommended offline navigation app. Unlike Google Maps, Maps.me is specifically designed for offline use, making it a reliable choice for travelers who anticipate spending time in areas with limited connectivity. The app offers detailed maps that include walking, driving, and public transportation directions, as well as information on nearby attractions, restaurants, and services. Maps.me is particularly useful for exploring neighborhoods outside of the main tourist areas, where internet access may be less reliable.

For those who prefer a more traditional approach to navigation, the Pocket Earth app offers detailed offline maps and travel guides that you can download and access without an internet connection. Pocket Earth includes topographic maps, hiking and biking trails, and comprehensive city guides, making it an excellent choice for both urban exploration and outdoor adventures. The app also allows you to create custom maps with your own points of interest, which can be particularly useful for planning a detailed itinerary.

In addition to navigation and language tools, managing your finances while traveling in New York City is essential for a stress-free trip. As mentioned earlier, it's important to inform your bank and credit card companies of your travel plans before arriving in the city. This helps prevent your cards from being flagged for suspicious activity when making transactions in the U.S. Many banks and credit card companies offer mobile apps that allow you to monitor your account activity, check balances, and receive alerts in real-time. These apps are invaluable for keeping track of your spending, ensuring that you stay within your budget and avoid any unexpected charges.

When using your credit card in New York, be aware of potential foreign transaction fees that may apply. Some credit card companies charge a fee, typically around 1-3% of the transaction amount, for purchases made in a foreign currency or processed through a foreign bank. To avoid these fees, consider using a credit card that offers no foreign transaction fees, which is often the case with travel-focused credit cards. These cards also typically offer additional perks, such as travel rewards, purchase protection, and emergency assistance services.

ATMs are widely available throughout New York City, making it easy to withdraw cash as needed. However, ATM fees can add up, especially if your home bank charges foreign transaction fees in addition to the fees imposed by the ATM operator. To minimize these costs, consider withdrawing larger amounts of cash at once rather than making multiple smaller withdrawals. Additionally, check with your bank before your trip to see if they have any partnerships with U.S. banks that allow you to use certain ATMs without incurring additional fees.

Lastly, consider using mobile payment options like Apple Pay, Google Pay, or Samsung Pay during your stay in New York City. These contactless payment methods are widely accepted at many retailers, restaurants, and transportation services, and they offer a more secure way to make transactions without exposing your credit card details.

Mobile payments are also convenient, as they eliminate the need to carry large amounts of cash or multiple cards.

Equipping yourself with the right applications and tools can greatly enhance your experience as a tourist in New York City. From must-have navigation and translation apps to offline maps and financial management tools, these resources will help you navigate the city with confidence, communicate effectively, and manage your finances efficiently. By staying informed and well-prepared, you can focus on enjoying all that New York City has to offer, making your visit both memorable and stress-free.

CHAPTER 5

UNDERSTANDING LOCAL RULES AND CULTURE

Local Customs and Laws

Understanding the local customs and laws of New York City is essential for any tourist who wants to navigate the city smoothly, avoid misunderstandings, and respect the local culture. New York City, often referred to as the melting pot of the United States, is a vibrant and diverse metropolis that attracts millions of visitors each year. The city's unique blend of cultures and its bustling urban environment create a set of unwritten social norms and legal regulations that can differ significantly from those in other parts of the world. Being aware of these customs and laws will help you have a more enjoyable and respectful experience during your stay.

One of the first things to understand about New York City is that it is a place where people are often in a hurry. The fast-paced lifestyle is evident in everything from the brisk walking speed of pedestrians to the quick service in restaurants and shops. As a visitor, it's important to be mindful of this pace, particularly when navigating crowded areas like sidewalks, subway stations, and busy streets. New Yorkers are known for their efficiency and can sometimes seem brusque or impatient, but this is usually not meant to be unfriendly. It's simply a reflection of the city's fast-moving culture. When walking, it's considered polite to keep to the right side of the sidewalk, allowing others to pass on the left, and to avoid stopping abruptly in the middle of a busy pathway. If you need to check your phone or take a moment to look around, it's best to step to the side to avoid disrupting the flow of foot traffic.

Tipping is another important custom in New York City, and it's something that visitors should be prepared for. In the United States, tipping is a standard practice in many service industries, and New York City is no exception. In restaurants, it is customary to tip your server between 15-20% of the total bill, depending on the quality of service. Some restaurants may automatically add a gratuity to the bill for larger groups, typically for parties of six or more, so be sure to check your receipt before adding an additional tip. Tipping is also expected in other situations, such as for taxi drivers (around 10-15% of the fare), hotel staff (typically $1-$2 per bag for bellhops and $1-$5 per day for housekeeping), and bartenders ($1-$2 per drink). If you're unsure about the appropriate amount to tip, it's generally better to err on the side of generosity, as many service workers in the city rely on tips as a significant part of their income.

When it comes to communication, New Yorkers are known for being direct and straightforward. This can sometimes be mistaken for rudeness, but it's usually just a way of getting to the point quickly. If you need directions or assistance, don't hesitate to ask—most New Yorkers are happy to help, but they may do so in a no-nonsense manner. It's also important to remember that New York is an incredibly diverse city, with people from all over the world living and working here. As such, you may encounter a wide range of languages, accents, and cultural practices. Showing respect for this diversity, being open-minded, and avoiding assumptions based on appearances or accents will help you navigate social interactions more smoothly.

Public transportation is a key part of life in New York City, and there are some unwritten rules that can make your experience more pleasant. When riding the subway, it's common courtesy to let passengers exit the train before you board, and to move into the car to make room for others as you enter. If you're carrying a large bag or backpack, it's polite to hold it in front of you or place it on the floor to avoid bumping into others. During rush hours, when trains are crowded, it's especially important to be mindful of your space and to avoid blocking the doors. On buses, it's customary to offer your seat to elderly passengers, people with disabilities, and pregnant women, particularly if you're seated in the priority seating area at the front of the bus.

New York City has a number of laws that are particularly relevant for tourists to be aware of. One of the most important is the city's strict smoking laws. Smoking is prohibited in all indoor public spaces, including restaurants, bars, theaters, and public transportation, as well as in many outdoor spaces such as parks, beaches, and pedestrian plazas. There are designated smoking areas in some locations, but these are increasingly rare. Violating smoking regulations can result in fines, so it's important to be mindful of where you're allowed to smoke. If you're unsure, it's best to ask a local or look for signage indicating whether smoking is permitted.

The legal drinking age in New York City is 21, which is strictly enforced. This means that anyone under the age of 21 is not allowed to purchase or consume alcoholic beverages in bars, restaurants, or stores. If you plan to drink alcohol during your visit, be prepared to show a valid government-issued ID, such as a passport or driver's license, as proof of age. Many establishments will check IDs at the door, especially in nightclubs and bars, so it's a good idea to carry your ID with you if you plan to visit these venues. It's also important to note that open containers of alcohol are not allowed in public spaces, such as streets, parks, or on public transportation. Drinking alcohol in public places can result in fines or other legal consequences, so it's best to keep any alcoholic beverages confined to licensed establishments.

Another important law to be aware of is the prohibition of jaywalking, which is crossing the street outside of a designated crosswalk or against a traffic signal. While jaywalking is common in New York City, it is technically illegal and can result in a fine if you're caught by the police. For your safety and to avoid legal trouble, it's best to cross streets at crosswalks and only when the pedestrian signal indicates that it's safe to do so. The city's traffic can be chaotic, and following the rules of the road will help keep you safe.

New York City also has strict laws regarding the possession and use of drugs. While the recreational use of marijuana has been legalized in New York State, there are still regulations governing where and how it can be used. It's legal for adults over the age of 21 to possess up to three ounces of marijuana for personal use, but smoking or consuming marijuana in public places is prohibited, similar to the city's smoking laws. Additionally, marijuana cannot be used in vehicles, and driving under the influence of marijuana is illegal. Other drugs, including those considered controlled substances, are strictly prohibited, and possession or use of these substances can result in serious legal consequences.

In terms of banking and credit card use, it's important for tourists to be prepared for the financial aspects of their trip to New York City. As mentioned previously, informing your bank and credit card companies of your travel plans is essential to avoid any issues with your cards being declined due to suspected fraud. Many banks offer mobile apps that allow you to monitor your account activity and receive alerts, which can help you keep track of your spending and detect any unauthorized transactions. When using your credit card in New York, be aware of potential foreign transaction fees that may apply, and consider using a credit card that offers no foreign transaction fees to save money.

ATMs are widely available throughout New York City, but it's important to be mindful of the fees associated with withdrawing cash. Some ATMs charge a fee for using a card issued by a different bank, and your home bank may also charge a foreign transaction fee. To minimize these fees, try to withdraw larger amounts of cash at once rather than making multiple smaller withdrawals. Additionally, using ATMs located inside banks or well-lit, busy areas can help reduce the risk of encountering skimming devices or other security threats.

Finally, when it comes to making purchases, contactless payment methods such as Apple Pay, Google Pay, or Samsung Pay are widely accepted in New York City. These payment options offer a convenient and secure way to make transactions without having to carry large amounts of cash or multiple cards. They also provide an added layer of security, as your payment information is encrypted and less vulnerable to theft.

Understanding the local customs and laws of New York City is key to having a safe, respectful, and enjoyable visit. By being aware of the city's fast-paced culture, adhering to tipping practices, following public transportation etiquette, and respecting local laws regarding smoking, drinking, and public behavior, you can navigate the city with confidence and avoid common pitfalls. Additionally, being prepared with banking and credit card tips will help ensure that your financial transactions go smoothly during your stay. With this knowledge in hand, you can focus on experiencing all that New York City has to offer, making the most of your time in this dynamic and diverse city.

Local Etiquette

Navigating the cultural nuances of New York City can greatly enhance your experience as a tourist and help you blend in more seamlessly with the local population. New York is a bustling metropolis with its own set of social norms, particularly in public places, restaurants, and shops. Understanding these unwritten rules of etiquette will not only make your visit more enjoyable but also ensure that you interact respectfully with both locals and other visitors. Whether you're walking through the city's busy streets, dining out, or shopping in one of its many stores, adhering to local etiquette can make a significant difference in how you're perceived and how smoothly your day-to-day interactions go.

In New York City, public spaces are always teeming with people—locals rushing to work, tourists taking in the sights, and street vendors selling their wares. Given the city's density, it's essential to be mindful of your behavior in public places. One of the most important aspects of local etiquette is respecting personal space, which can be challenging in a crowded city. New Yorkers, though often packed closely together on sidewalks, in subway cars, and in public venues, value their personal space. Avoid unnecessary physical contact, and try to keep a comfortable distance from others whenever possible.

When walking on busy sidewalks, it's crucial to keep moving. New Yorkers are known for their brisk pace, and the sidewalks in areas like Times Square or Midtown Manhattan can feel like highways for pedestrians. If you need to stop to check directions, take a photo, or simply take a break, be sure to step to the side, out of the main flow of foot traffic. Blocking the sidewalk or stopping suddenly in the middle of a busy path can be frustrating for others and is generally considered impolite.

Another key aspect of public etiquette in New York is noise. The city is loud by nature, but when it comes to personal noise levels, such as talking on the phone or playing music, it's important to be considerate. In public places like parks, museums, or on public transportation, keep your voice at a moderate level to avoid disturbing others. If you're using headphones, make sure the volume is low enough that it doesn't leak out and bother those around you. In some quieter areas, like libraries or certain public spaces, it's expected that you keep conversations to a minimum or speak in hushed tones.

Public transportation, particularly the subway, is a major part of life in New York City, and there are specific behaviors that are considered appropriate when using it. When boarding a subway train or bus, allow passengers to exit before you enter. This keeps the flow of people moving smoothly and prevents bottlenecks at the doors. Once inside, if the train or bus is crowded, remove your backpack and hold it in front of you to make more room for others. If you're seated, it's polite to offer your seat to elderly passengers, people with disabilities, or pregnant women. Additionally, avoid eating or drinking on public transportation, as this can be seen as inconsiderate, particularly in crowded conditions.

In restaurants, cafes, and shops, local etiquette emphasizes politeness and consideration for both staff and fellow customers. In New York City, dining out is often a quick and efficient affair, especially during busy lunch hours or in fast-casual eateries. When entering a restaurant, it's customary to wait to be seated unless there is a clear sign indicating that seating is open. If you're dining in a busy establishment, it's polite to be mindful of the time you spend at your table, particularly during peak hours when others may be waiting for a seat. Once you've finished your meal, signal for the check rather than lingering unnecessarily.

How you interact with service staff in restaurants is also an important aspect of local etiquette. New Yorkers generally appreciate efficiency, so when placing your order, it's helpful to know what you want before the server arrives. If you have questions about the menu or need recommendations, feel free to ask, but try to be decisive once you're ready to order. Being polite and courteous to servers, bartenders, and other staff is essential; a simple "please" and "thank you" go a long way in maintaining a positive interaction. It's also important to remember that servers in the U.S. often rely on tips as a significant part of their income, so tipping appropriately is not just polite—it's necessary.

Tipping in restaurants is typically between 15-20% of the total bill, depending on the quality of service. If you're dining in a group, particularly with six or more people, some restaurants may automatically add a gratuity to the bill. Be sure to check your receipt to see if a tip has already been included before adding more. In fast-casual restaurants or cafes where you order at the counter, tipping is still appreciated, though the amount can be smaller—often just a dollar or two in a tip jar or added to your payment when you sign the receipt. In bars, it's customary to tip the bartender $1-$2 per drink, or 15-20% of the total tab if you're running a tab. For takeout or delivery orders, tipping is also expected, usually around 10-15%, depending on the size of the order and the service provided.

Shopping in New York City can be an exciting experience, with everything from high-end boutiques to bustling street markets. When browsing in stores, it's important to handle merchandise with care, especially in upscale shops where items are often displayed meticulously. If you need assistance or have questions, don't hesitate to ask the staff, but be patient, especially in busy stores where staff may be attending to multiple customers. In smaller boutiques or specialty shops, it's customary to greet the staff when you enter, as these environments tend to be more personal than large department stores.

Haggling is not common in most stores in New York City, particularly in retail environments. Prices are typically fixed, and attempting to negotiate could be seen as rude or out of place. However, if you're shopping at a flea market or with street vendors, some level of negotiation might be expected, though it should be done politely and with a clear understanding of when to accept the price offered.

Another key aspect of local etiquette in New York City involves handling transactions and using credit cards. As mentioned earlier, it's important to inform your bank and credit card companies of your travel plans to avoid having your card declined due to suspected fraud. When making purchases, using a credit card is common and widely accepted, but it's important to be aware of potential foreign transaction fees. Some credit card companies charge a fee, typically around 1-3% of the transaction amount, for purchases made in a foreign currency or processed through a foreign bank. To avoid these fees, consider using a credit card that offers no foreign transaction fees, which is often the case with travel-focused credit cards. These cards also typically offer additional perks, such as travel rewards, purchase protection, and emergency assistance services.

When using your credit card, especially in restaurants or smaller shops, you may be asked whether you'd like to add a tip before signing the receipt. In most cases, you'll write the tip amount on the receipt and add it to the total before signing. This process is straightforward, but if you're unsure, don't hesitate to ask the staff how tipping is handled.

ATMs are widely available throughout New York City, but it's important to be mindful of the fees associated with withdrawing cash. Some ATMs charge a fee for using a card issued by a different bank, and your home bank may also charge a foreign transaction fee. To minimize these fees, try to withdraw larger amounts of cash at once rather than making multiple smaller withdrawals. Additionally, using ATMs located inside banks or well-lit, busy areas can help reduce the risk of encountering skimming devices or other security threats.

Lastly, consider using mobile payment options like Apple Pay, Google Pay, or Samsung Pay during your stay in New York City. These contactless payment methods are widely accepted at many retailers, restaurants, and transportation services, and they offer a more secure way to make transactions without exposing your credit card details. Mobile payments are also convenient, as they eliminate the need to carry large amounts of cash or multiple cards.

Understanding and respecting local etiquette in New York City will greatly enhance your experience as a tourist. From knowing how to navigate public spaces and transportation to interacting politely in restaurants and shops, these social norms will help you blend in with the local culture and avoid common faux pas. Additionally, being prepared with banking and credit card tips will ensure that your financial transactions go smoothly, allowing you to focus on enjoying all that New York City has to offer. By following these guidelines, you can make the most of your visit to this dynamic and diverse city, creating positive interactions and lasting memories along the way.

Cultural Etiquette and Taboos

When visiting New York City, understanding and respecting cultural etiquette and taboos is essential for navigating social interactions smoothly and avoiding any unintentional offenses. As one of the most diverse cities in the world, New York is a melting pot of cultures, languages, and traditions. This diversity is reflected in the city's customs and social norms, which can vary widely depending on the context and the people you're interacting with. By being aware of these cultural nuances, you can ensure that your visit is respectful and enjoyable for both yourself and those you encounter.

Respecting cultural differences is one of the most important aspects of cultural etiquette in New York City. The city is home to people from all over the world, and this diversity is a source of pride for many New Yorkers. As a visitor, it's important to approach this diversity with an open mind and a willingness to learn. You'll likely encounter people who speak different languages, follow different religious practices, and have different customs than you're used to. Showing respect for these differences is key to building positive interactions.

One way to demonstrate respect for cultural differences is by being mindful of how you speak and interact with others. Avoid making assumptions about someone's background based on their appearance, accent, or name. For example, don't assume that someone speaks English as their first language, and be patient if there are language barriers. If you're unsure about someone's cultural practices, it's perfectly acceptable to ask questions in a polite and curious manner, rather than making assumptions. Most people will appreciate your interest and respect.

When it comes to conversation, there are certain topics that are best avoided, particularly when speaking with people you've just met. New Yorkers, like many Americans, tend to value privacy, and certain subjects can be considered too personal or sensitive for casual conversation. Politics, for example, can be a particularly contentious topic. While New York City is generally known for its progressive political views, discussing politics with someone you don't know well can quickly become heated or uncomfortable. It's best to steer clear of political discussions unless you're in a setting where you know it's appropriate.

Religion is another topic that should be approached with caution. New Yorkers come from a wide variety of religious backgrounds, and while the city is known for its tolerance, religion can be a deeply personal subject. Avoid making assumptions about someone's beliefs or practices, and be respectful if the topic does come up. It's generally a good idea to avoid making jokes or offhand comments about religion, as these can easily be misunderstood or taken as disrespectful.

Personal finances, including questions about income, rent, or how much someone spends on something, are also generally considered off-limits in casual conversation. While you may be curious about the cost of living in New York or how much someone pays for their apartment, these questions can come across as intrusive. If you need information about costs, it's better to do some research online or ask a local in a more general way, such as inquiring about the average rent in a neighborhood rather than asking someone directly about their personal finances.

Another sensitive topic to avoid is race and ethnicity. New York City is one of the most racially and ethnically diverse cities in the world, and issues related to race can be complex and deeply felt. It's important to be aware of the potential for offense when discussing race, and to avoid making generalizations or assumptions based on someone's race or ethnicity. Instead, focus on treating everyone you meet with respect and as an individual, rather than as a representative of a particular group.

Customs around greetings and personal space in New York City can vary depending on the context and the individuals involved. In general, New Yorkers tend to be more reserved in their greetings compared to people in some other parts of the world. A simple "hello" or "hi" is usually sufficient when meeting someone for the first time, and there's no need for elaborate greetings or gestures. In more formal settings, such as a business meeting, a handshake is the standard form of greeting. Handshakes should be firm but not overly strong, and it's customary to make eye contact while shaking hands.

Hugging and kissing on the cheek are fewer common forms of greeting in New York, particularly among people who are not close friends or family. While these forms of greeting may be more common in some cultures, it's best to wait until you're more familiar with someone before offering a hug or a kiss on the cheek. In general, New Yorkers value their personal space, and it's important to be mindful of this in both greetings and everyday interactions. Standing too close to someone, especially in a crowded space like a subway car or elevator, can make others feel uncomfortable. Aim to maintain a comfortable distance when speaking with others, and be aware of cues that someone may need more space.

When it comes to queuing, or standing in line, New Yorkers take this seriously. Whether you're waiting for a subway train, buying coffee, or checking out at a store, it's important to respect the line and wait your turn. Cutting in line is considered rude and can lead to confrontations, so always be mindful of where the line starts and make sure to stand in the correct place. If you're unsure, it's okay to ask someone nearby if they're in line.

Tipping is an integral part of the culture in New York City, and understanding tipping etiquette is crucial for tourists. As mentioned earlier, tipping is customary in many service settings, including restaurants, bars, taxis, and hotels. The standard tipping rate in restaurants is between 15-20% of the total bill, depending on the level of service. Tipping is also expected in bars, where it's customary to tip $1-$2 per drink. In hotels, it's polite to tip the bellhop $1-$2 per bag for assistance with your luggage and to leave a small tip for housekeeping, usually $1-$5 per day, depending on the level of service.

When using taxis or ride-sharing services like Uber and Lyft, tipping is also expected. A tip of 10-15% of the fare is standard, and many ride-sharing apps now allow you to add a tip directly through the app. It's important to remember that tips are a significant part of the income for many service workers in New York, so tipping generously when appropriate is not only polite but also helps support those who provide these services.

Understanding these cultural norms and etiquette practices will help you navigate social interactions in New York City with confidence and respect. By being mindful of the city's diversity, avoiding sensitive topics in conversation, and respecting personal space and tipping customs, you can ensure that your visit is both enjoyable and respectful. These practices will help you build positive relationships with the people you meet, whether they're locals or fellow tourists, and allow you to fully appreciate the rich cultural tapestry that makes New York City such a unique and vibrant destination. Additionally, being prepared with banking and credit card tips will ensure that your financial transactions go smoothly, allowing you to focus on enjoying all that New York City has to offer without unnecessary stress.

The Language and Key Phrases

When traveling to New York City, having a grasp of the English language and understanding some local phrases can significantly enhance your experience. English is the primary language spoken in New York, and while the city is incredibly diverse, with residents and visitors from all over the world, most interactions will be in English. Being familiar with basic English phrases, local slang, and useful expressions will not only help you navigate the city more easily but also make your interactions with locals smoother and more enjoyable.

Starting with basic English phrases, it's important to have a set of simple, everyday expressions that can be used in a variety of situations. Even if you're not fluent in English, knowing these key phrases can help you with common interactions such as asking for directions, ordering food, or making small talk. Some essential phrases include:

Hello/Hi: A simple greeting that can be used in almost any situation.

Thank you: Expressing gratitude is always appreciated. You can also use "Thanks" as a more casual alternative.

Please: When making a request, adding "please" shows politeness.

- Use this phrase to get someone's attention or to politely ask someone to move.

I'm sorry: This is useful for apologizing, even for small things like accidentally bumping into someone.

Where is...? This phrase is helpful for asking directions, such as "Where is the subway station?" or "Where is Central Park?"

How much is this? Useful when shopping or dining out.

Can you help me? A polite way to ask for assistance, whether you need directions or help with something else.

I don't understand: This phrase lets the other person know you're having trouble following the conversation.

Do you speak (your language)? While English is the primary language, New York is home to many people who speak other languages. Asking if someone speaks your language can be helpful in some situations.

These basic phrases can be adapted to different contexts, making them versatile tools in your communication arsenal. It's also helpful to practice these phrases before your trip so that you feel more comfortable using them in real-life situations.

In addition to basic English phrases, understanding some local slang and expressions can give you a deeper insight into the way New Yorkers communicate. New York City has a unique linguistic culture, influenced by its diverse population and fast-paced lifestyle. While it's not necessary to learn all the local slang, being familiar with a few key expressions can help you understand conversations better and even impress the locals. Here are some common New York City slang terms and phrases:

The City: When New Yorkers refer to "The City," they're usually talking about Manhattan, the heart of New York City.

Uptown/Downtown: These terms refer to the general direction within Manhattan. "Uptown" means north, while "Downtown" means south. You might hear someone say, "I'm heading downtown," meaning they're going to the southern part of Manhattan.

The Subway: This is the term for New York City's underground train system. People might also refer to it as "the train."

Bodega: A small convenience store, often open 24/7, where you can buy snacks, drinks, and other essentials.

On line: In New York, people say they're "on line" instead of "in line" when they're waiting their turn, such as at a grocery store or a ticket booth.

Schlep: To carry something heavy or to travel with difficulty. For example, "I had to schlep my suitcase up the stairs."

Noho/Soho: These are neighborhood abbreviations. "Noho" stands for "North of Houston Street," and "Soho" stands for "South of Houston Street." Houston Street itself is pronounced "HOW-ston," not like the city in Texas.

The Village: Short for Greenwich Village, a well-known neighborhood in Manhattan.

The LIRR: Stands for the Long Island Rail Road, a commuter rail service that runs between Manhattan and Long Island.

Cabbie: A slang term for a taxi driver.

Bridge and Tunnel: Refers to people who commute into Manhattan from the outer boroughs or nearby suburbs, often used in a slightly derogatory way.

Understanding these terms can make it easier to follow conversations and directions while in New York City. It also shows that you've taken the time to learn about the local culture, which can endear you to the people you meet.

When it comes to navigating the city, certain phrases are particularly useful. Knowing how to ask for directions, interpret transportation announcements, and handle day-to-day situations will help you get around more efficiently. Here are some phrases that can come in handy while navigating New York City:

Which way is…? This phrase is helpful when you're looking for a specific location or direction. For example, "Which way is Times Square?" or "Which way is the nearest subway station?"

How do I get to…? Use this phrase when you need detailed directions. For instance, "How do I get to the Empire State Building?"

Is this the right train/bus for…? This phrase is essential when using public transportation. For example, "Is this the right train for Grand Central?"

Where do I buy a MetroCard? A MetroCard is the ticket you'll need to ride the subway and buses in New York City.

Can I walk there from here? This phrase is useful when you're trying to determine if a destination is within walking distance.

I need a cab/taxi: If you need to hail a taxi, this phrase will help you get one.

How long will it take? Use this phrase to ask about travel time, whether you're walking, taking a cab, or using public transportation.

What's the fare? Useful when asking about the cost of a taxi ride or a bus ticket.

Can you show me on the map? If you have a map or a phone, this phrase can be helpful when someone is giving you directions.

Where's the nearest bathroom/restroom? Public restrooms can be tricky to find in New York, so knowing this phrase is important.

Being familiar with these phrases will make it easier for you to get around and communicate your needs effectively. Whether you're asking for directions, hailing a cab, or purchasing a MetroCard, these expressions will help you navigate the city with confidence.

Having a good grasp of basic English phrases, local slang, and useful expressions will greatly enhance your experience in New York City. Whether you're asking for directions, ordering food, or simply making small talk, being able to communicate effectively will help you feel more confident and connected to the city. Understanding local slang and expressions can also give you deeper insights into the culture and make your interactions with locals more enjoyable.

Local Language Learning Resources

Learning the local language or improving your English skills can greatly enhance your experience as a tourist in New York City. Whether you're a non-English speaker looking to improve your language proficiency or someone interested in learning another language to connect with the city's diverse communities, New York offers a wealth of resources to help you achieve your goals. From language learning apps to classes, workshops, and online resources, there are many ways to immerse yourself in language learning both before and during your visit.

One of the most convenient and accessible ways to start learning or improving your language skills is through language learning apps. These apps are designed to help you practice speaking, listening, reading, and writing in a new language at your own pace. They are particularly useful for tourists who want to learn on the go, as they can be accessed from your smartphone or tablet. Some of the most popular language learning apps include:

Duolingo is one of the most widely used language learning apps in the world. It offers lessons in over 30 languages, including English, and is known for its user-friendly interface and gamified approach to learning. Duolingo breaks down language learning into small, manageable lessons that focus on vocabulary, grammar, and pronunciation. The app's engaging format, which includes earning points and rewards, makes it easy to stay motivated and track your progress. Duolingo also offers a feature called "Duolingo Stories," which are short, interactive stories designed to help you practice reading and listening in your target language.

Babbel is another highly regarded language learning app that offers lessons in 14 languages, including English. Babbel's lessons are designed by language experts and focus on real-life conversational skills, making it particularly useful for tourists who want to quickly learn practical phrases and expressions. The app's lessons are organized by topics, such as travel, shopping, and dining, allowing you to focus on the areas that are most relevant to your trip. Babbel also offers speech recognition technology to help you practice and improve your pronunciation.

Rosetta Stone is a well-known language learning platform that has been helping people learn new languages for decades. The Rosetta Stone app offers immersive lessons that focus on building a strong foundation in your target language. The app uses a method called "Dynamic Immersion," which teaches you new vocabulary and grammar through context and visual cues, rather than translation. This approach helps you think in the new language and develop your language skills more naturally. Rosetta Stone also offers live tutoring sessions with native speakers, providing an opportunity to practice speaking and get personalized feedback.

Memrise is an app that combines language learning with cultural immersion. It offers courses in a wide range of languages, including English, and focuses on teaching you practical phrases that you can use in real-life situations. Memrise's lessons include videos of native speakers using the language in context, helping you understand the nuances of pronunciation and cultural references. The app also uses spaced repetition to help reinforce your learning and ensure that you retain the new vocabulary and phrases you've learned.

While language learning apps are convenient and effective, there's also great value in taking in-person classes or workshops, especially if you're already in New York City. The city is home to numerous language schools and cultural institutions that offer classes for learners of all levels. These classes provide an opportunity to practice speaking with others, receive feedback from instructors, and immerse yourself in the language in a more structured setting.

One of the top language schools in New York City is the New York Language Center (NYLC). NYLC offers English as a Second Language (ESL) courses for non-native speakers, as well as courses in other languages. The school has multiple locations across Manhattan, Queens, and the Bronx, making it easily accessible to students in different parts of the city. NYLC's courses are designed to improve your speaking, listening, reading, and writing skills, and are available in both intensive and part-time formats. The school also offers cultural activities and excursions, allowing students to practice their language skills in real-world settings.

Another option is Fluent City, a language school that offers a wide range of language courses, including English, Spanish,

French, Italian, and more. Fluent City's courses are designed to be interactive and engaging, with a focus on conversational skills. The school offers small group classes, private lessons, and corporate training, as well as cultural events and workshops that provide additional opportunities for language practice. Fluent City's classes are available both in-person at their Manhattan location and online, making it a flexible option for learners with different schedules.

For those interested in a more cultural approach to language learning, The Instituto Cervantes in Manhattan offers Spanish language courses along with cultural workshops and events. The institute is part of a global network dedicated to promoting the Spanish language and Hispanic cultures, making it an excellent resource for anyone interested in learning Spanish or exploring Hispanic culture in New York City. The courses at Instituto Cervantes are taught by native speakers and cover a range of levels, from beginner to advanced. The institute also offers workshops on topics such as Spanish literature, cinema, and art, providing a deeper understanding of the cultural context in which the language is used.

In addition to classes and workshops, there are many books and online resources that can help you improve your language skills. Phrasebooks are a valuable resource for tourists, offering a quick reference for common phrases and expressions. Publishers like Lonely Planet and Berlitz offer phrasebooks in multiple languages, including English, that are specifically designed for travelers. These phrasebooks typically include sections on greetings, transportation, dining, and shopping, making them a handy tool for navigating everyday situations.

For a more in-depth approach, consider investing in a language textbook. Textbooks provide comprehensive lessons on grammar, vocabulary, and pronunciation, and often include exercises and quizzes to test your knowledge. Some popular English language textbooks for learners include the "English Grammar in Use" series by Raymond Murphy and "The Practice of English Language Teaching" by Jeremy Harmer. These textbooks are widely used in ESL courses and are highly regarded for their clear explanations and practical exercises.

Online resources also offer a wealth of language learning materials. Websites like BBC Learning English and VOA Learning English provide free lessons, articles, and videos designed to help non-native speakers improve their English skills. These resources are particularly useful for practicing listening and reading comprehension, as they often feature news stories, interviews, and other real-world content that can help you get used to the rhythm and flow of English as it's spoken in everyday life.

For those interested in practicing their language skills through reading, graded readers are an excellent option. Graded readers are books that have been adapted for language learners, with simplified vocabulary and grammar that matches your skill level. These books are available in a variety of genres, from classic literature to contemporary fiction, and can help you build your reading skills while enjoying a good story. Many graded readers also include comprehension questions and vocabulary exercises, making them a valuable tool for reinforcing your learning.

Podcasts and YouTube channels are also great resources for language learners. Podcasts like "The English We Speak" from the BBC and "All Ears English" provide short, engaging episodes on everyday English phrases, idioms, and cultural tips. These podcasts are a convenient way to practice listening skills and learn new expressions while on the go. YouTube channels like English Addict with Mr. Duncan and Rachel's English offer video lessons on pronunciation, vocabulary, and grammar, as well as insights into American culture. These videos can be watched at your own pace, allowing you to focus on the areas where you need the most practice.

Finally, language exchange programs offer a unique opportunity to practice speaking with native speakers in a relaxed and informal setting. Websites like ConversationExchange.com and Tandem connect language learners with native speakers around the world for one-on-one language practice. You can arrange to meet up with a language partner in person if you're in New York, or connect online via video chat. These exchanges allow you to practice speaking in a real-world context, ask questions about the language and culture, and make new friends along the way.

Whether you're looking to improve your English skills or learn a new language, New York City offers a wide range of resources to help you achieve your goals. From language learning apps and in-person classes to books, online resources, and language exchanges, there are many ways to immerse yourself in language learning both before and during your visit. By taking advantage of these resources, you can enhance your communication skills, gain a deeper understanding of the local culture, and make the most of your time in New York City. With dedication and practice, you'll be well on your way to becoming a more confident and capable speaker, ready to navigate the city and connect with its diverse communities.

CHAPTER 6

STAYING SAFE AND HEALTHY

Health Care and Safety

When visiting New York City, understanding how to access healthcare and ensure your safety is crucial for a worry-free trip. New York is a bustling metropolis with world-class medical facilities and resources, but as a tourist, navigating the healthcare system and knowing what to do in case of an emergency can be overwhelming. Additionally, being aware of common health concerns for tourists and taking appropriate precautions can help you avoid potential issues and enjoy your time in the city with peace of mind.

Accessing healthcare in New York City is straightforward, but it's important to know where to go and what to expect, especially if you're unfamiliar with the U.S. healthcare system. Unlike some countries with universal healthcare, the U.S. healthcare system is primarily private, and services can be expensive, particularly for those without insurance. As a tourist, having travel insurance that covers medical expenses is highly recommended to protect yourself from unexpected costs. Travel insurance policies typically cover emergency medical treatment, hospital stays, and sometimes even medical evacuation if necessary. Before your trip, review your policy to understand what is covered and how to access healthcare services in the event of illness or injury.

If you need medical attention while in New York City, there are several options available depending on the severity of your condition. For minor health concerns, such as colds, minor injuries, or prescription refills, urgent care clinics are a convenient and cost-effective option. Urgent care centers are walk-in clinics that provide immediate care for non-life-threatening conditions. They are typically open seven days a week, with extended hours, making them accessible outside of regular business hours. Some well-known urgent care providers in New York City include CityMD and MedRite Urgent Care. These clinics are located throughout the city, and many accept international travel insurance or offer affordable self-pay options.

For more serious conditions that require specialized care or diagnostic tests, you may need to visit a hospital emergency room. New York City is home to several top-ranked hospitals, including NewYork-Presbyterian Hospital, NYU Langone Health, and Mount Sinai Hospital. These hospitals offer comprehensive medical services, from emergency care to specialized treatments. If you need to visit an emergency room, be prepared for potentially long wait times, especially during busy periods. Emergency rooms prioritize patients based on the severity of their condition, so those with life-threatening conditions will be seen first.

In the event of a medical emergency, it's important to know how to access emergency services quickly. The emergency number in the United States is 911. You can dial 911 from any phone, including mobile phones, to request emergency assistance, whether it's for a medical emergency, fire, or crime. When you call 911, be prepared to provide your location and a brief description of the emergency. Emergency responders, including paramedics, firefighters, and police, will be dispatched to your location to provide assistance. In most cases, paramedics will transport you to the nearest hospital if you require medical attention.

If you experience a health issue that requires medication, there are numerous pharmacies throughout New York City where you can fill prescriptions or purchase over-the-counter medications. Major pharmacy chains such as CVS, Walgreens, and Duane Reade are conveniently located across the city, often with 24-hour locations. These pharmacies offer a wide range of products, including pain relievers, cold and flu medications, allergy treatments, and first aid supplies. If you need a prescription filled, you can take it to any pharmacy, and most will accept prescriptions from international doctors, though it's a good idea to carry your doctor's contact information in case the pharmacist needs to verify the prescription.

For travelers with chronic health conditions or those who require regular medication, it's important to plan ahead before your trip. Bring an adequate supply of your medication to last the duration of your stay, as well as a copy of your prescription in case you need a refill. Keep your medication in its original packaging, and carry it in your hand luggage to avoid any issues if your checked luggage is delayed or lost. If you have a medical condition that may require emergency treatment, such as diabetes or severe allergies, consider wearing a medical alert bracelet or carrying a medical ID card that details your condition and any necessary treatments.

In addition to knowing how to access healthcare, it's also important to be aware of common health concerns for tourists in New York City. One of the most prevalent issues is jet lag, particularly for travelers arriving from distant time zones. Jet lag can cause fatigue, insomnia, and difficulty concentrating, which can impact your ability to enjoy your trip. To minimize the effects of jet lag, try to adjust your sleep schedule before you travel, stay hydrated during your flight, and spend time outdoors in natural sunlight once you arrive to help reset your internal clock. If you're struggling with jet lag, over-the-counter sleep aids or melatonin supplements may help you adjust.

Another common concern for tourists is gastrointestinal issues related to changes in diet or water. While New York City's tap water is safe to drink and often praised for its quality, some travelers may experience mild digestive issues due to changes in food and drink. To avoid these problems, consider gradually introducing new foods into your diet, especially if you're trying local street food or unfamiliar cuisines. If you do experience stomach discomfort, over-the-counter remedies such as antacids, anti-diarrheal medications, or probiotics can help alleviate symptoms.

Seasonal allergies can also be a concern for visitors to New York City, particularly during the spring and fall when pollen counts are high. If you have a history of allergies, it's a good idea to bring your preferred allergy medication, whether it's an antihistamine, nasal spray, or eye drops. Check the local pollen forecast, which is often included in weather reports, and take your medication as needed to manage symptoms.

For those visiting New York City during the winter months, cold weather-related issues such as hypothermia and frostbite are potential risks, especially during severe cold snaps or blizzards. To protect yourself from the cold, dress in layers, including thermal underwear, a warm coat, gloves, a hat, and a scarf. If you plan to spend time outdoors, take frequent breaks indoors to warm up, and avoid prolonged exposure to extreme cold. Symptoms of hypothermia include shivering, confusion, and drowsiness, while frostbite can cause numbness, tingling, or discoloration of the skin. If you suspect you have hypothermia or frostbite, seek medical attention immediately.

Finally, personal safety is an important aspect of health and well-being while traveling. New York City is generally safe for tourists, but like any major city, it's important to take precautions to protect yourself from potential risks. When exploring the city, stay aware of your surroundings, particularly in crowded areas or at night. Keep your belongings secure, and avoid displaying large amounts of cash or expensive items, such as jewelry or electronics, that could attract attention. If you're using public transportation, be mindful of your belongings and avoid isolated subway stations late at night.

In case of an emergency that involves your personal safety, such as witnessing a crime or needing assistance, don't hesitate to call 911. The police in New York City are well-equipped to handle emergencies and can provide assistance if you're lost, injured, or in danger. It's also a good idea to know the location of the nearest police station, particularly if you're staying in the city for an extended period.

Being well-prepared for health and safety concerns during your trip to New York City will help ensure that your visit is both enjoyable and stress-free. By understanding how to access healthcare, knowing what to do in case of an emergency, and being aware of common health concerns, you can protect yourself from potential risks and focus on making the most of your time in the city. Whether you're dealing with minor health issues, navigating the healthcare system, or simply taking precautions to stay safe, having the right information and resources at your disposal will give you the confidence to explore New York City with peace of mind.

Emergency Contacts and Numbers

When traveling to New York City, being prepared with important emergency contacts and numbers is a critical aspect of ensuring your safety and well-being. While it's unlikely that you'll encounter a serious emergency during your visit, knowing how to quickly access help if needed can provide peace of mind and allow you to focus on enjoying your trip.

One of the most important things to remember when visiting New York City is the emergency phone number in the United States, which is 911. This number is used nationwide for emergencies, and you can call it from any phone, including mobile phones, even if you don't have a U.S. phone plan or your phone is locked. Dialing 911 will connect you to an emergency operator who will ask for details about your situation and dispatch the appropriate services, whether it's the police, ambulance, or fire department. It's crucial to only use 911 for true emergencies, such as life-threatening situations, serious injuries, fires, or crimes in progress. If you're unsure whether your situation constitutes an emergency, it's better to err on the side of caution and call. The operator can determine the severity of the situation and advise you accordingly.

When you call 911, the operator will typically ask for your location first, so it's important to know where you are or be able to describe your surroundings accurately. If you're in a public place, look for street signs, landmarks, or nearby businesses that can help identify your location. The operator will also ask for a brief description of the emergency, so be prepared to clearly and calmly explain what has happened. For example, if someone is injured, provide details about their condition, such as whether they are conscious, breathing, or bleeding. If you're reporting a fire, describe the location and whether anyone is inside the building. The more information you can provide, the better equipped the emergency responders will be to handle the situation.

In addition to 911, there are other important phone numbers you should have on hand during your visit to New York City. These include non-emergency numbers that can be useful for situations that don't require immediate assistance but still need attention. For example, the non-emergency number for the New York City Police Department (NYPD) is 311. This number can be used to report non-urgent issues such as noise complaints, minor accidents, or lost property. Calling 311 will connect you to a city operator who can assist with a wide range of municipal services and provide information on various city resources.

If you need to contact the police but it's not an emergency, you can also visit the nearest police precinct. New York City is divided into precincts, each with its own station and officers. You can find the closest precinct by searching online or asking a local. The precincts are open 24 hours a day, and you can visit them to file a report, seek assistance, or get information.

For medical emergencies that don't require calling 911, it's helpful to know the phone numbers of nearby hospitals or urgent care centers. Some of the major hospitals in New York City include NewYork-Presbyterian Hospital (phone: 212-746-5454), NYU Langone Health (phone: 212-263-7300), and Mount Sinai Hospital (phone: 212-241-6500). These hospitals are equipped to handle a wide range of medical emergencies and have emergency rooms that are open 24/7. If you need non-emergency medical care, such as treatment for minor injuries or illnesses, you can visit an urgent care center. Some well-known urgent care providers in New York City include CityMD and MedRite Urgent Care, both of which have multiple locations across the city.

For tourists, having access to embassy or consulate contact information is also essential. Embassies and consulates can provide assistance in various situations, such as if you lose your passport, need legal advice, or require emergency evacuation due to a natural disaster or political unrest. They can also assist with issues related to visas, travel documentation, and contacting family members in your home country. It's a good idea to locate the nearest embassy or consulate for your country before you travel and keep their contact information with you at all times.

For example, the Consulate General of the United Kingdom is located in Manhattan at 845 Third Avenue, New York, NY 10022, and their phone number is +1 212-745-0200. The Consulate General of Canada is located at 466 Lexington Avenue, 20th Floor, New York, NY 10017, and their phone number is +1 212-596-1700. The Consulate General of Australia is located at 150 East 42nd Street, 34th Floor, New York, NY 10017, and their phone number is +1 212-351-6500. Many other countries have consulates in New York City, and it's important to know where yours is located and how to reach them in case of an emergency.

In addition to having these phone numbers on hand, it's wise to have a plan for how you'll contact people in an emergency, especially if you're traveling with others. Make sure everyone in your group knows the emergency contact numbers and what to do if they get separated from the group or find themselves in an emergency situation. It's also a good idea to have a designated meeting spot in case you lose contact with each other, particularly if you're visiting a large, crowded area like Times Square or Central Park.

If you're using a mobile phone while in New York City, ensure that it's set up to make local calls. If you're using an international phone, check with your service provider before you leave to confirm that your phone will work in the U.S. and that you understand any potential charges for international roaming. Alternatively, you can purchase a local SIM card or use a global SIM card to make calls and access data while in New York.

Lastly, be aware of the importance of keeping a list of emergency contacts with you, including the contact information for friends or family members who should be notified if something happens to you. This list should include their phone numbers, email addresses, and any other relevant details. In addition, consider carrying a copy of your identification, such as your passport or driver's license, in case you lose your original documents.

Being prepared with the right emergency contacts and numbers can make all the difference in ensuring your safety and well-being while visiting New York City. By knowing how to contact emergency services, having important phone numbers on hand, and keeping embassy and consulate contact information readily available, you can navigate any situation that arises with confidence. Whether you're dealing with a medical emergency, reporting a crime, or seeking assistance from your embassy, having this information at your fingertips will help you respond quickly and effectively, allowing you to focus on enjoying your time in the city.

Weather-Related Safety Tips

When visiting New York City, it's essential to be prepared for the wide range of weather conditions that can occur throughout the year. The city experiences all four seasons, each with its own unique challenges, from the cold and snow of winter to the heat and humidity of summer. Being aware of these conditions and knowing how to stay safe can make your trip more enjoyable and help you avoid potential risks.

Preparing for the various weather conditions in New York City begins with understanding the seasonal climate patterns. New York's weather can change quickly, so it's important to pack accordingly and stay informed about the forecast during your stay. In general, the city experiences cold winters, mild to cool springs, warm and humid summers, and crisp autumns. Each season requires different preparations to ensure your comfort and safety.

Winter in New York City, typically from December through February, can be harsh, with temperatures often dropping below freezing. Snow, ice, and wind chill are common, making it necessary to dress warmly and take precautions against the cold. The key to staying warm in winter is layering your clothing. Start with a moisture-wicking base layer, such as thermal underwear, to keep sweat away from your skin. Add an insulating layer, like a sweater or fleece, to retain body heat, and finish with a waterproof and windproof outer layer, such as a down coat or parka, to protect against the elements. Accessories like a warm hat, gloves, scarf, and insulated boots are also essential for keeping extremities warm and dry.

Snow and ice can create slippery conditions on sidewalks and streets, so wearing appropriate footwear with good traction is important to prevent slips and falls. Consider bringing or purchasing ice cleats that can be attached to your shoes for added grip in icy conditions. When walking on snow or ice, take shorter steps, keep your center of gravity over your feet, and use handrails when available.

Winter storms, including snowstorms and blizzards, can occasionally disrupt travel plans and daily activities in New

York City. These storms can bring heavy snowfall, strong winds, and dangerously low temperatures. During a winter storm, it's important to stay indoors as much as possible. If you must go outside, limit your time in the cold, and seek shelter if you start to feel cold or wet. Frostbite and hypothermia are serious risks during extreme cold, so be aware of the symptoms, such as numbness, shivering, confusion, and drowsiness, and seek medical attention if necessary.

In addition to dressing appropriately, it's also important to stay informed about the weather forecast, especially during the winter months. Check local news or weather apps regularly for updates on storms, temperature changes, and travel advisories. New York City's Office of Emergency Management (OEM) provides real-time information on weather conditions, emergency alerts, and safety tips. You can sign up for emergency notifications through the city's Notify NYC service, which sends alerts via text message, email, or phone.

As the weather warms up in the spring, typically from March to May, the risk of snow diminishes, but rain becomes more common. Spring temperatures in New York City can vary widely, with mild days followed by chilly nights. It's important to dress in layers during this season, as the weather can change throughout the day. A lightweight jacket or raincoat, along with an umbrella, is advisable for unexpected rain showers. Spring in New York can also bring windy conditions, so be prepared for gusts, especially near tall buildings and along the waterfront.

Summer in New York City, from June through August, can be hot and humid, with temperatures often reaching the 80s and 90s Fahrenheit (27-35°C). Heatwaves, which are extended periods of unusually high temperatures, can pose significant health risks, particularly for those not accustomed to such conditions. To stay safe during a heatwave, it's important to stay hydrated by drinking plenty of water throughout the day. Avoid sugary drinks, caffeine, and alcohol, as they can contribute to dehydration. Carry a reusable water bottle with you, and refill it frequently at water fountains or cafes.

Wearing lightweight, breathable clothing is essential for staying cool in the summer heat. Choose fabrics like cotton or linen that allow air to circulate and help wick moisture away from your skin. A wide-brimmed hat and sunglasses can provide additional protection from the sun's rays, and applying sunscreen with a high SPF will help prevent sunburn. If you plan to spend extended time outdoors, seek shade whenever possible, especially during the peak heat of the day, typically between 10 a.m. and 4 p.m.

Heat exhaustion and heatstroke are serious conditions that can result from prolonged exposure to high temperatures. Symptoms of heat exhaustion include heavy sweating, weakness, dizziness, nausea, and headache. If you or someone else experiences these symptoms, move to a cooler place, drink water, and rest. If symptoms worsen or if the person becomes disoriented or loses consciousness, seek medical attention immediately, as this could indicate heatstroke, a life-threatening emergency.

Public spaces in New York City, such as parks and outdoor attractions, can become crowded during the summer months. When visiting these areas, be mindful of the heat and take breaks indoors in air-conditioned spaces like museums, shops, or restaurants. Many public buildings, including libraries and community centers, offer cooling centers where you can escape the heat. These centers are open to the public during heatwaves and provide a cool place to rest and rehydrate.

In the fall, from September through November, temperatures begin to cool, and the humidity decreases, making it one of the most pleasant times to visit New York City. However, fall weather can be unpredictable, with warm days followed by chilly evenings. Dressing in layers is once again advisable, as it allows you to adjust to the changing temperatures throughout the day. A light jacket or sweater is usually sufficient for most fall days, but be prepared for cooler temperatures as the season progresses.

Fall is also hurricane season on the East Coast, which runs from June through November, with the peak occurring in September and October. While hurricanes are relatively rare in New York City, they can happen, and it's important to be prepared. If a hurricane or tropical storm is forecasted, stay informed by monitoring weather reports and following any advisories or evacuation orders issued by local authorities. The city's OEM provides guidance on how to prepare for hurricanes, including creating an emergency plan, assembling a supply kit, and knowing the location of evacuation centers.

Being prepared for New York City's diverse weather conditions is key to ensuring your safety and comfort during your visit. By dressing appropriately, staying informed about the weather forecast, and taking precautions during extreme conditions like winter storms or heatwaves, you can enjoy all that the city has to offer without unnecessary risks. Whether you're navigating the cold of winter, the heat of summer, or the unpredictable weather of spring and fall, being well-prepared will allow you to make the most of your time in New York City, no matter what the weather brings.

Responsible Tourism

Visiting New York City offers a unique opportunity to explore a vibrant, diverse, and culturally rich metropolis. However, with this opportunity comes the responsibility to ensure that your actions as a tourist positively impact the environment, local communities, and the overall experience of the city. Responsible tourism in New York City involves being mindful of how your presence affects the city's resources, respecting the local culture and residents, supporting the economy by choosing local businesses, and adopting eco-friendly practices throughout your visit. By approaching your trip with these principles in mind, you can contribute to the sustainability and well-being of the city while enjoying a more meaningful and enriching travel experience.

One of the most important aspects of responsible tourism is respecting the environment and local communities. New York City, like any major urban center, faces challenges related to waste management, pollution, and the preservation of green spaces. As a visitor, you can play a role in mitigating these challenges by making conscious choices that reduce your environmental footprint. For instance, one of the simplest yet most impactful actions you can take is to be mindful of your waste. New York City has a comprehensive recycling program, with separate bins for paper, metal, glass, and plastic. Take the time to sort your waste correctly and dispose of it in the appropriate bins. Avoid littering at all costs, as it not only pollutes the environment but also detracts from the beauty and cleanliness of public spaces.

When visiting parks, gardens, and other natural areas, such as Central Park, the High Line, or the Brooklyn Botanic Garden, respect the rules and guidelines established to protect these spaces. Stay on designated paths, avoid picking flowers or plants, and do not feed wildlife. These guidelines help preserve the natural beauty and ecological balance of these areas, ensuring they remain enjoyable for future visitors. Additionally, consider participating in volunteer activities, such as park clean-up events or tree planting, which allow you to give back to the environment while enhancing your travel experience.

Being respectful of local communities is also essential to responsible tourism. New York City is home to a diverse population, with residents from all walks of life and cultural backgrounds. As a visitor, it's important to be mindful of how your behavior and actions impact those who live and work in the city. This includes being aware of noise levels, particularly in residential areas, and respecting the privacy and space of local residents. Avoid blocking sidewalks or building entrances, and be considerate when taking photographs, especially in residential neighborhoods. Always ask for permission before photographing people, especially if they are performing their work, such as street vendors or artists.

Supporting local businesses is another key component of responsible tourism. New York City is renowned for its small businesses, which are the backbone of the local economy and contribute to the city's unique character. By choosing to eat at local restaurants, shop at independent boutiques, and visit neighborhood markets, you are directly contributing to the livelihoods of local entrepreneurs and helping to sustain the city's vibrant culture. Whether you're enjoying a meal at a family-owned diner, purchasing a handmade item from a local artisan, or staying at a boutique hotel, your spending choices have a direct impact on the community.

Food is an integral part of New York City's culture, and supporting local eateries is a great way to immerse yourself in the city's culinary diversity while practicing responsible tourism. Instead of dining at chain restaurants, seek out neighborhood spots that serve authentic cuisine, such as a pizzeria in Little Italy, a deli in the Lower East Side, or a food truck in Queens offering dishes from around the world. These establishments often use locally sourced ingredients and employ local staff, making them a sustainable choice. Additionally, exploring local food markets like Union Square Greenmarket or Smorgasburg allows you to sample fresh, seasonal produce while supporting local farmers and producers.

Shopping at local businesses also extends to purchasing souvenirs and gifts. Rather than buying mass-produced items, look for unique, locally made products that reflect the city's creativity and craftsmanship. Many neighborhoods, such as Greenwich Village, Williamsburg, and SoHo, are known for their independent shops and galleries where you can find everything from handmade jewelry and clothing to original artwork and vintage goods. By choosing these one-of-a-kind items, you not only take home a meaningful memento of your trip but also support the city's artisans and creative community.

Eco-friendly travel tips are an essential part of practicing responsible tourism. Reducing your carbon footprint while exploring New York City not only benefits the environment but also enhances your overall experience by encouraging a slower, more thoughtful approach to travel. One of the most effective ways to minimize your environmental impact is by using public transportation. New York City's extensive subway and bus system is one of the most efficient and environmentally friendly ways to get around. The subway system, in particular, is powered by electricity, making it a lower-emission option compared to driving or taking taxis. Additionally, walking and biking are excellent ways to explore the city's neighborhoods, allowing you to experience the local culture and architecture up close while reducing your carbon footprint.

If you plan to rent a vehicle for part of your trip, consider choosing a hybrid or electric car to reduce your emissions. Many car rental companies in New York City offer eco-friendly vehicle options, and some hotels even provide charging stations for electric cars. When driving, try to carpool if possible, and plan your routes to minimize fuel consumption. Additionally, avoid idling your vehicle, as this contributes to unnecessary pollution.

Reducing energy and water consumption during your stay is another important aspect of eco-friendly travel. Simple actions, such as turning off lights, air conditioning, and electronics when not in use, can significantly reduce your energy footprint. Many hotels in New York City have adopted sustainable practices, such as using energy-efficient lighting, offering towel and linen reuse programs, and installing low-flow showerheads and faucets. Participating in these programs not only conserves resources but also supports the hotel's commitment to sustainability.

When it comes to water conservation, be mindful of your water usage by taking shorter showers, turning off the tap while brushing your teeth, and reusing towels. New York City's tap water is safe to drink, so consider bringing a reusable water bottle to refill throughout the day instead of purchasing bottled water. This reduces plastic waste and helps protect the environment.

Another way to practice responsible tourism is by reducing waste, particularly single-use plastics. Carrying a reusable shopping bag, coffee cup, and utensils can significantly decrease the amount of waste you generate during your trip. Many cafes and food vendors in New York City offer discounts for customers who bring their own cups or containers, making it both an eco-friendly and cost-effective choice. Additionally, avoid using plastic straws, and opt for biodegradable or reusable alternatives instead.

Participating in local environmental initiatives is a meaningful way to engage with the community and contribute to the city's sustainability efforts. New York City has numerous organizations dedicated to environmental conservation, urban gardening, and sustainable living. Volunteering with groups like the New York Restoration Project, which works to restore and maintain public green spaces, or GrowNYC, which promotes recycling and composting, allows you to give back to the city while learning more about its environmental challenges and solutions.

Finally, consider the impact of your travel choices beyond your time in New York City. Being a responsible tourist means thinking about how your actions affect not only the destination you visit but also the broader environment. This includes making conscious decisions about the mode of transportation you use to reach your destination, supporting sustainable tourism practices, and advocating for responsible travel in your own community. By sharing your experiences and encouraging others to adopt eco-friendly and community-focused travel habits, you can help promote a more sustainable and responsible approach to tourism worldwide.

In conclusion, responsible tourism in New York City involves making thoughtful choices that respect the environment, support local communities, and promote sustainability. By being mindful of your actions, whether it's reducing waste, supporting local businesses, or participating in eco-friendly travel practices, you can contribute to the city's well-being and ensure that it remains a vibrant and welcoming destination for future generations. Your commitment to responsible tourism not only enhances your own travel experience but also helps protect and preserve the unique character and beauty of New York City.

Travel Scams and How to Avoid Them

When visiting New York City, it's essential to be aware of the potential for travel scams that target tourists. While the city is generally safe and welcoming, it, like many other major tourist destinations, attracts individuals looking to take advantage of unsuspecting visitors. Understanding the types of scams that are common in New York City, learning how to recognize them, and knowing what to do if you fall victim to a scam are all crucial aspects of ensuring a safe and enjoyable trip.

Travel scams can take many forms, ranging from small-scale cons to more elaborate schemes. These scams often prey on the unfamiliarity of tourists with the local environment, taking advantage of their eagerness to explore the city and their potential lack of awareness about certain risks. To avoid falling victim to these scams, it's important to educate yourself about the most common types of scams targeting tourists in New York City and to develop strategies for recognizing and avoiding them.

One of the most common scams in New York City involves phony taxi drivers. These individuals often wait outside major transportation hubs, such as airports, train stations, and bus terminals, offering rides to tourists who may be unfamiliar with the city's official taxi system. They may approach you directly, offering a ride at a seemingly reasonable rate, but once you're in the vehicle, the fare may suddenly increase, or they may take a longer route to inflate the cost. To avoid this scam, always use official yellow cabs, which are easily recognizable and regulated by the city. Look for the taxi's medallion number displayed on the roof, and ensure that the driver starts the meter as soon as your journey begins. Alternatively, you can use ride-sharing apps like Uber or Lyft, which allow you to track your ride and know the cost upfront.

Another scam that targets tourists in New York City is the fake ticket seller scam. This often occurs near popular attractions such as Broadway theaters, museums, or sightseeing tours, where individuals may offer to sell you discounted or last-minute tickets. While the offer may seem like a great deal, the tickets are often counterfeit or invalid. To avoid this scam, always purchase tickets from official vendors, either directly at the box office, through authorized websites, or from reputable third-party sellers. Be cautious of anyone selling tickets on the street, as these are rarely legitimate.

Street performers and "characters" posing for photos in popular tourist areas like Times Square can also be a source of scams. While many street performers and costumed characters are legitimate entertainers who earn a living through tips, some may pressure or even demand money from tourists after posing for a photo, sometimes asking for an exorbitant amount. If you choose to take a photo with a street performer or character, be sure to ask beforehand if a tip is expected and how much. It's best to agree on a reasonable amount before taking the photo to avoid any misunderstandings or pressure tactics.

Pickpocketing is another risk that tourists should be aware of in crowded areas such as subway stations, busy streets, and popular attractions. Pickpockets often work in teams and use distraction techniques to divert your attention while they steal your belongings. Common tactics include bumping into you, creating a commotion, or asking for directions. To protect yourself, keep your belongings secure by using a crossbody bag or a money belt worn under your clothing. Avoid keeping valuables in easily accessible pockets, and be especially cautious when someone gets too close or tries to engage you in conversation in a crowded area.

Another scam that tourists should be aware of is the fake charity collector. Scammers posing as charity workers may approach you on the street, in subway stations, or near tourist attractions, asking for donations to support a cause. They may carry fake identification or display materials that look legitimate, but the money collected often goes directly into their pockets. To avoid this scam, if you wish to donate to a charity, do so through official channels or reputable organizations that you can verify. Be cautious of anyone asking for donations on the street, especially if they are insistent or use guilt tactics.

ATM and credit card skimming is a more sophisticated scam that involves tampering with ATM machines or credit card readers to steal your card information. Skimmers, devices that capture card data, are often placed over the legitimate card slot, making them difficult to detect. To protect yourself from this scam, use ATMs located inside banks or well-lit, busy areas, as these are less likely to be tampered with. Before using an ATM, inspect the card slot for any loose or suspicious-looking attachments, and cover the keypad with your hand when entering your PIN. If possible, use contactless payment methods like Apple Pay or Google Pay, which reduce the risk of your card information being compromised.

Fake tour guides are another common scam targeting tourists in New York City. These individuals may approach you near popular landmarks, offering guided tours at a discounted rate. However, the tours they provide are often of poor quality, and they may take you to locations where they receive kickbacks from certain businesses. To avoid this scam, book tours through reputable companies or your hotel, and be wary of anyone offering tours on the street without proper credentials.

Recognizing and avoiding scams requires a combination of awareness, caution, and skepticism. Trust your instincts—if something feels off or too good to be true, it probably is. Be cautious of offers that seem unusually cheap, free, or urgent, as scammers often use these tactics to lure in unsuspecting victims. When approached by someone on the street offering services or asking for money, it's okay to say no and walk away.

If you do fall victim to a scam, it's important to take immediate action. First, try to remain calm and assess the situation. If you've been scammed out of money or belongings, contact the local authorities by calling 911 to report the incident. Provide as much information as possible, including a description of the scammer, the location, and any other relevant details. The police can help you file a report, which may be necessary for insurance claims or further investigation.

If your credit card information has been compromised, contact your bank or credit card company immediately to report the fraudulent activity and have your card canceled. Many credit card companies offer fraud protection, which can help you recover lost funds or prevent further unauthorized charges. If you suspect that an ATM has been tampered with, notify the bank or business where the ATM is located, and consider filing a report with the police.

In the case of identity theft or other serious scams, you may also need to report the incident to additional authorities, such as the Federal Trade Commission (FTC) in the United States. The FTC provides resources and guidance for victims of identity theft, including steps to protect your personal information and credit.

While New York City is a vibrant and exciting destination, it's important to be aware of potential travel scams that can target tourists. By educating yourself about common scams, recognizing red flags, and taking steps to protect yourself, you can minimize the risk of falling victim to these schemes. Should you encounter a scam, knowing how to respond and where to seek help will ensure that you can address the situation effectively and continue to enjoy your visit. Responsible and informed travel is key to making the most of your time in New York City while keeping yourself and your belongings safe.

CHAPTER 7

WHERE TO STAY IN NEW YORK CITY

Accommodations (by traveler type, price, and location)

Budget-Friendly Hostels and Hotels

Finding budget-friendly accommodations in New York City can seem challenging, given the city's reputation for high prices. However, with some careful planning and research, you can discover a range of affordable hostels and hotels that offer comfortable stays without breaking the bank. These options not only provide a place to rest after a day of exploring but also offer a variety of amenities and conveniences that enhance your overall experience.

One of the popular budget-friendly options in New York City is The Local NYC, a hostel located in Long Island City, Queens. This hostel is known for its modern design, friendly atmosphere, and convenient location just a short subway ride from Manhattan. The price range for dormitory-style rooms at The Local NYC typically falls between $50 and $80 per night, depending on the season and room type. Private rooms are also available, with rates starting around $150 per night. The Local NYC offers amenities such as free Wi-Fi, a rooftop terrace with stunning views of the city skyline, a communal kitchen, and a bar and café on-site. Guests can also take advantage of the hostel's social events, which include movie nights, trivia, and live music performances.

To reach The Local NYC from major airports, travelers arriving at John F. Kennedy International Airport (JFK) can take the AirTrain to Jamaica Station, then transfer to the E subway line toward Manhattan, getting off at Court Square-23rd Street. From there, it's a short walk to the hostel. Those arriving at LaGuardia Airport (LGA) can take the Q70 bus to Jackson Heights-Roosevelt Avenue, then transfer to the E subway line, following the same directions to Court Square-23rd Street. If you're arriving at Newark Liberty International Airport (EWR), you can take the AirTrain to Newark Liberty Airport Station, then catch an NJ Transit train to Penn Station in Manhattan. From Penn Station, take the E subway line to Court Square-23rd Street.

Booking a stay at The Local NYC can be done directly through the hostel's website, where you'll often find the best rates and availability. You can also book through popular travel websites such as Booking.com, Hostelworld, or Expedia, which offer customer reviews and additional booking options.

Another budget-friendly accommodation option in New York City is HI New York City Hostel, part of Hostelling International's global network. Located on the Upper West Side of Manhattan, this hostel is housed in a historic building and offers a range of affordable dormitory-style rooms, with prices starting around $50 per night. Private rooms are also available, with rates typically starting at $120 per night. The hostel provides a variety of amenities, including free Wi-Fi, a large outdoor patio, a communal kitchen, and organized activities such as walking tours, pub crawls, and comedy nights. HI New York City Hostel is especially popular among solo travelers and groups looking to meet other tourists.

To get to HI New York City Hostel from JFK Airport, you can take the AirTrain to Howard Beach, then transfer to the A subway line toward Manhattan. Get off at 59th Street-Columbus Circle, then transfer to the 1 subway line, getting off at 103rd Street. The hostel is a short walk from the station. From LGA Airport, take the M60 bus to 125th Street and Broadway, then transfer to the 1 subway line and get off at 103rd Street. If arriving from EWR Airport, take the AirTrain to Newark Liberty Airport Station, then take an NJ Transit train to Penn Station. From Penn Station, take the 1 subway line to 103rd Street.

You can book a stay at HI New York City Hostel through the official Hostelling International website, where you can also sign up for a membership to receive discounts on your stay. Additionally, the hostel is listed on major booking platforms like Hostelworld and Booking.com, which allow you to compare prices and read reviews from other travelers.

For those seeking a budget-friendly hotel rather than a hostel, Pod 51 is an excellent option. Located in Midtown Manhattan, Pod 51 offers compact, efficiently designed rooms at an affordable price, with rates typically ranging from $100 to $200 per night, depending on the room type and season. The hotel features amenities such as free Wi-Fi, a rooftop garden with city views, a communal lounge, and an on-site café. Pod 51 is particularly well-suited for travelers who prioritize location and convenience, as it is within walking distance of major attractions like Rockefeller Center, Times Square, and the Museum of Modern Art.

To reach Pod 51 from JFK Airport, take the AirTrain to Jamaica Station, then transfer to the E subway line toward Manhattan. Get off at Lexington Avenue-53rd Street, and the hotel is a short walk from the station. From LGA Airport, take the Q70 bus to Jackson Heights-Roosevelt Avenue, then transfer to the E subway line, following the same directions to Lexington Avenue-53rd Street. For travelers arriving at EWR Airport, take the AirTrain to Newark Liberty Airport Station, then take an NJ Transit train to Penn Station. From Penn Station, take the E subway line to Lexington Avenue-53rd Street.

Pod 51 can be booked directly through the hotel's website, where you can find special offers and package deals. It's also available on major booking sites such as Expedia, Booking.com, and Hotels.com, where you can compare rates and read reviews.

Another budget-friendly hotel in New York City is The Jane Hotel, located in the trendy West Village neighborhood. The Jane Hotel is known for its historic charm and unique room design, inspired by ship cabins. Rooms at The Jane are small but affordable, with rates starting around $100 per night for a single cabin. The hotel offers amenities such as free Wi-Fi, a rooftop bar with views of the Hudson River, and bike rentals for exploring the city. The Jane Hotel is a great choice for travelers who appreciate historic architecture and want to stay in a vibrant, artsy neighborhood.

To get to The Jane Hotel from JFK Airport, take the AirTrain to Howard Beach, then transfer to the A subway line toward Manhattan. Get off at 14th Street, then transfer to the L subway line and get off at 8th Avenue. The hotel is a short walk from the station. From LGA Airport, take the M60 bus to Astoria-Ditmars Boulevard, then transfer to the N subway line, getting off at 8th Avenue. If arriving from EWR Airport, take the AirTrain to Newark Liberty Airport Station, then take an NJ Transit train to Penn Station. From Penn Station, take the 1 subway line to 14th Street, then walk or take a taxi to the hotel.

Booking a stay at The Jane Hotel can be done directly through the hotel's website, where you may find exclusive deals and promotions. It's also available on travel booking platforms like Booking.com and Expedia, where you can read guest reviews and compare prices.

Lastly, The Bowery House offers a unique budget-friendly option in the Nolita neighborhood of Manhattan. This hostel-style accommodation features cabin-like rooms and a rooftop garden with views of the city. Prices for single cabins typically start around $60 per night, with larger rooms available at higher rates. The Bowery House provides amenities such as free Wi-Fi, a communal lounge, and a café. The hostel's location in Nolita, known for its boutique shops, restaurants, and art galleries, makes it an ideal choice for travelers who want to experience New York City's creative scene.

To reach The Bowery House from JFK Airport, take the AirTrain to Howard Beach, then transfer to the A subway line toward Manhattan. Get off at West 4th Street-Washington Square, then transfer to the F subway line and get off at 2nd Avenue. The hostel is a short walk from the station. From LGA Airport, take the Q70 bus to Jackson Heights-Roosevelt Avenue, then transfer to the F subway line, following the same directions to 2nd Avenue. If arriving from EWR Airport, take the AirTrain to Newark Liberty Airport Station, then take an NJ Transit train to Penn Station. From Penn Station, take the 1 subway line to 14th Street, then transfer to the F subway line to 2nd Avenue.

You can book a stay at The Bowery House through their official website, where you may find discounted rates for longer stays. The hostel is also listed on popular booking sites like Hostelworld and Booking.com, where you can compare prices and read reviews from other travelers.

New York City offers a variety of budget-friendly hostels and hotels that cater to different preferences and needs. Whether you're looking for a social atmosphere, historic charm, or a convenient location, there are affordable options available that provide comfort and value. By choosing accommodations that align with your budget, you can enjoy all that New York City has to offer without overspending. When booking, consider using the hotel or hostel's official website for the best rates, or compare prices on major booking platforms to ensure you're getting the best deal. With the right planning, you can find a comfortable and budget-friendly place to stay while exploring the vibrant and diverse city of New York.

Mid-Range Hotels and B&Bs

Finding the perfect accommodation in New York City can significantly enhance your travel experience, especially when you're looking for something that offers a balance between comfort, amenities, and cost. Mid-range hotels and bed and breakfasts (B&Bs) provide an excellent option for travelers who want to enjoy a comfortable stay with additional perks without venturing into the higher price brackets typical of luxury accommodations. These options offer a great combination of value and quality, allowing you to enjoy your time in the city while staying within your budget. In this detailed explanation, you will find information about five mid-range hotels and B&Bs in New York City, including their price ranges, amenities, locations, and how to get there from the major airports.

One excellent mid-range option in New York City is the Arlo NoMad, located in the bustling NoMad (North of Madison Square Park) neighborhood of Manhattan. This boutique hotel offers modern, compact rooms with a focus on smart design and functionality. The price range for a stay at Arlo NoMad typically falls between $200 and $300 per night, depending on the season and room type. The hotel features a rooftop bar with stunning views of the Empire State Building, a cozy lobby lounge, and complimentary Wi-Fi throughout the property. Guests can also enjoy the hotel's on-site restaurant, which serves a variety of locally sourced dishes. The rooms are thoughtfully designed with comfortable bedding, rain showers, and floor-to-ceiling windows that provide plenty of natural light and city views.

To reach Arlo NoMad from John F. Kennedy International Airport (JFK), you can take the AirTrain to Jamaica Station, then transfer to the E subway line toward Manhattan. Get off at 34th Street-Herald Square, and the hotel is a short walk from the station. From LaGuardia Airport (LGA), take the Q70 bus to Jackson Heights-Roosevelt Avenue, then transfer to the F subway line and get off at 34th Street-Herald Square. If arriving from Newark Liberty International Airport (EWR), take the AirTrain to Newark Liberty Airport Station, then take an NJ Transit train to Penn Station. From Penn Station, you can either walk to the hotel, which is about 10 minutes away, or take a short taxi ride.

Booking a stay at Arlo NoMad can be done directly through the hotel's official website, where you may find exclusive offers and package deals. Additionally, the hotel is listed on major booking platforms like Expedia, Booking.com, and Hotels.com, where you can compare prices and read reviews from other travelers.

Another great mid-range option is the Hotel Edison, a historic hotel located in the heart of the Theater District, just steps away from Times Square. The Hotel Edison offers a range of room types, from standard rooms to suites, with prices typically ranging from $180 to $350 per night. The hotel features Art Deco design elements, a 24-hour fitness center, and two on-site restaurants, including Bond 45, which serves Italian-American cuisine. Guests can also enjoy live jazz music in the hotel's lobby bar, The Rum House, which adds to the hotel's classic New York charm. The rooms at Hotel Edison are spacious and well-appointed, with modern amenities such as flat-screen TVs, complimentary Wi-Fi, and plush bedding.

To get to Hotel Edison from JFK Airport, take the AirTrain to Jamaica Station, then transfer to the E subway line toward Manhattan. Get off at 50th Street, and the hotel is just a short walk from the station. From LGA Airport, take the Q70 bus to Jackson Heights-Roosevelt Avenue, then transfer to the E subway line, following the same directions to 50th Street. If arriving from EWR Airport, take the AirTrain to Newark Liberty Airport Station, then take an NJ Transit train to Penn Station. From Penn Station, take the 1 subway line to 50th Street, or take a quick taxi ride to the hotel.

You can book a stay at Hotel Edison through the hotel's official website, where you can often find special discounts for direct bookings. The hotel is also available on popular travel booking websites like Booking.com, Expedia, and Hotels.com, where you can check availability and compare prices.

For those seeking a more intimate and personalized experience, Incentra Village House in the West Village is a charming B&B-style accommodation that offers a cozy retreat in one of Manhattan's most desirable neighborhoods. The price range for a stay at Incentra Village House typically falls between $250 and $350 per night, depending on the room type and season. This historic 19th-century guesthouse features individually decorated rooms with antique furnishings, private bathrooms, and kitchenettes, providing a home-like atmosphere. The B&B also offers complimentary Wi-Fi, daily housekeeping, and a small garden courtyard where guests can relax. The West Village location is perfect for exploring nearby attractions, such as the High Line, Washington Square Park, and the vibrant dining and shopping scene of Greenwich Village.

To reach Incentra Village House from JFK Airport, take the AirTrain to Jamaica Station, then transfer to the E subway line toward Manhattan. Get off at 14th Street, and from there, it's a short walk to the guesthouse. From LGA Airport, take the Q70 bus to Jackson Heights-Roosevelt Avenue, then transfer to the F subway line and get off at 14th Street. If arriving from EWR Airport, take the AirTrain to Newark Liberty Airport Station, then take an NJ Transit train to Penn Station. From Penn Station, you can take a taxi to the guesthouse or take the 1 subway line to 14th Street.

Booking a stay at Incentra Village House is best done directly through their official website, where you can check availability and make reservations. The B&B is also listed on Booking.com and Expedia, where you can read reviews and compare rates.

Another excellent mid-range hotel option is the Hotel Giraffe by Library Hotel Collection, located in the Flatiron District. This boutique hotel offers a combination of luxury and affordability, with room rates typically ranging from $250 to $400 per night. Hotel Giraffe is known for its elegant décor, complimentary continental breakfast, and evening wine and cheese receptions, making it a popular choice for both leisure and business travelers. The hotel also features a rooftop garden, a fitness center, and free Wi-Fi throughout the property. The spacious rooms are designed with a warm, modern aesthetic and include amenities such as plush bedding, flat-screen TVs, and marble bathrooms.

To get to Hotel Giraffe from JFK Airport, take the AirTrain to Jamaica Station, then transfer to the E subway line toward Manhattan. Get off at 23rd Street, and the hotel is a short walk from the station. From LGA Airport, take the Q70 bus to Jackson Heights-Roosevelt Avenue, then transfer to the 7-subway line and get off at 5th Avenue-Bryant Park. From there, it's a short taxi ride or a walk to the hotel. If arriving from EWR Airport, take the AirTrain to Newark Liberty Airport Station, then take an NJ Transit train to Penn Station. From Penn Station, take the 1 subway line to 23rd Street, or take a taxi directly to the hotel.

You can book a stay at Hotel Giraffe through the hotel's official website, where you can often find exclusive deals and packages. The hotel is also available on booking platforms like Expedia, Booking.com, and Hotels.com, where you can compare rates and read guest reviews.

Lastly, The Franklin Hotel on the Upper East Side offers a stylish and comfortable mid-range option for travelers looking to stay in a quieter, residential part of Manhattan. The Franklin Hotel is known for its boutique charm and intimate atmosphere, with room rates typically ranging from $200 to $350 per night. The hotel offers amenities such as free Wi-Fi, complimentary breakfast, and evening wine and cheese receptions. The rooms are elegantly decorated with warm tones, luxurious linens, and marble bathrooms, providing a relaxing environment after a day of exploring the city. The hotel's location near Central Park, the Metropolitan

Museum of Art, and the upscale shopping along Madison Avenue makes it an ideal choice for culture enthusiasts and shoppers.

To reach The Franklin Hotel from JFK Airport, take the AirTrain to Jamaica Station, then transfer to the E subway line toward Manhattan. Get off at Lexington Avenue-63rd Street, and the hotel is a short walk from the station. From LGA Airport, take the Q70 bus to Jackson Heights-Roosevelt Avenue, then transfer to the F subway line and get off at Lexington Avenue-63rd Street. If arriving from EWR Airport, take the AirTrain to Newark Liberty Airport Station, then take an NJ Transit train to Penn Station. From Penn Station, take the E subway line to Lexington Avenue-63rd Street, or take a taxi to the hotel.

You can book a stay at The Franklin Hotel through the hotel's official website, where you can often find special promotions for direct bookings. The hotel is also listed on popular travel booking sites like Booking.com, Expedia, and Hotels.com, where you can compare prices and read reviews from other travelers.

New York City offers a variety of mid-range hotels and B&Bs that cater to different tastes and preferences, providing a comfortable and affordable stay without compromising on quality. Whether you're looking for a boutique hotel with modern amenities, a historic B&B with personalized service, or a centrally located property with easy access to the city's attractions, there are plenty of options to choose from. By booking directly through the hotel's website or using reputable booking platforms, you can ensure that you find the best rates and availability for your stay. With careful planning and the right accommodation, you can enjoy all the excitement and charm of New York City while staying within your budget.

Luxury Hotels and Resorts

For those seeking a truly exceptional experience during their stay in New York City, luxury hotels and resorts offer unparalleled comfort, service, and amenities. These accommodations provide more than just a place to rest—they are destinations in their own right, offering world-class dining, exquisite design, and personalized attention that make your visit unforgettable. Whether you're celebrating a special occasion, traveling for business, or simply indulging in the finest that the city has to offer, New York City's luxury hotels and resorts cater to every need and desire.

One of the most iconic luxury hotels in New York City is The Plaza Hotel, located at Fifth Avenue and Central Park South. This historic hotel, which first opened its doors in 1907, is synonymous with luxury and elegance. The Plaza offers a range of accommodations, from opulent guest rooms to lavish suites, with prices typically starting around $800 per night and reaching well into the thousands for the more exclusive suites. The hotel's amenities include the famed Palm Court, where guests can enjoy afternoon tea, the elegant Champagne Bar, a luxurious spa, and 24-hour butler service. The Plaza's location provides easy access to Central Park, Fifth Avenue shopping, and cultural institutions such as The Museum of Modern Art (MoMA).

To reach The Plaza Hotel from John F. Kennedy International Airport (JFK), take the AirTrain to Jamaica Station, then transfer to the E subway line toward Manhattan. Get off at 5th Avenue-53rd Street, and the hotel is just a short walk from the station. From LaGuardia Airport (LGA), take the Q70 bus to Jackson Heights-Roosevelt Avenue, then transfer to the F subway line and get off at 57th Street. If arriving from Newark Liberty International Airport (EWR), take the AirTrain to Newark Liberty Airport Station, then take an NJ Transit train to Penn Station. From Penn Station, you can take the 1 subway line to 59th Street-Columbus Circle, or take a taxi directly to the hotel.

Booking a stay at The Plaza Hotel can be done directly through the hotel's official website, where you may find exclusive offers and packages tailored to your preferences. Additionally, The Plaza is listed on luxury travel booking platforms like Virtuoso, where you can access special amenities such as room upgrades, late check-out, and dining credits when booking through a Virtuoso travel advisor.

Another top luxury option is The St. Regis New York, located on East 55th Street, just steps from Fifth Avenue. The St. Regis is known for its timeless elegance, impeccable service, and signature St. Regis Butler Service, which is available to all guests. Room rates at The St. Regis typically start around $900 per night, with suites priced significantly higher. The hotel offers a range of amenities, including the iconic King Cole Bar, which is home to the original Bloody Mary, a full-service spa, a state-of-the-art fitness center, and a collection of curated experiences designed to enhance your stay. The rooms and suites are luxuriously appointed with custom furnishings, marble bathrooms, and high-end technology, providing a perfect blend of classic and modern design.

To reach The St. Regis New York from JFK Airport, take the AirTrain to Jamaica Station, then transfer to the E subway line toward Manhattan. Get off at 5th Avenue-53rd Street, and the hotel is just a short walk from the station. From LGA Airport, take the Q70 bus to Jackson Heights-Roosevelt Avenue, then transfer to the F subway line and get off at 57th Street. If arriving from EWR Airport, take the AirTrain to Newark Liberty Airport Station, then take an NJ Transit train to Penn Station. From Penn Station, you can take the E subway line to 5th Avenue-53rd Street, or take a taxi to the hotel.

Booking a stay at The St. Regis New York can be done directly through the hotel's website, where you can explore a variety of packages and special offers. The hotel is also part of the Marriott Bonvoy loyalty program, allowing members to earn and redeem points during their stay. Additionally, The St. Regis is available on luxury travel sites like American Express Fine Hotels & Resorts, where booking through the platform can provide additional benefits, including complimentary breakfast, late check-out, and a resort credit.

The Ritz-Carlton New York, Central Park is another premier luxury hotel that offers a serene retreat in the heart of the city. Located on Central Park South, this hotel combines the timeless elegance of a classic New York hotel with modern amenities and personalized service. Room rates at The Ritz-Carlton typically start around $1,000 per night, with suites commanding even higher prices. The hotel's amenities include a full-service spa, a well-equipped fitness center, and Auden Bistro & Bar, which serves contemporary American cuisine with a focus on seasonal ingredients. Many of the rooms and suites offer breathtaking views of Central Park, and the hotel's Club Lounge provides an exclusive experience for guests, with continuous culinary offerings throughout the day.

To get to The Ritz-Carlton New York, Central Park from JFK Airport, take the AirTrain to Jamaica Station, then transfer to the E subway line toward Manhattan. Get off at 7th Avenue, and the hotel is a short walk from the station. From LGA Airport, take the Q70 bus to Jackson Heights-Roosevelt Avenue, then transfer to the F subway line and get off at 57th Street. If arriving from EWR Airport, take the AirTrain to Newark Liberty Airport Station, then take an NJ Transit train to Penn Station. From Penn Station, you can take the 1 subway line to 59th Street-Columbus Circle, or take a taxi to the hotel.

Booking a stay at The Ritz-Carlton New York, Central Park can be done through the hotel's official website, where you can explore various packages and offers, including romantic getaways, wellness retreats, and family experiences. The Ritz-Carlton is part of the Marriott Bonvoy program, allowing guests to earn and redeem points. For those looking for additional perks, booking through a luxury travel advisor with access to Virtuoso or American Express Fine Hotels & Resorts can provide complimentary benefits such as room upgrades, daily breakfast, and late check-out.

For a modern and sophisticated luxury experience, The Langham, New York, Fifth Avenue is an excellent choice. Located between Bryant Park and the Empire State Building, The Langham offers contemporary luxury with spacious accommodations and attentive service. Room rates typically start around $700 per night, with suites and specialty accommodations available at higher rates. The hotel features Ai Fiori, a Michelin-starred restaurant serving Italian and French Riviera-inspired cuisine, a wellness center with a fully-equipped gym, and The Langham Club, an exclusive lounge offering complimentary breakfast, refreshments, and evening cocktails. The rooms and suites at The Langham are designed with a sleek, modern aesthetic, featuring luxurious bedding, marble bathrooms, and floor-to-ceiling windows that offer views of the city skyline.

To reach The Langham, New York, Fifth Avenue from JFK Airport, take the AirTrain to Jamaica Station, then transfer to the E subway line toward Manhattan. Get off at 34th Street-Herald Square, and the hotel is just a short walk from the station. From LGA Airport, take the Q70 bus to Jackson Heights-Roosevelt Avenue, then transfer to the F subway line and get off at 34th Street-Herald Square. If arriving from EWR Airport, take the AirTrain to Newark Liberty Airport Station, then take an NJ Transit train to Penn Station. From Penn Station, you can walk to the hotel or take a short taxi ride.

Booking a stay at The Langham, New York, Fifth Avenue can be done directly through the hotel's official website, where you can find special offers and packages tailored to your needs. The Langham is also available on luxury travel booking platforms such as Virtuoso and American Express Fine Hotels & Resorts, which offer additional amenities when booking through their services.

Finally, The Peninsula New York offers a luxurious and tranquil escape on Fifth Avenue, just steps away from some of the city's most iconic landmarks, including Rockefeller Center and St. Patrick's Cathedral. The Peninsula New York is known for its timeless elegance and exceptional service, with room rates typically starting around $900 per night. The hotel's amenities include The Peninsula Spa, which offers a range of treatments and an indoor pool with views of the city, as well as Clement, a restaurant serving contemporary American cuisine, and Salon de Ning, a rooftop bar with panoramic views of Manhattan. The rooms and suites at The Peninsula are beautifully appointed with luxurious linens, marble bathrooms, and state-of-the-art technology, providing a perfect blend of comfort and sophistication.

To reach The Peninsula New York from JFK Airport, take the AirTrain to Jamaica Station, then transfer to the E subway line toward Manhattan. Get off at 5th Avenue-53rd Street, and the hotel is a short walk from the station. From LGA Airport, take the Q70 bus to Jackson Heights-Roosevelt Avenue, then transfer to the F subway line and get off at 57th Street. If arriving from EWR Airport, take the AirTrain to Newark Liberty Airport Station, then take an NJ Transit train to Penn Station. From Penn Station, you can take the E subway line to 5th Avenue-53rd Street, or take a taxi to the hotel.

Booking a stay at The Peninsula New York can be done through the hotel's official website, where you can explore various packages and promotions. The

Peninsula is also part of The Leading Hotels of the World, which offers exclusive benefits to members of its Leaders Club loyalty program. Additionally, the hotel is listed on luxury travel booking platforms like Virtuoso and American Express Fine Hotels & Resorts, where booking through these platforms can provide added value, including room upgrades, complimentary breakfast, and late check-out.

New York City's luxury hotels and resorts offer an unparalleled experience of comfort, service, and sophistication. Whether you choose the historic elegance of The Plaza, the timeless charm of The St. Regis, the serene luxury of The Ritz-Carlton, the modern sophistication of The Langham, or the refined tranquility of The Peninsula, each of these accommodations provides a unique and unforgettable stay. By booking through the hotel's official website or using luxury travel platforms, you can access exclusive offers and additional perks that enhance your experience. With careful planning and the right accommodation choice, your stay in New York City will be nothing short of extraordinary.

Family-Friendly Accommodation Options

When planning a family trip to New York City, finding the right accommodation is key to ensuring a comfortable and enjoyable experience for everyone. The city offers a wide range of family-friendly hotels that cater to the needs of both parents and children, providing amenities that make traveling with kids easier and more fun. Whether you're looking for spacious rooms, convenient locations, or special features like play areas and family-oriented services, New York City has something to offer. Below, you'll find detailed information about five family-friendly accommodation options, including their price ranges, amenities, locations, and how to get there from the major airports. This information will help you make an informed decision that best suits your family's needs, ensuring a memorable stay in the city.

One of the top choices for families visiting New York City is Residence Inn by Marriott New York Manhattan/Times Square. This hotel offers spacious suites with fully equipped kitchens, making it ideal for families who prefer the convenience of preparing their own meals. The price range for a stay at Residence Inn typically falls between $250 and $400 per night, depending on the season and suite type. The hotel provides a complimentary breakfast buffet each morning, which is a great perk for families with children. Other amenities include free Wi-Fi, a fitness center, and a laundry facility. The location is central, just a short walk from Times Square, Bryant Park, and several subway lines, making it easy to explore the city's attractions.

To reach Residence Inn by Marriott New York Manhattan/Times Square from John F. Kennedy International Airport (JFK), take the AirTrain to Jamaica Station, then transfer to the E subway line toward Manhattan. Get off at 42nd Street-Port Authority Bus Terminal, and the hotel is a short walk from the station. From LaGuardia Airport (LGA), take the Q70 bus to Jackson

Heights-Roosevelt Avenue, then transfer to the 7 subway line and get off at Times Square-42nd Street. If arriving from Newark Liberty International Airport (EWR), take the AirTrain to Newark Liberty Airport Station, then take an NJ Transit train to Penn Station. From Penn Station, you can walk to the hotel, which is about 10 minutes away, or take a short taxi ride.

You can book a stay at Residence Inn by Marriott through the hotel's official website, where you can often find family packages that include additional perks such as free parking or late check-out. The hotel is also listed on major travel booking sites like Expedia, Booking.com, and Hotels.com, where you can compare prices and read reviews from other families.

Another excellent family-friendly option is Loews Regency New York Hotel, located on Park Avenue in the Upper East Side. This luxury hotel is known for its spacious rooms and suites, which are perfect for families. The price range for a stay at Loews Regency typically starts around $400 per night and can go up depending on the room type and season. The hotel offers a variety of family-oriented amenities, including complimentary cribs, rollaway beds, and children's bath products. The on-site restaurant, The Regency Bar & Grill, offers a kids' menu, and the hotel's concierge can arrange babysitting services, making it easier for parents to enjoy a night out. The hotel's location near Central Park, the Metropolitan Museum of Art, and the American Museum of Natural History makes it a convenient base for family adventures.

To get to Loews Regency New York Hotel from JFK Airport, take the AirTrain to Jamaica Station, then transfer to the E subway line toward Manhattan. Get off at Lexington Avenue-63rd Street, and the hotel is a short walk from the station. From LGA Airport, take the Q70 bus to Jackson Heights-Roosevelt Avenue, then transfer to the F subway line and get off at Lexington Avenue-63rd Street. If arriving from EWR Airport, take the AirTrain to Newark Liberty Airport Station, then take an NJ Transit train to Penn Station. From Penn Station, you can take the E subway line to Lexington Avenue-63rd Street, or take a taxi to the hotel.

Booking a stay at Loews Regency New York Hotel can be done through the hotel's official website, where you can explore various family packages and special offers. The hotel is also available on luxury travel booking platforms such as Virtuoso, where booking through the platform can provide additional benefits like room upgrades, complimentary breakfast, and late check-out.

For families looking for a unique and kid-friendly experience, The Benjamin Hotel in Midtown East is a great choice. The Benjamin offers a special "Winks' Kidzzz Club" program, which includes a variety of services and amenities tailored to young guests. These include custom-designed children's pillows, bedtime snacks, and a library of family-friendly books and games. The price range for a stay at The Benjamin typically starts around $300 per night. The hotel also offers suites with kitchenettes, which are perfect for families who want the option to prepare simple meals. Other amenities include free Wi-Fi, a fitness center, and room service. The hotel's location provides easy access to Rockefeller Center, St. Patrick's Cathedral, and the Theater District.

To reach The Benjamin Hotel from JFK Airport, take the AirTrain to Jamaica Station, then transfer to the E subway line toward Manhattan. Get off at Lexington Avenue-53rd Street, and the hotel is a short walk from the station. From LGA Airport, take the Q70 bus to Jackson Heights-Roosevelt Avenue, then transfer to the F subway line and get off at 57th Street. If arriving from EWR Airport, take the AirTrain to Newark Liberty Airport Station, then take an NJ Transit train to Penn Station. From Penn Station, take the E subway line to Lexington Avenue-53rd Street, or take a taxi directly to the hotel.

You can book a stay at The Benjamin Hotel through the hotel's official website, where you can find special offers tailored to families, including packages that include tickets to nearby attractions. The hotel is also listed on major booking sites like Booking.com, Expedia, and Hotels.com, where you can compare prices and read reviews from other families who have stayed at the property.

The Kimberly Hotel in Midtown East is another family-friendly option that offers spacious suites and a variety of amenities that cater to families. The Kimberly Hotel is known for its large rooms, some of which include kitchenettes and private balconies, making it a comfortable choice for families who need extra space. The price range for a stay at The Kimberly typically falls between $350 and $600 per night, depending on the room type and season. The hotel also offers complimentary Wi-Fi, a fitness center, and a rooftop lounge with views of the city. The location is ideal for families, with easy access to attractions like the United Nations Headquarters, Rockefeller Center, and the shops along Fifth Avenue.

To get to The Kimberly Hotel from JFK Airport, take the AirTrain to Jamaica Station, then transfer to the E subway line toward Manhattan. Get off at Lexington Avenue-53rd Street, and the hotel is just a short walk from the station. From LGA Airport, take the Q70 bus to Jackson Heights-Roosevelt Avenue, then transfer to the F subway line and get off at 57th Street. If arriving from EWR Airport, take the AirTrain to Newark Liberty Airport Station, then take an NJ Transit train to Penn Station. From Penn Station, take the E subway line to Lexington Avenue-53rd Street, or take a taxi to the hotel.

Booking a stay at The Kimberly Hotel can be done through the hotel's official website, where you can find special family packages that include perks like complimentary breakfast or tickets to nearby attractions. The hotel is also available on travel booking platforms like Expedia, Booking.com, and Hotels.com, where you can compare rates and read reviews from other travelers.

Finally, The Peninsula New York is a luxury hotel that also offers a range of family-friendly amenities, making it an excellent choice for those who want to combine luxury with family convenience. The Peninsula offers spacious rooms and suites, many of which include connecting rooms for larger families. The price range for a stay at The Peninsula typically starts around $900 per night. The hotel offers a dedicated children's program, which includes welcome amenities for kids, children's bathrobes and slippers, and special dining options tailored to young guests. The Peninsula also features a rooftop pool, a full-service spa, and multiple dining options, including a kids' menu at Clement restaurant. The hotel's location on Fifth Avenue makes it easy to explore Central Park, the Rockefeller Center, and the city's top museums.

To reach The Peninsula New York from JFK Airport, take the AirTrain to Jamaica Station, then transfer to the E subway line toward Manhattan. Get off at 5th Avenue-53rd Street, and the hotel is just a short walk from the station. From LGA Airport, take the Q70 bus to Jackson Heights-Roosevelt Avenue, then transfer to the F subway line and get off at 57th Street. If arriving from EWR Airport, take the AirTrain to Newark Liberty Airport Station, then take an NJ Transit train to Penn Station. From Penn Station, you can take the E subway line to 5th Avenue-53rd Street, or take a taxi directly to the hotel.

Booking a stay at The Peninsula New York can be done through the hotel's official website, where you can explore family packages and special offers. The hotel is also part of The Leading Hotels of the World, which provides exclusive benefits to members of its Leaders Club loyalty program. Additionally, The Peninsula is listed on luxury travel booking platforms like Virtuoso and American Express Fine Hotels & Resorts, where booking through these platforms can provide added value, including room upgrades, complimentary breakfast, and late check-out.

New York City offers a wide range of family-friendly accommodation options that cater to the needs of travelers with children. Whether you're looking for a luxury experience, spacious suites with kitchenettes, or special amenities designed for kids, there are plenty of choices that provide comfort, convenience, and value. By booking through the hotel's official website or using reputable travel booking platforms, you can ensure that you find the best rates and availability for your stay. With the right accommodation, your family can enjoy all the excitement and wonder that New York City has to offer, creating memories that will last a lifetime.

CHAPTER 8

EXPLORING NEW YORK CITY

Activities for Different Types of Travelers

Family-Friendly Activities

New York City is a vibrant and bustling metropolis that offers countless activities for visitors of all ages, making it an ideal destination for families. Whether you're traveling with young children, teenagers, or a mix of both, there are plenty of family-friendly activities that can keep everyone entertained while also providing educational and cultural experiences. From iconic landmarks to interactive museums, parks, and even boat rides, New York City has something for every family to enjoy. Exploring these attractions together not only creates lasting memories but also allows children to experience the diverse and dynamic culture of one of the world's most exciting cities.

One of the most popular and must-visit attractions for families in New York City is Central Park. This sprawling urban oasis offers a wide variety of activities that cater to all ages, making it a perfect spot for families to spend an entire day. Central Park features playgrounds, open spaces for picnics, and scenic walking paths where children can run around and explore. Families can rent bikes, take a horse-drawn carriage ride, or even rent rowboats at the Loeb Boathouse for a relaxing time on the lake. One of the park's highlights is the Central Park Zoo, where kids can see a variety of animals, including sea lions, penguins, and tropical birds. The Tisch Children's Zoo within the zoo allows children to get up close with farm animals like goats, sheep, and pigs. Additionally, the park hosts the historic Central Park Carousel, which has been a favorite among children for generations.

For families looking to introduce their children to art and culture, The American Museum of Natural History is a must-visit. Located on the Upper West Side, this iconic museum offers an array of exhibits that captivate the imagination of both children and adults. The museum is home to the famous dinosaur skeletons, including the towering Tyrannosaurus rex and the massive Apatosaurus. The Hall of Ocean Life features a life-size model of a blue whale suspended from the ceiling, which is always a hit with kids. The museum also offers hands-on exhibits where children can learn about the natural world through interactive displays and activities. The Discovery Room is a special area designed for young explorers, offering activities like fossil digging, examining animal specimens, and solving puzzles. With its vast collection and engaging exhibits, the American Museum of Natural History provides a fun and educational experience that the whole family can enjoy.

Another fantastic family-friendly attraction is The Statue of Liberty and Ellis Island. A visit to these iconic landmarks is both educational and inspiring, offering children a glimpse into the history of the United States. Families can take a ferry from Battery Park to Liberty Island, where they can explore the grounds and learn about the history and significance of the Statue of Liberty. The pedestal of the statue offers panoramic views of the New York Harbor, and visitors can also visit the museum inside the pedestal, which features exhibits on the statue's history and symbolism. Afterward, the ferry continues to Ellis Island, where families can explore the Ellis Island National Museum of Immigration. Here, children can learn about the immigrant experience and the role Ellis Island played as the gateway to America for millions of people. The museum offers interactive exhibits and artifacts that bring history to life, making it a meaningful and educational experience for children and adults alike.

For a more interactive experience, The Children's Museum of Manhattan is an excellent choice for families with young children. Located on the Upper West Side, this museum is designed specifically for children aged 0-10 and offers a variety of hands-on exhibits that encourage learning through play. The museum's exhibits cover topics like art, science, culture, and health, with activities that allow children to explore, create, and discover. The "PlayWorks" exhibit is particularly popular with toddlers, offering a safe and stimulating environment where they can engage in sensory play, build with blocks, and explore a mock fire truck. Older children will enjoy the "Adventures with Dora and Diego" exhibit, where they can go on interactive adventures with their favorite characters from the popular children's show. The museum also hosts special events and workshops, such as art classes, storytime, and music performances, making it a fun and dynamic place for families to visit.

For families who enjoy the outdoors and want to take in some breathtaking views of the city, a visit to The Brooklyn Bridge is a must. Walking across this historic bridge provides a unique perspective of the New York City skyline and the East River. The bridge's pedestrian walkway is wide and safe, making it a great activity for families with children of all ages. As you stroll across the bridge, you can stop to take photos of the skyline, the Statue of Liberty in the distance, and the iconic bridge itself. The walk from Manhattan to Brooklyn (or vice versa) takes about 30-45 minutes at a leisurely pace, and once you reach the Brooklyn side, you can explore Brooklyn Bridge Park. This waterfront park offers playgrounds, picnic areas, and even a carousel, making it a perfect place to relax after the walk. The park also offers stunning views of Manhattan, and families can enjoy an ice cream from the famous Brooklyn Ice Cream Factory while taking in the scenery.

The New York Aquarium in Coney Island is another great option for a family day out. The aquarium is home to a wide variety of marine life, including sharks, sea otters, sea lions, and penguins. Children can watch sea lions perform tricks at the Aquatheater, explore the "Sharks! Predators of the Deep" exhibit, and learn about conservation efforts to protect marine habitats. The aquarium also features touch tanks where kids can get hands-on with marine creatures like starfish and sea urchins. After visiting the aquarium, families can spend some time at the Coney Island boardwalk, which offers amusement rides, games, and beach access, providing a full day of fun and entertainment.

For families who want to experience the excitement of New York City's entertainment scene, attending a Broadway Show is a must. Many Broadway shows offer performances that are family-friendly, with themes, characters, and stories that appeal to children and adults alike. Shows like "The Lion King," "Aladdin," and "Frozen" are particularly popular with families, offering stunning visuals, memorable music, and captivating performances that keep audiences of all ages engaged. Attending a Broadway show is not only entertaining but also provides children with an introduction to the world of theater and the performing arts. Families can purchase tickets in advance through official Broadway websites or at the TKTS booth in Times Square, which offers discounted tickets for same-day performances.

For a unique experience that combines education with fun, The Intrepid Sea, Air & Space Museum is a fantastic destination for families. Located on the west side of Manhattan along the Hudson River, this museum is housed on the USS Intrepid, a retired aircraft carrier that served in World War II and the Vietnam War. The museum features a wide range of exhibits, including historic aircraft, a space shuttle, a submarine, and various interactive displays. Children can explore the ship's decks, climb into a helicopter, and learn about the history of aviation and space exploration. The museum also offers special programs and events for children, such as "Kids Week," where families can participate in hands-on activities, demonstrations, and workshops. The Intrepid Museum is a great place for children to learn about history, science, and technology in an engaging and immersive environment.

New York City is a treasure trove of family-friendly activities that offer something for everyone, from toddlers to teenagers. Whether your family is interested in exploring the city's parks, visiting museums, or enjoying entertainment and cultural experiences, there are endless opportunities to create lasting memories together. By planning your itinerary with these activities in mind, you can ensure that your family has a fun, enriching, and unforgettable time in the city. Whether it's walking across the Brooklyn Bridge, marveling at the dinosaurs at the American Museum of Natural History, or taking in a Broadway show, New York City provides a wide range of experiences that will captivate and delight both children and adults alike.

Romantic Spots for Couples

New York City is often considered one of the most romantic destinations in the world, offering countless spots where couples can create cherished memories together. Whether you're strolling through a peaceful garden, enjoying a sunset on the waterfront, or dining at an intimate restaurant, the city provides endless opportunities for romance. Its unique blend of iconic landmarks, hidden gems, and breathtaking views makes it the perfect place for couples to experience something special.

One of the most iconic and romantic places in New York City is Central Park. This sprawling urban oasis offers a variety of picturesque spots where couples can enjoy each other's company in a tranquil setting. A classic romantic activity in Central Park is taking a leisurely stroll along the winding paths, surrounded by lush greenery and scenic views. The park's many bridges, such as Bow Bridge and Gapstow Bridge, provide beautiful backdrops for couples looking to capture a romantic moment on camera. The Bethesda Terrace and Fountain is another romantic spot within the park, offering stunning views of the lake and the surrounding landscape. Couples can also rent a rowboat from the Loeb Boathouse and spend some peaceful time on the water, enjoying the serene atmosphere of the park.

For those who prefer a more secluded and intimate setting, the Conservatory Garden within Central Park is an ideal spot. This formal garden is divided into three sections, each with its own unique charm. The Italian Garden features a large lawn surrounded by vibrant flowers and neatly trimmed hedges, while the French Garden boasts a stunning display of seasonal blooms and a beautiful fountain. The English Garden is perhaps the most romantic of the three, with its winding paths, lush greenery, and secluded benches where couples can sit and enjoy the beauty of the garden in peace. The Conservatory Garden is especially lovely in the spring when the cherry blossoms are in full bloom, creating a magical and romantic atmosphere.

Another romantic spot in New York City is Top of the Rock at Rockefeller Center. This observation deck offers panoramic views of the city, including the iconic Empire State Building and Central Park. Visiting Top of the Rock at sunset is a particularly romantic experience, as the sky changes color and the city lights begin to twinkle below. The experience of watching the sun set over the city together is one that couples are sure to remember. For those who want to add an extra touch of romance, the Top of the Rock offers special packages that include champagne and priority access to the observation deck.

For couples who enjoy breathtaking views and waterfront settings, a visit to Brooklyn Bridge Park is a must. This park stretches along the East River, offering stunning views of the Manhattan skyline and the Brooklyn Bridge. Couples can take a romantic walk along the waterfront promenade, stopping to admire the views or sit on one of the park's many benches to watch the boats pass by. The park also features several piers, each with its own unique attractions, such as gardens, playgrounds, and even a carousel. One of the most romantic spots within the park is the Pebble Beach area, where couples can sit on the rocks and enjoy the sound of the waves while taking in the stunning view of the bridge and the city. As the sun sets, the lights of the Manhattan skyline reflect on the water, creating a truly magical and romantic scene.

DUMBO (Down Under the Manhattan Bridge Overpass) is another romantic neighborhood in Brooklyn that offers couples a mix of stunning views, charming streets, and unique experiences. The area is known for its cobblestone streets, art galleries, and trendy cafes, making it a perfect place for a romantic stroll. One of the most iconic views in DUMBO is the view of the Manhattan Bridge framed by the buildings on Washington Street, which is a popular spot for couples to take photos. After exploring the neighborhood, couples can head to the nearby Empire Fulton Ferry park, where they can relax on the grassy lawn, enjoy a picnic, and take in the views of the Brooklyn and Manhattan Bridges. As the sun sets, the view of the city from DUMBO becomes even more romantic, with the lights of the skyline and the bridges reflecting on the water.

For couples looking for a romantic dining experience, New York City offers a plethora of options, but one that stands out is One if by Land, Two if by Sea in the West Village. This historic restaurant is housed in a former carriage house that dates back to the 18th century, and it exudes a romantic and elegant ambiance. The restaurant is known for its candlelit tables, fireplaces, and live piano music, creating a perfect setting for a romantic dinner. The menu features classic American cuisine with a focus on seasonal ingredients, and the wine list is extensive, offering a wide selection of wines to complement the meal. Dining at One if by Land, Two if by Sea is an experience that couples will cherish, making it an ideal choice for a special occasion or a romantic night out.

For a more casual yet equally romantic experience, couples can visit The High Line, an elevated park that runs along the west side of Manhattan. The High Line is built on a former railway line, and it offers a unique perspective of the city, with views of the Hudson River, the Meatpacking District, and the Chelsea neighborhood. The park is lined with gardens, art installations, and seating areas, providing plenty of opportunities for couples to sit and enjoy the surroundings. Walking along The High Line at dusk, as the city lights begin to glow, is a particularly romantic experience. The park also hosts various events and activities throughout the year, such as stargazing, guided tours, and art installations, making it a dynamic and engaging place for couples to explore together.

For those who want to combine romance with a bit of adventure, a sail around New York Harbor is a perfect choice. Several companies offer sailing tours that take couples on a scenic journey around the harbor, providing stunning views of the Statue of Liberty, Ellis Island, and the Manhattan skyline. Some tours are offered on historic sailboats, adding a touch of nostalgia and charm to the experience. Sunset sails are particularly popular, as they offer the chance to watch the sun set over the city while enjoying a glass of wine or champagne. The gentle rocking of the boat, the sound of the waves, and the breathtaking views create a romantic and serene atmosphere that couples are sure to enjoy.

Another romantic experience in New York City is visiting the Met Cloisters in Upper Manhattan. This museum is dedicated to medieval art and architecture, and it is located in Fort Tryon Park, overlooking the Hudson River. The Met Cloisters is housed in a building designed to resemble a medieval European monastery, complete with cloistered gardens, stone arches, and ancient artifacts. The peaceful and serene setting of the museum makes it a perfect place for couples to explore together, taking in the art and history while enjoying the tranquil surroundings. After visiting the museum, couples can take a walk through Fort Tryon Park, which offers beautiful views of the river and the George Washington Bridge, as well as peaceful gardens and wooded paths.

Finally, no romantic trip to New York City would be complete without a visit to Times Square at night. While Times Square is known for its hustle and bustle, it also offers a unique and exhilarating experience for couples who want to immerse themselves in the energy of the city. The bright lights, giant billboards, and constant movement of people create a vibrant and dynamic atmosphere that is unlike anywhere else in the world. Couples can walk hand-in-hand through Times Square, take in the sights and sounds, and perhaps even catch a Broadway show. As you stand in the middle of Times Square, surrounded by the dazzling lights and the excitement of the city, you'll feel the magic and romance of New York City come alive.

New York City offers an abundance of romantic spots and experiences for couples, whether you're looking for peaceful gardens, breathtaking views, or intimate dining. The city's diverse and dynamic landscape provides the perfect backdrop for creating unforgettable memories with your partner. By exploring these romantic spots together, you'll not only deepen your connection but also experience the beauty and magic of New York City in a way that you'll both cherish forever. Whether it's a walk-through Central Park, a sunset sail around the harbor, or a candlelit dinner at a historic restaurant, New York City has something to offer every couple looking for a romantic escape.

Solo Traveler Experiences

New York City is a remarkable destination for solo travelers, offering a vast array of experiences that cater to individual interests and preferences. Whether you're seeking cultural enrichment, adventure, or quiet moments of reflection, the city provides countless opportunities to explore at your own pace. Traveling alone in New York allows you to fully immerse yourself in the vibrant energy of the city, with the freedom to design your itinerary exactly as you wish. From iconic landmarks to hidden gems, New York City is a place where solo travelers can discover new passions, meet like-minded people, and enjoy the thrill of independence.

One of the great joys of traveling solo in New York City is the freedom to explore its rich cultural landscape. The Metropolitan Museum of Art, often referred to as The Met, is an absolute must-visit for any solo traveler with an interest in art, history, and culture. The Met is one of the largest and most comprehensive art museums in the world, with a collection that spans over 5,000 years of art from every corner of the globe. As a solo traveler, you can wander through the museum's vast galleries at your own pace, taking in the masterpieces that resonate with you the most. From ancient Egyptian artifacts to European paintings and contemporary art, The Met offers something for everyone. The museum's serene atmosphere also provides a perfect setting for quiet contemplation, allowing you to fully absorb the beauty and significance of the works on display.

For those who prefer a more interactive experience, The American Museum of Natural History on the Upper West Side is another fantastic destination. This museum is known for its fascinating exhibits on natural history, including the famous dinosaur skeletons, the Hall of Ocean Life, and the Rose Center for Earth and Space. As a solo traveler, you can spend as much time as you like exploring the museum's various halls, learning about the wonders of the natural world. The museum also offers a variety of special exhibitions and events throughout the year, providing additional opportunities for discovery and engagement. Whether you're interested in paleontology, astronomy, or anthropology, the

American Museum of Natural History offers a wealth of knowledge and inspiration.

One of the great advantages of solo travel is the opportunity to fully immerse yourself in the local scene, and there is no better place to do this than in Greenwich Village. This historic neighborhood is known for its bohemian atmosphere, charming streets, and vibrant arts scene. As you stroll through the Village, you'll encounter a mix of trendy cafes, independent bookstores, and intimate music venues, each offering a unique glimpse into the neighborhood's creative spirit. The Village is also home to Washington Square Park, a popular gathering place for locals and visitors alike. Here, you can sit on a bench, watch street performers, and perhaps strike up a conversation with a fellow traveler or a friendly New Yorker. The Village's relaxed vibe and welcoming community make it an ideal place for solo travelers to explore and connect with the city's cultural heartbeat.

For solo travelers who enjoy the outdoors, Central Park offers a peaceful retreat from the hustle and bustle of the city. This expansive park is an oasis of green in the heart of Manhattan, providing countless opportunities for relaxation and recreation. As you explore Central Park, you can discover hidden gems like the Shakespeare Garden, the Conservatory Garden, and the Ramble, a wooded area with winding paths that are perfect for a quiet walk. The park also offers a variety of activities, such as bike rentals, rowboat rentals at the Loeb Boathouse, and even yoga classes on the Great Lawn. Whether you're looking to enjoy a leisurely picnic, go for a run, or simply sit and watch the world go by, Central Park provides a serene and picturesque setting for solo travelers to unwind and recharge.

Another quintessential New York experience for solo travelers is taking in the city's breathtaking views from one of its iconic observation decks. The Empire State Building and Top of the Rock at Rockefeller Center both offer stunning panoramic views of the city, allowing you to see New York's skyline in all its glory. Visiting these observation decks alone allows you to fully appreciate the grandeur of the city without any distractions. You can take your time admiring the views, taking photos, and reflecting on your journey. If you're an early riser, consider visiting the Empire State Building at sunrise for a truly unforgettable experience. The sight of the city awakening in the early morning light is a moment that will stay with you long after your trip is over.

For solo travelers who enjoy exploring diverse neighborhoods, Chinatown offers a fascinating and immersive experience. As you wander through the bustling streets of Chinatown, you'll encounter a vibrant mix of shops, markets, and restaurants, each offering a taste of Chinese culture. The neighborhood is known for its authentic cuisine, and as a solo traveler, you can sample a variety of dishes at different eateries, from dim sum to hand-pulled noodles. Be sure to visit Columbus Park, where you can watch locals playing chess or practicing tai chi, and stop by the Museum of Chinese in America to learn about the history and contributions of Chinese immigrants in the United States. Chinatown's lively atmosphere and rich cultural heritage make it a perfect destination for solo travelers looking to experience a different side of New York City.

For those who appreciate the arts, Broadway is a must-see, and catching a show on your own can be a liberating experience. The energy of live theater, combined with the talent of world-class performers, creates an unforgettable experience. As a solo traveler, you can easily find last-minute tickets to popular shows or explore off-Broadway productions that offer unique and often more intimate performances. The experience of watching a Broadway show alone allows you to fully immerse yourself in the story and performances, free from distractions. Whether you're a fan of musicals, dramas, or comedies, Broadway has something to offer every theater lover, making it a highlight of any solo trip to New York.

For a more offbeat experience, solo travelers can visit The High Line, an elevated park built on a former railway line that runs along Manhattan's west side. The High Line offers a unique perspective of the city, with views of the Hudson River, the Meatpacking District, and the Chelsea neighborhood. As you walk along the park's pathways, you'll encounter public art installations, gardens, and seating areas where you can relax and take in the surroundings. The High Line is also a great place for people-watching, as locals and visitors alike come to enjoy this urban oasis. The park hosts various events and activities throughout the year, including guided tours, stargazing, and art exhibitions, making it a dynamic and engaging place for solo travelers to explore.

For solo travelers who enjoy shopping, SoHo is a neighborhood that should not be missed. SoHo is known for its trendy boutiques, art galleries, and designer stores, offering a shopping experience that is both stylish and eclectic. As you explore SoHo's cobblestone streets, you'll find a mix of high-end fashion, unique jewelry, and one-of-a-kind art pieces. The neighborhood is also home to a variety of cafes and restaurants, where you can take a break from shopping and enjoy a meal or a cup of coffee. SoHo's vibrant atmosphere and diverse offerings make it a great place for solo travelers to indulge in some retail therapy and discover unique finds.

For a quieter and more contemplative experience, solo travelers can visit The New York Public Library's main branch at Bryant Park. This iconic library, with its grand architecture and historic reading rooms, is a haven for book lovers and history enthusiasts. The library offers free tours that provide insights into the building's history, art, and architecture. After exploring the library, you can relax in Bryant Park, which is located right behind the library. The park offers a peaceful setting with gardens, fountains, and plenty of seating areas where you can read, write, or simply enjoy the tranquility. Bryant Park also hosts various events throughout the year, including outdoor movie nights, ice skating in the winter, and yoga classes, making it a versatile destination for solo travelers.

For a unique and immersive experience, solo travelers can explore DUMBO (Down Under the Manhattan Bridge Overpass) in Brooklyn. This neighborhood offers stunning views of the Manhattan skyline, the Brooklyn Bridge, and the East River. DUMBO is known for its art galleries, independent shops, and trendy cafes, making it a great place to wander and explore. One of the highlights of DUMBO is the opportunity to walk across the Brooklyn Bridge, which connects the neighborhood to Manhattan. Walking across the bridge is a quintessential New York experience, offering breathtaking views of the city and the river. Once you reach the Manhattan side, you can explore the Financial District or take a ferry to the Statue of Liberty and Ellis Island.

New York City offers a wealth of experiences for solo travelers, allowing you to explore the city on your own terms and at your own pace. Whether you're interested in art, culture, history, or simply enjoying the energy of the city, there is something for everyone in New York. The city's diverse neighborhoods, iconic landmarks, and vibrant cultural scene provide endless opportunities for discovery and adventure. Traveling alone in New York City allows you to fully immerse yourself in the experiences that matter most to you, creating memories that will last a lifetime. Whether you're visiting a world-class museum, strolling through a historic neighborhood, or taking in the views from an observation deck, New York City is a place where solo travelers can find inspiration, excitement, and a sense of connection to one of the world's most dynamic and captivating cities.

Activities for Seniors

New York City offers a rich tapestry of activities that cater to visitors of all ages, including seniors who are looking for experiences that are both engaging and comfortable. The city's vast cultural resources, historic landmarks, and serene parks make it an ideal destination for senior tourists who wish to explore at a leisurely pace while still immersing themselves in the vibrant energy that New York City has to offer. Whether it's visiting world-renowned museums, enjoying a peaceful stroll in a beautiful garden, or taking in a Broadway show, the city provides a wealth of options that allow seniors to enjoy their visit fully.

One of the most enjoyable activities for seniors visiting New York City is exploring its world-class museums. The Metropolitan Museum of Art, known simply as The Met, is a must-see for anyone interested in art, history, and culture. The Met houses an expansive collection that spans 5,000 years, featuring everything from ancient Egyptian artifacts to modern American art. What makes The Met particularly appealing for seniors is its spacious galleries, which allow for easy movement and exploration at a comfortable pace. The museum also offers plenty of seating throughout its exhibits, making it easy to rest and take in the art without feeling rushed. Additionally, The Met provides guided tours that are tailored to seniors, focusing on key highlights of the collection and offering in-depth explanations that enhance the experience. Audio guides are also available, allowing visitors to explore the museum independently while still gaining insight into the art and history on display. For those who prefer a more personal experience, private tours can be arranged, offering an even more tailored exploration of the museum's vast collection.

Another wonderful option for seniors is the American Museum of Natural History. Located on the Upper West Side, this museum offers a fascinating journey through the natural world, with exhibits that include dinosaur fossils, gems and minerals, and a life-sized model of a blue whale. The museum is known for its accessibility, with elevators and ramps making it easy to navigate the various exhibits. Seniors can spend hours exploring the museum's halls, learning about everything from the history of the planet to the intricacies of the human body. The Rose Center for Earth and Space is a particular highlight, offering immersive exhibits on astronomy and the universe. The museum also offers senior discounts on admission, as well as special programming and events that are designed to be both educational and entertaining. Whether you're interested in the natural sciences, anthropology, or the stars, the American Museum of Natural History provides an enriching experience that is both engaging and accessible.

For seniors who appreciate history and architecture, a visit to St. Patrick's Cathedral is a must. This iconic Gothic-style cathedral, located on Fifth Avenue in Midtown Manhattan, is one of the most beautiful and historically significant churches in the United States. St. Patrick's is open to visitors daily, and seniors can take a self-guided tour to admire the stunning stained glass windows, intricate woodwork, and impressive altars. The cathedral also offers guided tours that provide detailed information about its history, architecture, and the role it has played in the spiritual life of the city. The peaceful atmosphere of the cathedral makes it an ideal place for reflection and quiet contemplation. Additionally, St. Patrick's hosts daily masses and special events, providing opportunities for spiritual enrichment. The cathedral is fully accessible, with ramps and elevators available for those who may have mobility concerns.

Central Park is another excellent destination for seniors visiting New York City. This vast green space in the heart of Manhattan offers a peaceful retreat from the hustle and bustle of the city, with plenty of opportunities for leisurely strolls, picnics, and birdwatching. The park is home to numerous walking paths, gardens, and ponds, each offering a unique experience. Seniors can enjoy a relaxing walk around the Jacqueline Kennedy Onassis Reservoir, which offers beautiful views of the city skyline and the surrounding park. The Shakespeare Garden is another lovely spot, with its meticulously landscaped flower beds and benches where visitors can sit and enjoy the serene surroundings. For those who prefer a more guided experience, Central Park offers various walking tours that focus on the park's history, architecture, and natural beauty. These tours are led by knowledgeable guides and are designed to be easygoing, making them accessible to seniors who may prefer a slower pace.

One of the best ways for seniors to experience the city's skyline and waterfront is by taking a New York Harbor cruise. Several companies offer sightseeing cruises that take passengers around Manhattan Island, providing stunning views of the Statue of Liberty, Ellis Island, the Brooklyn Bridge, and the iconic skyline of Lower Manhattan. These cruises are a relaxing way to see the city's most famous landmarks without the need for extensive walking. Many of the boats are equipped with comfortable seating, climate control, and onboard amenities such as food and beverage service, making the experience both enjoyable and convenient. Some cruises offer narration that provides historical context and interesting facts about the sights, adding an educational element to the experience. For those who prefer a more intimate setting, private boat tours can also be arranged, offering a more personalized exploration of New York Harbor.

For seniors who enjoy theater and the performing arts, attending a Broadway show is an essential part of the New York City experience. Broadway offers a wide variety of shows, from classic musicals to contemporary plays, ensuring that there is something to suit every taste. Many theaters offer matinee performances, which are often less crowded and can be more comfortable for those who prefer to avoid evening crowds. Additionally, Broadway theaters are committed to accessibility, with many offering services such as wheelchair seating, assistive listening devices, and captioning for those with hearing impairments. For seniors who are looking for discounted tickets, the TKTS booth in Times Square offers same-day tickets at reduced prices, allowing for a more affordable theater experience. Whether you're a fan of timeless classics like "The Phantom of the Opera" or new hits like "Hamilton," attending a Broadway show is a memorable experience that showcases the best of New York City's vibrant performing arts scene.

For a more tranquil experience, seniors can visit The New York Botanical Garden in the Bronx. This 250-acre garden is a National Historic Landmark and offers a peaceful escape from the city's hustle and bustle. The garden features a variety of themed gardens, including the Enid A. Haupt Conservatory, which houses tropical plants and flowers from around the world. The Rose Garden, with its stunning display of roses in full bloom, is a favorite spot for visitors, offering both beauty and fragrance. The Thain Family Forest, a 50-acre old-growth forest, provides a serene setting for a leisurely walk along its shaded paths. The New York Botanical Garden also offers tram tours that allow visitors to see the highlights of the garden without extensive walking. These tours provide a comfortable and informative way to explore the garden's many attractions. In addition, the garden hosts seasonal exhibitions, workshops, and special events that cater to a variety of interests.

For seniors interested in history and immigration, a visit to Ellis Island and the Statue of Liberty offers a fascinating journey through America's past. Ellis Island was the gateway for millions of immigrants who came to the United States in search of a better life, and today it serves as a museum dedicated to their stories. The Ellis Island National Museum of Immigration features exhibits that explore the immigrant experience, with personal stories, photographs, and artifacts that bring history to life. Seniors can take a self-guided tour of the museum or join a guided tour that provides deeper insights into the exhibits. The ferry ride to Ellis Island also includes a stop at Liberty Island, where visitors can see the Statue of Liberty up close and learn about its history and significance. Both islands are accessible, with ramps and elevators available for those with mobility concerns. The ferry ride itself offers beautiful views of the New York Harbor, making it an enjoyable and scenic part of the experience.

For seniors who enjoy music and the arts, attending a performance at Carnegie Hall is a must. This world-renowned concert venue has hosted some of the greatest musicians and performers in history, and it continues to be a premier destination for classical music, jazz, and more. Carnegie Hall offers a variety of performances throughout the year, ranging from symphony orchestras to solo recitals. The venue is known for its exceptional acoustics and elegant atmosphere, providing a truly memorable experience for music lovers. Carnegie Hall is also committed to accessibility, offering services such as wheelchair seating, assistive listening devices, and accessible restrooms. For those interested in learning more about the history of the venue, Carnegie Hall offers guided tours that explore its rich history, architecture, and the legendary performers who have graced its stage.

New York City offers a diverse array of activities that cater to the interests and needs of senior tourists. Whether you're interested in exploring world-class museums, enjoying the serenity of a botanical garden, or taking in a Broadway show, the city provides countless opportunities for enrichment and enjoyment. With its rich cultural heritage, beautiful parks, and vibrant arts scene, New York City is a destination where seniors can explore, learn, and relax at their own pace. By taking advantage of the city's many accessible and senior-friendly attractions, visitors can create a trip that is both fulfilling and memorable. Whether it's a peaceful walk-through Central Park, a visit to a historic landmark, or a night at the theater, New York City offers experiences that will inspire and delight seniors, making it an ideal destination for travelers of all ages.

Free Tourist Attractions

New York City, often seen as one of the most expensive cities in the world, surprisingly offers a wide range of free attractions that allow visitors to experience the essence of the city without spending a dime. Whether you are interested in iconic landmarks, peaceful parks, or rich cultural experiences, New York has something to offer for everyone. Exploring the city's free attractions not only provides an opportunity to save money but also allows you to connect with the city's vibrant culture, history, and natural beauty.

One of the most iconic free attractions in New York City is the Statue of Liberty and the Staten Island Ferry. While visiting Liberty Island and Ellis Island requires a paid ferry ticket, you can still enjoy breathtaking views of the Statue of Liberty for free by taking a ride on the Staten Island Ferry. The ferry runs 24 hours a day, seven days a week, and offers stunning views of the Statue of Liberty, Ellis Island, and the Manhattan skyline. The ferry departs from the Whitehall Terminal in Lower Manhattan, located at 4 Whitehall Street, and takes approximately 25 minutes to reach Staten Island. To get to the ferry terminal, you can take the 1 or R subway line to South Ferry Station or the 4 or 5 line to Bowling Green Station. Once on board, find a spot on the right side of the ferry for the best views of the Statue of Liberty. The ferry is free, making it an excellent option for visitors who want to experience one of New York's most iconic sights without spending money.

Another must-visit free attraction is Central Park, a sprawling 843-acre green space in the heart of Manhattan. Central Park is one of the most famous urban parks in the world, offering a wide range of activities and sights for visitors to enjoy. The park is home to beautiful landscapes, scenic walking paths, and historic landmarks, making it a perfect place to spend a day outdoors. Some of the park's highlights include Bethesda Terrace and Fountain, Bow Bridge, and the Central Park Mall. Visitors can also explore the tranquil Conservatory Garden, take a leisurely walk around the Jacqueline Kennedy Onassis Reservoir, or enjoy a peaceful moment at the Shakespeare Garden. To get to Central Park, you can take the A, B, C, D, 1, or 2 subway lines to 59th Street-Columbus Circle, or the N, R, or W lines to 5th Avenue-59th Street. Once in the park, take your time exploring the various paths, gardens, and landmarks at your own pace. Whether you're interested in birdwatching, people-watching, or simply relaxing in a natural setting, Central Park offers countless opportunities to enjoy the outdoors.

For those who are interested in history and architecture, St. Patrick's Cathedral is another excellent free attraction in New York City. Located on 5th Avenue between 50th and 51st Streets, St. Patrick's Cathedral is the largest Gothic-style Catholic cathedral in the United States and a stunning example of 19th-century architecture. Visitors are welcome to explore the cathedral's interior, which features intricate stained glass windows, soaring ceilings, and beautifully detailed altars. The cathedral also houses the crypt of New York's archbishops, adding to its historical significance. To get to St. Patrick's Cathedral, you can take the E or M subway lines to 5th Avenue-53rd Street, or the 6 line to 51st Street. Once inside, take your time to admire the craftsmanship of the architecture and perhaps light a candle in one of the side chapels. The cathedral also offers free guided tours at certain times of the day, providing more in-depth insights into its history and design.

Another fantastic free attraction is the Brooklyn Bridge, an iconic symbol of New York City that connects Manhattan and Brooklyn. Walking across the Brooklyn Bridge is a quintessential New York experience that offers stunning views of the Manhattan skyline, the East River, and the Statue of Liberty in the distance. The pedestrian walkway, located above the car lanes, provides a safe and scenic path for walkers and cyclists. The bridge is especially beautiful at sunrise or sunset, when the city is bathed in golden light. To get to the Manhattan side of the Brooklyn Bridge, you can take the 4, 5, or 6 subway lines to Brooklyn Bridge-City Hall

Station, or the J, Z, or A lines to Fulton Street. From the Brooklyn side, the A or C lines will take you to High Street-Brooklyn Bridge Station. Once on the bridge, take your time to enjoy the views, take photos, and soak in the experience of walking across one of the world's most famous bridges.

For those who enjoy art and culture, The High Line is a unique and free attraction that offers a blend of nature, art, and urban design. The High Line is an elevated park built on a former railway line that runs along Manhattan's west side, from Gansevoort Street in the Meatpacking District to 34th Street near Hudson Yards. The park features beautifully landscaped gardens, public art installations, and seating areas where visitors can relax and enjoy the views of the city and the Hudson River. The High Line is also home to a variety of events and programs, including free guided tours, art exhibitions, and performances, making it a dynamic and engaging place to visit. To get to The High Line, you can take the A, C, or E subway lines to 14th Street, or the L line to 8th Avenue. Once on The High Line, take your time to explore the various sections of the park, stopping to admire the art, enjoy the gardens, or simply watch the city go by from above.

For those interested in museums, many of New York City's top museums offer free admission days or pay-what-you-wish hours, allowing visitors to experience world-class art and history without breaking the bank. The Museum of Modern Art (MoMA), located at 11 West 53rd Street in Midtown Manhattan, offers free admission on Fridays from 5:30 p.m. to 9:00 p.m. MoMA is home to an impressive collection of modern and contemporary art, including works by Picasso, Van Gogh, and Warhol. To get to MoMA, you can take the

E or M subway lines to 5th Avenue-53rd Street, or the B, D, F, or M lines to 47th-50th Streets-Rockefeller Center. During your visit, be sure to explore the museum's various galleries, as well as its sculpture garden, which provides a peaceful outdoor space to enjoy the art.

Another museum that offers free admission is The American Museum of Natural History, located at Central Park West and 79th Street on the Upper West Side. The museum offers a "pay-what-you-wish" admission policy for New York State residents, but for non-residents, the museum offers free admission during certain special events and programs. The museum is famous for its dinosaur fossils, the Hall of Ocean Life, and the Rose Center for Earth and Space, among other exhibits. To get to the museum, you can take the B or C subway lines to 81st Street-Museum of Natural History. Once inside, take your time to explore the various halls and exhibits, learning about the natural world and the history of our planet.

For those who enjoy outdoor spaces, Washington Square Park is a vibrant and historic park located in the heart of Greenwich Village. The park is known for its iconic Washington Square Arch, its lively fountain area, and its rich history as a gathering place for artists, musicians, and activists. Washington Square Park is a great place to relax, people-watch, or enjoy a picnic. The park often hosts live music performances, chess games, and other cultural events, making it a dynamic and engaging place to visit. To get to Washington Square Park, you can take the A, B, C, D, E, F, or M subway lines to West 4th Street-Washington Square, or the N, Q, R, or W lines to 8th Street-NYU. Once in the park, take your time to explore its various paths, watch the street performers, or simply sit by the fountain and enjoy the lively atmosphere.

Grand Central Terminal is another free attraction that offers a glimpse into New York City's history and architecture. Located at 42nd Street and Park Avenue in Midtown Manhattan, Grand Central is one of the most famous train stations in the world, known for its stunning Beaux-Arts architecture and its iconic celestial ceiling. Visitors can explore the terminal's main concourse, visit the Whispering Gallery, or browse the shops and restaurants located within the terminal. Grand Central also offers free walking tours that provide insights into the history and design of the building. To get to Grand Central, you can take the 4, 5, 6, or 7 subway lines to Grand Central-42nd Street. During your visit, be sure to look up at the terminal's ceiling, which features a beautiful mural of the constellations, and explore the various nooks and crannies of this historic landmark.

Finally, for those who enjoy cultural events, New York City hosts a variety of free festivals and events throughout the year that offer a taste of the city's diverse culture. One such event is SummerStage, a free performing arts festival that takes place in Central Park and other parks throughout the city. SummerStage features a wide range of performances, including music, dance, theater, and spoken word, with artists from around the world. The festival is a great way to experience New York City's vibrant arts scene while enjoying the outdoors. To attend a SummerStage event, check the festival's schedule online and arrive early to secure a good spot.

Another free event is Bryant Park's Winter Village, which transforms the park into a festive holiday market with ice skating, food vendors, and holiday shopping. The Winter Village is free to enter, and while ice skating and shopping come with a cost, simply strolling through the market and enjoying the holiday atmosphere is a delightful experience. To get to Bryant Park, you can take the B, D, F, or M subway lines to 42nd Street-Bryant Park, or the 7 line to 5th Avenue. The Winter Village is a great place to soak in the holiday spirit, with twinkling lights, festive decorations, and the sound of carolers filling the air.

New York City offers an abundance of free attractions that allow visitors to experience the best of the city without spending money. Whether you're interested in exploring iconic landmarks, enjoying peaceful parks, or experiencing world-class art and culture, there are countless opportunities to make your visit to New York City both enjoyable and memorable. By taking advantage of these free attractions, you can immerse yourself in the city's rich history, vibrant culture, and natural beauty, creating lasting memories of your time in the Big Apple. Whether it's a walk across the Brooklyn Bridge, a visit to Central Park, or a ride on the Staten Island Ferry, New York City offers endless possibilities for exploration and adventure, all without costing a cent.

Paid Tourist Attractions

New York City is renowned for its vast array of world-class tourist attractions, many of which come with an admission fee that is well worth the experience they offer. From iconic landmarks to cutting-edge museums and thrilling observation decks, the city provides countless opportunities to immerse yourself in its rich history, culture, and unparalleled views. While some of these attractions require an entry fee, there are ways to make the most of your visit by planning ahead, taking advantage of combo tickets and passes, and exploring various options to save money.

One of the most iconic paid attractions in New York City is the Empire State Building, a symbol of the city's architectural grandeur and a must-visit for any traveler. The Empire State

Building, located at 350 5th Avenue in Midtown Manhattan, offers breathtaking views of the city from its 86th-floor open-air observation deck and the 102nd-floor indoor observatory. From these heights, you can see the entire cityscape, including Central Park, the Statue of Liberty, and the Hudson River. The experience of standing atop one of the most famous buildings in the world is both thrilling and awe-inspiring. To get to the Empire State Building, you can take the B, D, F, M, N, Q, R, or W subway lines to 34th Street-Herald Square, or the 1, 2, or 3 lines to 34th Street-Penn Station. Once you arrive, consider purchasing a ticket that includes access to both the 86th and 102nd floors for the full experience. To make your visit even more memorable, try to arrive early in the morning or late in the evening to avoid the crowds and enjoy the stunning views with fewer people around.

Another must-see attraction is the Statue of Liberty and Ellis Island. This experience allows you to delve into the history of American immigration and witness one of the most enduring symbols of freedom. The ferry to Liberty Island and Ellis Island departs from Battery Park in Lower Manhattan, located at the southern tip of the island. To get to Battery Park, you can take the 4 or 5 subway lines to Bowling Green, or the 1 line to South Ferry. Once on the ferry, you'll be treated to stunning views of the Statue of Liberty as you approach the island. Upon arrival, you can explore the grounds of Liberty Island, visit the museum inside the statue's pedestal, and take in panoramic views of the city and harbor from the observation deck. The ferry then continues to Ellis Island, where you can visit the Ellis Island National Museum of Immigration. Here, you can explore exhibits that tell the stories of the millions of immigrants who passed through the island on their way to a new life in America. The museum also offers an interactive experience where you can search for your ancestors in the passenger records database. To enhance your visit, consider booking a guided tour or an audio tour, which provides in-depth information about the history and significance of these iconic landmarks.

For those who appreciate art and culture, The Museum of Modern Art (MoMA) is an essential destination. Located at 11 West 53rd Street in Midtown Manhattan, MoMA is home to one of the most comprehensive collections of modern and contemporary art in the world. The museum features works by iconic artists such as Van Gogh, Picasso, Warhol, and Pollock, as well as rotating exhibitions that showcase the latest developments in the art world. To get to MoMA, you can take the E or M subway lines to 5th Avenue-53rd Street, or the B, D, F, or M lines to 47th-50th Streets-Rockefeller Center. Once inside, take your time to explore the museum's various galleries, which include paintings, sculptures, photography, and design. The museum's sculpture garden, located on the ground floor, is a peaceful outdoor space where you can relax and enjoy the art in a natural setting. MoMA offers free admission on Friday evenings from 5:30 p.m. to 9:00 p.m., but if you prefer to visit during less crowded times, purchasing a ticket in advance is recommended. For an even more enriching experience, consider taking a guided tour or renting an audio guide to learn more about the artworks on display.

Another top attraction that is worth the admission fee is the Top of the Rock Observation Deck at Rockefeller Center.

Located at 30 Rockefeller Plaza in Midtown Manhattan, Top of the Rock offers spectacular 360-degree views of New York City from its three observation decks, including an outdoor deck on the 70th floor. From this vantage point, you can see Central Park, the Empire State Building, and the Chrysler Building, as well as the city's rivers and bridges. The experience of seeing the city from such heights is truly unforgettable, especially during sunrise or sunset when the light transforms the skyline. To get to Rockefeller Center, you can take the B, D, F, or M subway lines to 47th-50th Streets-Rockefeller Center. Once you arrive, consider purchasing a combination ticket that includes access to both Top of the Rock and a guided tour of Rockefeller Center, which provides insights into the history and architecture of this iconic complex. If you're visiting during the holiday season, don't miss the chance to see the famous Rockefeller Center Christmas Tree and the ice skating rink below.

For visitors interested in history and science, the American Museum of Natural History is a must-visit attraction. Located at Central Park West and 79th Street on the Upper West Side, this museum is one of the largest and most renowned natural history museums in the world. The museum's extensive exhibits cover a wide range of topics, including dinosaur fossils, human evolution, the oceans, and outer space. One of the museum's highlights is the Hall of Ocean Life, which features a life-sized model of a blue whale suspended from the ceiling. Another popular exhibit is the Hall of Dinosaurs, which showcases the museum's impressive collection of dinosaur fossils, including the iconic Tyrannosaurus rex. To get to the museum, you can take the B or C subway lines to 81st Street-Museum of Natural

History, or the 1 line to 79th Street. Once inside, be sure to visit the Rose Center for Earth and Space, which includes the Hayden Planetarium and exhibits on the cosmos. The museum offers various ticket options, including general admission and special exhibition tickets, as well as combo tickets that include admission to the planetarium. For an even more immersive experience, consider attending one of the museum's special events, such as stargazing nights at the planetarium or sleepovers at the museum, where you can explore the exhibits after hours.

For those looking to experience New York's performing arts scene, attending a Broadway show is an experience not to be missed. Broadway theaters, located primarily in the Theater District around Times Square, offer a wide range of shows, from timeless classics like "The Phantom of the Opera" to contemporary hits like "Hamilton" and "Wicked." Watching a Broadway show is a quintessential New York experience, and the quality of the performances, the production values, and the atmosphere make it well worth the ticket price. To get to the Theater District, you can take the 1, 2, 3, N, Q, R, or W subway lines to Times Square-42nd Street, or the B, D, F, or M lines to 42nd Street-Bryant Park. Tickets can be purchased online through official Broadway websites, at the theater box offices, or at the TKTS booth in Times Square, which offers discounted tickets for same-day performances. For a truly memorable experience, consider booking tickets to a show that is well-reviewed and recommended by other theatergoers, or opt for a backstage tour to see what goes on behind the scenes.

For those who want to explore multiple attractions while saving money, purchasing a combo ticket or city pass is an excellent option. The New York CityPASS is a popular choice, offering discounted admission to six of the city's top attractions, including the Empire State Building, the American Museum of Natural History, and the Top of the Rock Observation Deck. The CityPASS is valid for nine days, giving you plenty of time to visit the included attractions at your own pace. Another option is the New York Pass, which offers access to over 100 attractions, including the Statue of Liberty, MoMA, and the 9/11 Memorial & Museum. The New York Pass is available for durations ranging from one to ten days, allowing you to choose the option that best fits your itinerary. By using a combo ticket or city pass, you can save money on admission fees while enjoying the convenience of having access to multiple attractions with a single pass.

When planning your visit to paid attractions in New York City, there are also several ways to save money on entry fees. Many attractions offer discounts for seniors, students, and military personnel, so be sure to bring appropriate identification to take advantage of these offers. Some museums and cultural institutions also offer pay-what-you-wish admission days or free admission hours, allowing you to visit at a reduced cost or for free. Additionally, purchasing tickets online in advance can often result in savings, as many attractions offer discounted rates for advance purchases. If you're visiting New York City during a special event or holiday, such as Museum Day or Open House New York, you may also find that certain attractions offer free or reduced admission as part of the celebration.

Museums

New York City is home to a rich tapestry of museums that cater to every interest and passion, offering visitors an unparalleled opportunity to explore art, history, science, and culture in all its forms. Whether you're a seasoned museum-goer or simply looking to spend an afternoon immersed in a world of knowledge and beauty, the city's diverse array of museums promises something for everyone. From world-renowned institutions that house masterpieces of art and history to specialty museums that explore niche topics, New York's museums are integral to the city's cultural fabric.

One of the most famous and iconic museums in New York City is The Metropolitan Museum of Art, commonly known as The Met. Located on Fifth Avenue along the eastern edge of Central Park, The Met is one of the largest and most comprehensive art museums in the world, boasting a collection that spans 5,000 years of art from across the globe. The museum's vast collection includes everything from ancient Egyptian artifacts and European masterpieces to modern American art and decorative arts. To get to The Met, you can take the 4, 5, or 6 subway lines to 86th Street and walk west towards Fifth Avenue, or take the M1, M2, M3, or M4 buses, which stop directly in front of the museum. Once inside, visitors can explore the museum's many galleries at their own pace, with highlights including the Temple of Dendur, the European Paintings galleries, and the American Wing. The Met also offers special exhibitions, guided tours, and audio guides that provide deeper insights into the art on display. For a truly unique experience, consider visiting The

Met Cloisters, a branch of the museum located in Fort Tryon Park in Upper Manhattan, which is dedicated to medieval European art and architecture.

Another must-see museum in New York City is the American Museum of Natural History. Located on the Upper West Side of Manhattan, across from Central Park, this museum is a favorite among visitors of all ages, offering a fascinating exploration of the natural world. The museum's exhibits cover a wide range of topics, including dinosaurs, human evolution, the oceans, and outer space. One of the museum's most famous exhibits is the Hall of Saurischian Dinosaurs, which features the towering skeleton of a Tyrannosaurus rex, as well as other prehistoric creatures. The Hall of Ocean Life, with its life-sized model of a blue whale, is another highlight that captivates visitors. To get to the American Museum of Natural History, you can take the B or C subway lines to 81st Street-Museum of Natural History, or the 1 line to 79th Street. Once inside, visitors can explore the museum's extensive exhibits, attend a show at the Hayden Planetarium, or participate in one of the museum's many educational programs and events. The museum also offers a variety of tours, including self-guided, audio, and guided tours, that provide a deeper understanding of the exhibits and their significance.

For those who appreciate modern and contemporary art, The Museum of Modern Art (MoMA) is a must-visit destination. Located in Midtown Manhattan at 11 West 53rd Street, MoMA is one of the most influential modern art museums in the world, featuring an extensive collection of paintings, sculptures, photography, design, and media. The museum is home to iconic works such as Vincent van Gogh's "Starry Night," Pablo Picasso's "Les Demoiselles d'Avignon," and Andy Warhol's "Campbell's Soup Cans." To get to MoMA, you can take the E or M subway lines to 5th Avenue-53rd Street, or the B, D, F, or M lines to 47th-50th Streets-Rockefeller Center. Once inside, visitors can explore the museum's galleries, enjoy a meal at the museum's café, or relax in the sculpture garden, which provides a peaceful outdoor space to reflect on the art. MoMA also hosts special exhibitions, film screenings, and educational programs that offer visitors a deeper engagement with modern and contemporary art.

While the city's famous museums are undoubtedly impressive, New York is also home to a number of specialty museums and hidden gems that offer unique and engaging experiences. One such museum is the Tenement Museum, located at 103 Orchard Street on the Lower East Side. This museum is dedicated to the history of immigration in New York City, with a focus on the lives of the working-class immigrants who lived in the tenement buildings of the Lower East Side in the 19th and early 20th centuries. The museum offers guided tours of the restored tenement apartments, where visitors can learn about the challenges and triumphs of the immigrant experience. To get to the Tenement Museum, you can take the F subway line to Delancey Street, or the J, M, or Z lines to Essex Street. The museum's tours are led by knowledgeable guides who bring the stories of the immigrants to life, making it a moving and educational experience.

Another hidden gem is the Museum of the Moving Image, located in Astoria, Queens, at 36-01 35th Avenue. This museum is dedicated to the art, history, and technology of film, television, and digital media. The museum's exhibits explore the history of cinema, from the early days of silent films to the latest in digital effects, and feature artifacts such as costumes, props, and behind-the-scenes footage. To get to the Museum of the Moving Image, you can take the R or M subway lines to Steinway Street, or the N or W lines to 36th Avenue. The museum also offers interactive exhibits where visitors can create their own stop-motion animations or experiment with sound effects, making it a fun and engaging experience for visitors of all ages. The museum's film screenings and special events provide additional opportunities to explore the world of film and media.

For those interested in the history of New York City, the New-York Historical Society is a must-visit museum. Located at 170 Central Park West at 77th Street, the New-York Historical Society is the city's oldest museum, offering a comprehensive exploration of New York's history from its founding to the present day. The museum's exhibits cover a wide range of topics, including the American Revolution, the Civil War, and the history of slavery in New York. The museum is also home to the Center for Women's History, which explores the contributions of women to the city's history and culture. To get to the New-York Historical Society, you can take the B or C subway lines to 81st Street-Museum of Natural History, or the 1 line to 79th Street. The museum offers a variety of guided tours, lectures, and educational programs that provide a deeper understanding of the exhibits and their significance. The New-York Historical

Society also houses the DiMenna Children's History Museum, which offers interactive exhibits and activities designed specifically for young visitors, making it a family-friendly destination.

Speaking of family-friendly museums, New York City offers several options that are perfect for visitors with children. One of the most popular family-friendly museums is the Children's Museum of Manhattan (CMOM), located at 212 West 83rd Street on the Upper West Side. This museum is designed specifically for children, offering a variety of hands-on exhibits and activities that encourage learning through play. The museum's exhibits cover topics such as art, science, culture, and health, with activities that allow children to explore, create, and discover. To get to the Children's Museum of Manhattan, you can take the 1 subway line to 79th Street, or the B or C lines to 81st Street-Museum of Natural History. The museum also offers special programs, workshops, and performances that provide additional opportunities for fun and learning.

Another great family-friendly museum is the Intrepid Sea, Air & Space Museum, located at Pier 86 on the Hudson River, at 12th Avenue and 46th Street. This museum is housed on the USS Intrepid, a retired aircraft carrier, and features exhibits on aviation, space exploration, and military history. Visitors can explore the ship's decks, climb into a cockpit, and see historic aircraft up close. The museum is also home to the Space Shuttle Pavilion, which houses the space shuttle Enterprise. To get to the Intrepid Sea, Air & Space Museum, you can take the A, C, or E subway lines to 42nd Street-Port Authority Bus Terminal, and then walk west to 12th Avenue.

The museum offers interactive exhibits, simulators, and educational programs that make it an exciting and engaging destination for visitors of all ages.

For a unique experience, families can visit the New York Transit Museum, located in a historic subway station at 99 Schermerhorn Street in Downtown Brooklyn. This museum is dedicated to the history of public transportation in New York City, with exhibits that explore the development of the city's subway, bus, and trolley systems. The museum features vintage subway cars, interactive exhibits, and a variety of educational programs that provide a fun and informative experience for visitors of all ages. To get to the New York Transit Museum, you can take the 2, 3, 4, or 5 subway lines to Borough Hall, or the A, C, or F lines to Jay Street-MetroTech. The museum offers special events and programs for children, making it a great destination for families interested in learning more about the history of New York's transportation system.

New York City's museums offer a wealth of opportunities for exploration, learning, and enjoyment. Whether you're interested in art, history, science, or culture, the city's museums provide something for everyone. From the world-famous Metropolitan

Museum of Art and the American Museum of Natural History to the hidden gems like the Tenement Museum and the Museum of the Moving Image, each museum offers a unique experience that allows visitors to connect with the city's rich cultural heritage. For families, the city's family-friendly museums provide fun and educational experiences that are sure to be memorable for visitors of all ages. Whether you're a first-time visitor or a seasoned New Yorker, exploring the city's museums is an essential part of experiencing the richness and diversity of New York City.

Off the Beaten Paths

New York City is a sprawling metropolis that offers countless well-known attractions, but for those willing to venture off the beaten path, the city reveals hidden gems that showcase its unique character and vibrant diversity. These lesser-known neighborhoods, attractions, and experiences offer a more intimate glimpse into the city's soul, providing visitors with opportunities to explore areas and sites that many tourists overlook.

One of the most fascinating neighborhoods to explore off the beaten path is Red Hook in Brooklyn. Red Hook is a waterfront neighborhood that has retained much of its industrial charm while evolving into a hub for artists, makers, and food enthusiasts. Located on the western edge of Brooklyn, Red Hook offers stunning views of the Statue of Liberty and the Manhattan skyline, making it a perfect destination for those who appreciate both history and modern creativity. To get to Red Hook, you can take the F or G subway lines to Smith-9th Streets and then transfer to the B61 bus, which will take you directly into the heart of the neighborhood. Once there, you can explore the Red Hook waterfront, visit the Red Hook Winery for a wine tasting, and enjoy delicious seafood at local eateries like Red Hook Lobster Pound. The neighborhood is also home to a variety of art galleries, studios, and the historic Red Hook Grain Terminal, which offers a glimpse into the area's industrial past. A walk along the waterfront at sunset is particularly memorable, as you can watch the sun dip below the horizon with the Statue of Liberty in the distance.

Another unique neighborhood that offers a more local experience is Jackson Heights in Queens. Jackson Heights is one of the most culturally diverse neighborhoods in New York City, with residents hailing from all over the world, including South Asia, Latin America, and Southeast Asia. This diversity is reflected in the neighborhood's vibrant street life, colorful markets, and delicious food offerings. To get to Jackson Heights, you can take the 7, E, F, M, or R subway lines to Jackson Heights-Roosevelt Avenue. Once there, you can explore the bustling 74th Street, often referred to as "Little India," where you'll find shops selling traditional Indian clothing, jewelry, and spices. The area is also known for its authentic South Asian cuisine, with restaurants offering dishes like biryani, dosa, and chaat. For a true taste of the neighborhood, visit the Jackson Heights Greenmarket, held on Sundays, where you can sample fresh produce and homemade goods from local vendors. Jackson Heights is also home to a number of beautiful pre-war garden apartments and co-ops, making it a lovely area for a leisurely stroll.

For those interested in exploring the rich history and charm of old New York, the neighborhood of Greenwood Heights in Brooklyn offers a quiet retreat from the city's hustle and bustle. Greenwood Heights is located south of Park Slope and is named after Green-Wood Cemetery, a sprawling and historic cemetery that dates back to 1838. Green-Wood

Cemetery is not just a burial ground but also a beautiful and serene park that offers stunning views, lush landscapes, and a fascinating glimpse into New York's past. To get to Greenwood Heights, you can take the R subway line to 25th Street, and from there, it's a short walk to the cemetery entrance. Once inside Green-Wood, you can explore its winding paths, visit the graves of famous New Yorkers such as Jean-Michel Basquiat and Leonard Bernstein, and admire the impressive Gothic Revival architecture of the cemetery's chapel. The cemetery also offers guided tours and special events, including nighttime tours that highlight the cemetery's history and architecture under the moonlight. After your visit, you can explore the surrounding neighborhood, which is home to charming cafes, local eateries, and a growing number of art studios.

In Manhattan, the neighborhood of East Harlem offers a rich cultural experience that is often overlooked by tourists. Also known as "El Barrio," East Harlem is a vibrant neighborhood with a strong Puerto Rican and Latino heritage, as well as a growing Mexican and Central American community. To get to East Harlem, you can take the 6-subway line to 103rd Street or the 2 or 3 lines to 116th Street. Once there, you can explore the area's many murals and street art, which reflect the neighborhood's cultural pride and history. East Harlem is also home to the El Museo del Barrio, a museum dedicated to Latin American and Caribbean art, culture, and history. The museum offers a variety of exhibits, workshops, and events that celebrate the contributions of the Latino community to New York City. While in East Harlem, be sure to visit local restaurants like La Fonda Boricua and El Paso Taqueria, where you can enjoy authentic Puerto Rican and Mexican cuisine. The neighborhood's rich cultural history, vibrant street life, and welcoming community make it a must-visit for those looking to experience a different side of Manhattan.

For those interested in lesser-known attractions and sites, the City Island in the Bronx offers a charming and unexpected escape from the city. City Island is a small, picturesque island that feels more like a New England fishing village than a part of New York City. To get to City Island, you can take the 6 subway line to Pelham Bay Park and then transfer to the Bx29 bus, which will take you across the bridge to the island. Once on City Island, you can explore its quaint streets, visit local art galleries, and enjoy fresh seafood at one of the many waterfront restaurants. The island is also home to the City Island Nautical Museum, which offers a glimpse into the island's maritime history. A walk along the island's shores provides beautiful views of Long Island Sound and is a perfect way to spend a relaxing afternoon. City Island is also known for its community events, such as the annual City Island Art and Craft Fair, where you can browse handmade goods and meet local artists.

Another lesser-known site that offers a unique experience is the Elevated Acre, a hidden park located in the Financial District. The Elevated Acre is a one-acre park located on the roof of a parking garage at 55 Water Street, offering stunning views of the East River, the Brooklyn Bridge, and the city skyline. To get to the Elevated Acre, you can take the 2, 3, 4, or 5 subway lines to Wall Street, or the J or Z lines to Broad Street. The park is a peaceful retreat from the hustle and bustle of the Financial District, with beautifully landscaped gardens, seating areas, and an amphitheater where free performances are sometimes held. The Elevated Acre is a great spot to relax, have a picnic, or simply enjoy the view. The park's hidden location and tranquil atmosphere make it a perfect escape for those looking to take a break from the city's crowded streets.

For those interested in alternative tours and experiences, New York City offers a variety of options that allow you to explore the city in unique and unconventional ways. One such experience is a bike tour of Governors Island, a small island located just off the southern tip of Manhattan. Governors Island is a former military base that has been transformed into a public park, offering stunning views, historic sites, and plenty of green space for outdoor activities. To get to Governors Island, you can take a ferry from the Battery Maritime Building in Lower Manhattan or from Pier 6 in Brooklyn Bridge Park. Once on the island, you can rent a bike and explore its many paths, visit historic buildings like Fort Jay and Castle Williams, and enjoy a picnic on the Great Lawn. The island also hosts a variety of events and festivals throughout the year, making it a lively and engaging destination.

Another alternative experience is a food tour of Flushing, Queens, a neighborhood known for its incredible diversity and delicious cuisine. Flushing is home to one of the largest and most vibrant Asian communities in New York City, with a wide variety of restaurants, markets, and food stalls offering dishes from China, Korea, Japan, and beyond. To get to Flushing, you can take the 7-subway line to Flushing-Main Street. Once there, you can join a guided food tour that will take you to some of the best and most authentic eateries in the neighborhood, where you can sample everything from dim sum and hand-pulled noodles to Korean barbecue and bubble tea. A food tour of Flushing is a delicious and immersive way to experience the neighborhood's rich culinary traditions and cultural diversity.

For those interested in exploring New York City's natural beauty, a kayak tour on the Hudson River offers a unique perspective of the city. Several organizations, including the Downtown Boathouse and the Brooklyn Bridge Park Boathouse, offer free and low-cost kayaking programs that allow you to paddle along the Hudson River, taking in views of the Manhattan skyline, the Statue of Liberty, and the Brooklyn Bridge. To participate, simply show up at one of the designated launch sites, such as Pier 26 in Tribeca or Pier 4 in Brooklyn Bridge Park, during the scheduled program times. Kayaking on the Hudson River is a fun and refreshing way to experience the city's waterfront, and it's suitable for both beginners and experienced paddlers.

New York City is a treasure trove of unique neighborhoods, lesser-known attractions, and alternative experiences that offer a deeper and more authentic connection to the city. Whether you're exploring the industrial charm of Red Hook, the cultural richness of Jackson Heights, or the serene beauty of Greenwood Heights, these off-the-beaten-path destinations provide a fresh perspective on New York's diverse and vibrant character. By venturing beyond the usual tourist spots, you'll discover a side of the city that is rich with history, culture, and local flavor, making your visit to New York City truly unforgettable. Whether you're biking around Governors Island, sampling food in Flushing, or kayaking on the Hudson River, these unique experiences offer a chance to see the city in a whole new light, creating lasting memories and a deeper appreciation for all that New York has to offer.

Hidden Gems

New York City is full of iconic landmarks and tourist attractions, but for those who want to experience the city like a local, there are countless hidden gems waiting to be discovered. These secret spots, tucked-away restaurants, and unusual attractions offer a more intimate and unique experience, revealing the city's lesser-known treasures that are often overlooked by tourists.

One of the most fascinating hidden gems in New York City is The Elevated Acre, a secluded rooftop park located in the Financial District. This one-acre park, nestled between skyscrapers at 55 Water Street, offers a peaceful retreat from the hustle and bustle of the city below. The Elevated Acre features beautifully landscaped gardens, a grassy lawn, and an amphitheater with stunning views of the East River, the Brooklyn Bridge, and the city skyline. Despite its central location, the park is often overlooked by tourists, making it a perfect spot for a quiet picnic, a relaxing break, or even a small event. To get to The Elevated Acre, you can take the 2, 3, 4, or 5 subway lines to Wall Street, or the J or Z lines to Broad Street. Once there, enter the Water Street building and take the escalator to the park, which is situated on the elevated platform above the parking garage. The park's hidden location and serene atmosphere make it a true hidden gem, providing a unique perspective of the city.

Another secret spot that only locals tend to know about is The Garden at St. Luke in the Fields, a hidden oasis in the heart of the West Village. This lush, walled garden, located at 487 Hudson Street, is part of the St. Luke in the Fields Episcopal Church and offers a tranquil escape from the busy streets of Manhattan. The garden is beautifully maintained, with flowering plants, shady trees, and benches where visitors can sit and enjoy the peaceful surroundings. The garden is especially lovely in the spring and summer when the flowers are in full bloom, attracting birds and butterflies. To get to the Garden at St. Luke in the Fields, you can take the 1 subway line to Christopher Street-Sheridan Square, or the A, C, E, B, D, F, or M lines to West 4th Street-Washington Square. The garden is open to the public during daylight hours and is free to visit, making it a perfect spot for a quiet moment of reflection or a leisurely stroll.

For those interested in hidden restaurants and bars, Please Don't Tell (PDT) is a must-visit speakeasy located in the East Village. PDT is one of New York City's most famous secret bars, hidden behind a phone booth inside the hot dog joint Crif Dogs at 113 St. Marks Place. To enter, you must step into the phone booth, pick up the receiver, and dial the number to be granted access to the bar. Once inside, you'll find a cozy, dimly lit space with a menu of creative cocktails and gourmet hot dogs. PDT is known for its intimate atmosphere, expertly crafted drinks, and the sense of exclusivity that comes with finding this hidden gem. To get to PDT, you can take the 6 subway line to Astor Place, or the L line to 1st Avenue. Due to its popularity, it's recommended to make a reservation in advance, as the bar fills up quickly, especially on weekends. A visit to PDT offers a unique and memorable nightlife experience, combining the nostalgia of Prohibition-era speakeasies with the modern creativity of New York's cocktail scene.

Another hidden culinary gem is Freemans, a restaurant tucked away at the end of a narrow alley off the Bowery. Located at the end of Freemans Alley, between Rivington and Stanton Streets, Freemans offers a rustic, cozy atmosphere with a menu of hearty American fare. The restaurant's entrance is easy to miss, as it's located at the back of the alley, but once you find it, you'll be greeted by a warm and inviting space filled with antique furnishings, taxidermy, and soft candlelight. The menu features dishes like roasted bone marrow, lamb shepherd's pie, and a variety of seasonal vegetables, all prepared with care and attention to detail. To get to Freemans, you can take the F subway line to 2nd Avenue, or the J, Z, 6, B, D, or M lines to Bowery. Freemans is open for brunch, lunch, and dinner, making it a great spot for any meal. The restaurant's hidden location and charming ambiance make it a favorite among locals and a must-visit for those looking to experience a true New York hidden gem.

For those who enjoy unusual attractions and activities, the Museum of the American Gangster offers a unique glimpse into New York City's Prohibition-era history. Located at 80 St. Marks Place in the East Village, this small museum is housed in a former speakeasy and explores the history of organized crime in America, with a focus on the rise of the mafia and the impact of Prohibition. The museum features exhibits on famous gangsters like Al Capone and Lucky Luciano, as well as artifacts such as tommy guns, bootlegged liquor, and original Prohibition-era documents. To get to the

Museum of the American Gangster, you can take the 6 subway line to Astor Place, or the L line to 1st Avenue. The museum offers guided tours that provide in-depth information about the exhibits and the history of organized crime in New York City. After your visit, you can explore the surrounding East Village neighborhood, which is filled with historic buildings, vintage shops, and unique eateries.

Another unusual attraction worth visiting is the Mmuseumm, a tiny museum located in a freight elevator in a narrow alley in Tribeca. Mmuseumm is a "modern natural history museum" that showcases a rotating collection of everyday objects and artifacts from around the world. The museum's exhibits are quirky and eclectic, featuring items like a collection of cornflakes, counterfeit objects, and artifacts from the 2008 financial crisis. Despite its small size, Mmuseumm offers a thought-provoking exploration of the mundane and the overlooked, inviting visitors to reconsider the significance of everyday objects. To get to Mmuseumm, you can take the 1, 2, 3, A, C, or E subway lines to Chambers Street, or the N, Q, R, W, J, or Z lines to Canal Street. The museum is located in Cortlandt Alley, and visitors can view the exhibits through the windows of the freight elevator or step inside for a closer look. Mmuseumm is open on weekends and by appointment, and admission is free, making it a perfect stop for those interested in unconventional art and culture.

For a truly unique experience, consider taking a Secret Subway Tour of the abandoned City Hall Station, one of New York City's most beautiful and historic subway stations. City Hall Station, which opened in 1904, was the original southern terminus of the city's first subway line and features stunning architecture, including arched ceilings, skylights, and ornate tile work. The station was closed to the public in 1945 but can still be visited on special tours offered by the New York Transit Museum. To get to City Hall Station, you can take the 4, 5, 6, J, or Z subway lines to Brooklyn Bridge-City Hall, and then board a 6 train to see the station as the train loops around before heading uptown. The Secret Subway Tour provides a rare opportunity to explore this hidden architectural gem and learn about the history of New York's subway system. The tour is only available to members of the New York Transit Museum, so it's recommended to join the museum in advance if you're interested in this unique experience.

New York City is filled with hidden gems that offer a more intimate and unique experience for those willing to venture off the beaten path. From secret parks and gardens to hidden restaurants, speakeasies, and unusual museums, the city's lesser-known treasures reveal a side of New York that is often overlooked by tourists. Whether you're enjoying a quiet moment at The Elevated Acre, savoring a cocktail at Please Don't Tell, or exploring the quirky exhibits at Mmuseumm, these hidden gems provide a deeper connection to the city's rich history, culture, and diversity. By seeking out these secret spots, you'll discover a New York that is full of surprises and unforgettable experiences, making your visit truly special and one-of-a-kind.

Historical Landmarks and Monuments

New York City, with its rich and storied history, is home to an array of historical landmarks and monuments that serve as lasting reminders of the city's past. These sites not only reflect the architectural and cultural heritage of the city but also tell the stories of the people, events, and movements that have shaped New York into what it is today. From iconic statues that symbolize freedom to historic buildings that have witnessed centuries of change, these landmarks are integral to understanding the city's history.

One of the most significant historical landmarks in New York City is the Statue of Liberty, a symbol of freedom and democracy recognized around the world. Located on Liberty Island in New York Harbor, the Statue of Liberty was a gift from France to the United States in 1886 to celebrate the centennial of American independence and to symbolize the enduring friendship between the two nations. The statue, designed by French sculptor Frédéric Auguste Bartholdi and engineered by Gustave Eiffel, stands at 305 feet tall, including its pedestal, and depicts a robed female figure representing Libertas, the Roman goddess of freedom. The statue holds a torch in her right hand, symbolizing enlightenment, and a tablet in her left hand inscribed with the date of the American Declaration of Independence, July 4, 1776. To visit the Statue of Liberty, you can take a ferry from Battery Park in Lower Manhattan, which also stops at Ellis Island. The ferry ride offers stunning views of the Manhattan skyline and the harbor. Once on Liberty Island, visitors can explore the grounds, visit the museum located inside the pedestal, and, with a special ticket, climb to the crown for panoramic views of the city and harbor. The Statue of Liberty is not just a monumental piece of art but also a powerful symbol of hope and freedom, making it an essential stop for anyone interested in American history.

Another landmark of great historical importance is Ellis Island, which served as the primary immigration station for the United States from 1892 to 1954. Located just a short ferry ride from the Statue of Liberty, Ellis Island was the entry point for millions of immigrants seeking a new life in America. The island's main building, now the Ellis Island National Museum of Immigration, has been meticulously restored and houses exhibits that tell the stories of the immigrants who passed through its halls. The museum's exhibits include photographs, documents, and personal artifacts that provide a poignant look at the immigrant experience, including the challenges and triumphs of starting a new life in a foreign land. To get to Ellis Island, you can take the same ferry that services the Statue of Liberty, departing from Battery Park. Once on the island, visitors can take a self-guided tour of the museum, explore the restored Great Hall where immigrants were processed, and search for their ancestors in the museum's passenger records database. Ellis Island is a place of deep historical significance, offering a moving and insightful look at the immigrant experience that has shaped the United States.

In the heart of Manhattan stands Federal Hall National Memorial, a site of immense historical importance as the location where George Washington took the oath of office as the first President of the United States in 1789. Located at 26 Wall Street, Federal Hall was originally built as New York's City Hall in 1703 and later became the first capitol of the United States under the Constitution. The current building, constructed in the Greek Revival style in 1842, serves as a museum and memorial to the early history of the United States. Inside, visitors can view exhibits on the early government of the United States, including Washington's inauguration, the drafting of the Bill of Rights, and the nation's first Congress. The building also features a rotunda with a marble statue of George Washington, a replica of the Bible used during his inauguration, and other artifacts related to the founding of the nation. To visit Federal Hall, you can take the 2, 3, 4, or 5 subway lines to Wall Street. Federal Hall is open to the public and offers free admission, making it an accessible and educational stop for anyone interested in the early history of the United States. The site's rich history and its role in the birth of the nation make it a must-visit for history enthusiasts.

Another iconic historical site in New York City is The Empire State Building, an enduring symbol of American ingenuity and ambition. Completed in 1931 during the Great Depression, the Empire State Building was the tallest building in the world for nearly 40 years and remains one of the most recognizable skyscrapers globally. Located at 350 Fifth Avenue in Midtown Manhattan, the building stands 1,454 feet tall, including its antenna, and offers breathtaking views of the city from its observation decks on the 86th and 102nd floors. The construction of the Empire State Building was a remarkable feat, completed in just over a year, and it quickly became an icon of the New York skyline. Visitors can learn about the building's history and construction through exhibits located in the lobby and on the observation deck floors. To visit, you can take the B, D, F, M, N, Q, R, or W subway lines to 34th Street-Herald Square, or the 1, 2, or 3 lines to 34th Street-Penn Station. The Empire State Building offers both daytime and nighttime visits, each providing a unique perspective of the city below. The building's historical significance, architectural beauty, and stunning views make it a must-see landmark in New York City.

In the southern part of Manhattan, The 9/11 Memorial & Museum stands as a powerful tribute to the nearly 3,000 people who lost their lives in the September 11, 2001, terrorist attacks, as well as the six people killed in the 1993 World Trade Center bombing. Located at the site of the former World Trade Center complex, the 9/11 Memorial consists of two large reflecting pools set within the footprints of the Twin Towers, with the names of the victims inscribed on bronze panels surrounding the pools. The adjacent museum tells the story of 9/11 through artifacts, photographs, and personal stories, providing a deeply moving and educational experience. The museum's exhibits include remnants of the original World Trade Center, recordings of emergency calls, and personal items recovered from the site, all of which help to convey the impact of the events on individuals and the nation as a whole. To visit the 9/11 Memorial & Museum, you can take the A, C, E, 1, 2, or 3 subway lines to Chambers Street, or the R, W lines to Cortlandt Street. The memorial is free to visit, while the museum requires an admission fee. The 9/11 Memorial & Museum is a place of reflection, remembrance, and learning, offering visitors a chance to honor the lives lost and understand the events that shaped the world we live in today.

One of the most famous and visited monuments in New York City is The Washington Square Arch, located in the heart of Greenwich Village at the northern end of Washington Square Park. The arch was erected in 1892 to commemorate the centennial of George Washington's inauguration as the first President of the United States. Designed by Stanford White, the arch is modeled after the Arc de Triomphe in Paris and features sculptures of George Washington in both his military and civilian roles. Washington Square Park itself is a vibrant and lively space, known for its bohemian history and as a gathering place for artists, musicians, and performers. The arch and park have long been symbols of free expression and cultural diversity in New York City. To visit the Washington Square Arch, you can take the A, B, C, D, E, F, or M subway lines to West 4th Street-Washington Square, or the 1 subway line to Christopher Street-Sheridan Square. Visitors can enjoy a stroll through the park, relax on a bench, and take in the lively atmosphere while admiring the historic architecture of the arch.

Another important historical monument in New York City is the African Burial Ground National Monument, located in Lower Manhattan at 290 Broadway. This site marks the location of a burial ground used by free and enslaved Africans from the 1690s until 1794. Discovered during construction in the 1990s, the burial ground is one of the most significant archaeological finds in New York City's history, providing a tangible link to the African community in colonial New York. The monument includes an outdoor memorial, as well as an interpretive center that explores the history and significance of the site. The memorial, designed by architect Rodney Leon, features a large granite monument with symbols and inscriptions that honor the African ancestors buried there. The interpretive center offers exhibits on the history of slavery in New York, the African community in the city, and the process of discovering and preserving the burial ground. To visit the African Burial Ground National Monument, you can take the 4, 5, J, or Z subway lines to Brooklyn Bridge-City Hall, or the A, C, 2, 3 subway lines to Chambers Street. The site is open to the public and offers free admission, making it a deeply meaningful and educational destination for visitors interested in learning more about the history of African Americans in New York City.

New York City's historical landmarks and monuments offer a wealth of opportunities to explore the city's rich past and understand the events and people that have shaped its history. From the towering Statue of Liberty to the solemn 9/11 Memorial, these sites serve as reminders of the city's resilience, diversity, and enduring significance in American history. By visiting these landmarks, you'll gain a deeper appreciation for the history and culture of New York City, making your trip not only enjoyable but also enlightening and memorable. Whether you're exploring the immigrant stories at Ellis Island, standing in the shadow of the Empire State Building, or reflecting on the history of slavery at the African Burial Ground, each site offers a unique and powerful connection to the city's past.

Self-Guided Tours and Walks

Exploring New York City on foot is one of the best ways to truly immerse yourself in its rich history, diverse culture, and vibrant neighborhoods. The city's layout, with its grid system and numerous parks, makes it ideal for walking tours and self-guided explorations. Whether you're interested in discovering the unique character of different neighborhoods, following a themed route that highlights specific aspects of the city's history and culture, or simply enjoying a leisurely stroll through iconic areas, New York City offers countless opportunities for unforgettable walks.

One of the most iconic walking tours in New York City is a stroll across the Brooklyn Bridge, which offers breathtaking views of the Manhattan skyline and the East River. The Brooklyn Bridge, completed in 1883, is one of the oldest suspension bridges in the United States and a symbol of New York's engineering prowess. To start your walk, you can enter the pedestrian pathway from the Manhattan side at City Hall Park, near the entrance at Centre Street. The closest subway stations are the 4, 5, 6, J, or Z lines to Brooklyn Bridge-City Hall, or the A, C lines to Chambers Street. As you walk across the bridge, take your time to enjoy the views of the Statue of Liberty, the Empire State Building, and the towering skyscrapers of Lower Manhattan. The bridge's Gothic-style towers and web of cables create a stunning architectural backdrop for photos. Once you reach the Brooklyn side, you can continue your walk into the vibrant neighborhood of DUMBO (Down Under the Manhattan Bridge Overpass), where you'll find cobblestone streets, art galleries, and excellent dining options. From DUMBO, you can explore Brooklyn Bridge Park, a waterfront green space that offers even more stunning views and activities like kayaking and picnicking. The walk across the Brooklyn Bridge is a must-do for any visitor to New York City, providing both a historical and scenic experience.

Another popular walking tour is through Central Park, an urban oasis in the heart of Manhattan that spans 843 acres. Central Park is one of the most famous parks in the world and offers a diverse range of landscapes, from manicured gardens to wooded areas and open meadows. To begin your self-guided tour, you can enter the park at its southernmost point at 59th Street and 5th Avenue, accessible by the N, R, W subway lines to 5th Avenue-59th Street, or the A, B, C, D, 1 lines to 59th Street-Columbus Circle. As you explore Central Park, be sure to visit iconic landmarks such as Bethesda Terrace and Fountain, where you can enjoy views of the Lake and listen to live performances by musicians. Continue north to the Central Park Mall, a grand promenade lined with American elm trees that leads to the Bethesda Terrace. The park's many bridges, statues, and fountains offer countless photo opportunities and a chance to relax in a peaceful setting. Other highlights include the Central Park Zoo, where you can see animals from around the world, and the Bow Bridge, an elegant cast-iron bridge that spans the Lake and offers picturesque views. For a more serene experience, visit the Conservatory Garden, a formal garden located on the east side of the park at 105th Street. Central Park is a place where you can spend hours exploring, whether you're interested in nature, art, or simply enjoying a walk in a beautiful setting.

For those interested in exploring New York's diverse neighborhoods, a walking tour of Greenwich Village offers a fascinating journey through one of the city's most historic and culturally rich areas. Greenwich Village, often simply called "the Village," is known for its bohemian history, charming streets, and vibrant arts scene. To start your tour, you can take the A, B, C, D, E, F, or M subway lines to West 4th Street-Washington Square and begin at Washington Square Park, the heart of the Village. The park is dominated by the Washington Square Arch, a grand monument that has long been a gathering place for artists, musicians, and activists. From the park, you can wander the narrow, tree-lined streets of the Village, where you'll find historic brownstones, small independent shops, and cozy cafes. Be sure to visit MacDougal Street, known for its lively atmosphere and historic venues like the Comedy Cellar, a famous comedy club that has hosted some of the biggest names in stand-up. Another highlight is the Stonewall Inn on Christopher Street, a National Historic Landmark that was the site of the 1969 Stonewall Riots, a pivotal event in the LGBTQ+ rights movement. The Village's blend of history, culture, and creativity makes it a must-see neighborhood for any visitor to New York City.

If you're looking for a themed self-guided tour, a Harlem Renaissance Walking Tour offers a deep dive into the cultural history of Harlem, a neighborhood that was the center of African American culture and arts in the early 20th century. The Harlem Renaissance was a period of flourishing arts, literature, and music that produced some of the most influential figures in American culture, including Langston Hughes, Zora Neale Hurston, and Duke Ellington. To begin your tour, you can take the 2, 3 subway lines to 125th Street and start at the Apollo Theater, located at 253 West 125th Street. The Apollo is one of the most famous music venues in the world and has been a launching pad for legendary artists like Ella Fitzgerald, James Brown, and Aretha Franklin. From there, you can explore the surrounding streets, where you'll find historic churches, jazz clubs, and landmarks like the Schomburg Center for Research in Black Culture, a research library dedicated to the study of African American history and culture. The Schomburg Center is located at 515 Malcolm X Boulevard (Lenox Avenue), and offers exhibits and events that highlight the contributions of African Americans to the arts, politics, and society. A Harlem Renaissance Walking Tour provides a rich and educational experience, allowing you to connect with the cultural legacy of one of New York City's most vibrant neighborhoods.

For those who prefer to explore New York's history, a Lower Manhattan Walking Tour offers a journey through the city's oldest and most historically significant area. Lower Manhattan, also known as Downtown, is where New York

City began, and it's home to some of the city's most important landmarks and monuments. To start your tour, you can take the 4, 5, J, Z subway lines to Brooklyn Bridge-City Hall and begin at the Brooklyn Bridge entrance. From there, walk south to Wall Street, the financial heart of the city and home to the New York Stock Exchange and Federal Hall. Federal Hall, located at 26 Wall Street, is where George Washington took the oath of office as the first President of the United States. Continue your walk to Trinity Church, one of the oldest churches in New York, where you can visit the grave of Alexander Hamilton, one of the Founding Fathers of the United States. From Trinity Church, walk down Broadway to the Charging Bull statue, a symbol of Wall Street and financial optimism. Your tour can end at Battery Park, where you can enjoy views of the Statue of Liberty and Ellis Island. A Lower Manhattan Walking Tour offers a deep connection to the city's history and provides a fascinating look at the events and people that have shaped New York.

For those who enjoy scenic walks, the High Line offers a unique and elevated perspective of the city. The High Line is a linear park built on a former elevated railroad track that runs along Manhattan's West Side, from Gansevoort Street in the Meatpacking District to 34th Street near Hudson Yards. The park is beautifully landscaped with gardens, public art installations, and seating areas, making it a popular spot for both locals and tourists. To start your walk, you can enter the High Line at its southernmost point at Gansevoort Street, accessible by the A, C, E, or L subway lines to 14th Street-8th Avenue. As you walk north along the High Line, you'll pass through neighborhoods like Chelsea and Hell's Kitchen, with views of the Hudson River, the Empire State

Building, and the modern architecture of Hudson Yards. The High Line also offers access to attractions like the Whitney Museum of American Art, located at the southern entrance, and Chelsea Market, a food hall and shopping destination located just below the park. Walking the High Line is a relaxing and scenic experience that allows you to see the city from a different angle while enjoying the beauty of urban green space.

New York City's self-guided tours and walks offer countless opportunities to explore the city's diverse neighborhoods, rich history, and scenic beauty on foot. Whether you're crossing the Brooklyn Bridge, wandering through Central Park, or discovering the cultural history of Harlem, these walking tours provide a deeper connection to the city and allow you to experience New York at your own pace. By exploring on foot, you'll have the chance to see the city up close, discover hidden gems, and create lasting memories of your visit. Whether you're following a themed route, exploring a historic neighborhood, or simply enjoying a leisurely stroll through one of the city's iconic parks, New York City's walking tours offer an unforgettable experience for visitors of all interests and ages.

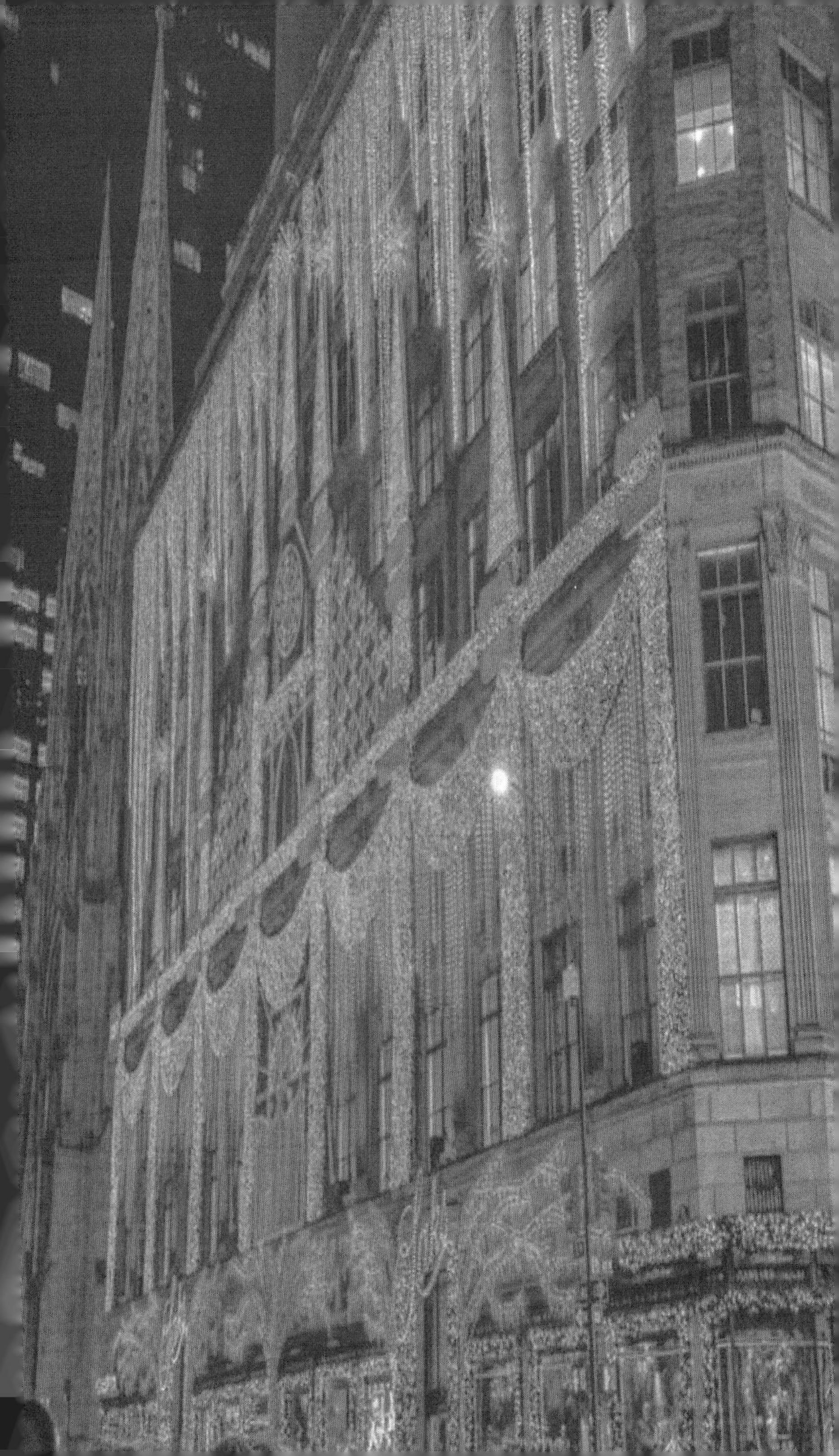

CHAPTER 9

EXPERIENCING LOCAL CULTURE AND EVENTS

Festivals and Celebrations Throughout the Year

New York City is a cultural melting pot, and throughout the year, it hosts a wide array of festivals and celebrations that reflect its diverse population and vibrant spirit. From iconic parades that draw millions of spectators to local street fairs that bring neighborhoods to life, the city offers endless opportunities to experience its rich cultural tapestry. These events not only showcase the city's traditions but also provide visitors with a chance to participate in local festivities, whether by watching a parade, dancing at a street festival, or savoring the flavors of global cuisines.

One of the most famous annual festivals in New York City is the Macy's Thanksgiving Day Parade, a beloved tradition that has been delighting audiences since 1924. Held on Thanksgiving Day, which falls on the fourth Thursday of November, the parade features giant balloons, floats, marching bands, and performances by Broadway casts and musical artists. The parade route starts at 77th Street and Central Park West, continues down to Columbus Circle, and then travels along 6th Avenue before ending at Macy's Herald Square on 34th Street. To get a good spot to watch the parade, it's recommended to arrive early in the morning, as the streets fill up quickly with spectators. The best viewing spots are along Central Park West and 6th Avenue, and you can easily access the route by taking the B, C subway lines to 72nd Street or the 1, 2, 3 lines to 66th Street-Lincoln Center. The Macy's Thanksgiving Day Parade is an iconic New York event that marks the start of the holiday season, and it's a must-see for anyone visiting the city in November.

Another major event that draws large crowds is the New York City Pride March, held every June in celebration of LGBTQ+ pride and equality. The Pride March is the centerpiece of NYC Pride, a month-long series of events that commemorate the 1969 Stonewall Riots, which were a pivotal moment in the LGBTQ+ rights movement. The march typically starts in Midtown Manhattan and travels down 5th Avenue, passing by the historic Stonewall Inn in Greenwich Village before ending in the West Village. The closest subway stations to the route include 14th Street-Union Square (4, 5, 6, L, N, Q, R, W), Christopher Street-Sheridan Square (1), and West 4th Street-Washington Square (A, B, C, D, E, F, M). The Pride March is known for its colorful floats, lively music, and enthusiastic participants, making it one of the most joyous and vibrant events in the city. Visitors can participate by joining the march, attending one of the many Pride parties and events, or simply watching the parade and enjoying the festive atmosphere.

For those who appreciate cultural celebrations, the Chinese New Year Parade in Chinatown is a vibrant and colorful event that showcases Chinese traditions and heritage. The parade, which typically takes place in January or February depending on the lunar calendar, features dragon and lion dances, elaborate costumes, firecrackers, and traditional music. The parade route winds through the narrow streets of Chinatown, with the main festivities centered around Mott Street, Canal Street, and East Broadway. To get to Chinatown, you can take the 6, J, N, Q, R, W, or Z subway lines to Canal Street, or the B, D lines to Grand Street. In addition to the parade, visitors can enjoy delicious Chinese cuisine at the many restaurants in the area, participate in cultural activities like calligraphy and paper cutting, and shop for traditional Chinese New Year decorations and gifts. The Chinese New Year Parade is a lively and festive celebration that offers a glimpse into one of New York's most vibrant communities.

New York City also hosts numerous seasonal celebrations and events that bring the city to life throughout the year. In the winter, the Rockefeller Center Christmas Tree Lighting is a quintessential New York holiday tradition that attracts visitors from around the world. The tree lighting ceremony usually takes place in late November or early December and features live performances by popular artists, culminating in the illumination of the massive Christmas tree, which is adorned with thousands of twinkling lights. The tree remains lit through early January, and visitors can enjoy ice skating at the Rockefeller Center rink, located just below the tree. To get to Rockefeller Center, you can take the B, D, F, or M subway lines to 47th-50th Streets-Rockefeller Center, or the E, M lines to 5th Avenue-53rd Street. The Rockefeller Center Christmas Tree Lighting is a magical event that captures the holiday spirit and is a must-see for anyone visiting New York City during the winter season.

In the spring, the Tribeca Film Festival is a major cultural event that celebrates the art of film and storytelling. Founded by Robert De Niro, Jane Rosenthal, and Craig Hatkoff in 2002, the Tribeca Film Festival showcases a diverse range of films, including independent features, documentaries, shorts, and virtual reality experiences. The festival takes place at various venues throughout Lower Manhattan, including the Tribeca Performing Arts Center, the SVA Theatre, and the BMCC Tribeca Performing Arts Center. To get to the festival, you can take the 1, 2, 3 subway lines to Chambers Street, or the A, C, E lines to Canal Street. In addition to film screenings, the festival offers panel discussions, Q&A sessions with filmmakers, and special events like outdoor screenings and interactive exhibits. The Tribeca Film Festival is a must-attend event for film lovers and offers a unique opportunity to see cutting-edge films and engage with the creative minds behind them.

For a taste of summer in New York, the Fourth of July Fireworks display is a spectacular event that lights up the city's skyline in celebration of Independence Day. The fireworks are launched from barges along the East River, with the main viewing areas located in Midtown Manhattan, Long Island City in Queens, and along the Brooklyn waterfront. To get to the best viewing spots, you can take the 4, 5, 6, 7 subway lines to Grand Central-42nd Street, the N, Q, R, W lines to Lexington Avenue-59th Street, or the L, G lines to Long Island City-Court Square. In addition to the fireworks, many neighborhoods host their own Fourth of July celebrations, including barbecues, block parties, and concerts. Visitors can also enjoy a traditional American picnic in one of the city's many parks, such as Central Park or Prospect Park, before heading to the fireworks display. The Fourth of July Fireworks in New York City is an unforgettable experience that captures the patriotic spirit and excitement of the holiday.

Autumn in New York brings the New York City Marathon, one of the most prestigious marathons in the world. Held on the first Sunday in November, the marathon attracts over 50,000 runners from around the globe, who race through all five boroughs of the city—Staten Island, Brooklyn, Queens, the Bronx, and Manhattan. The marathon route offers stunning views of the city's diverse neighborhoods, iconic landmarks, and enthusiastic crowds of spectators who line the streets to cheer on the runners. To watch the marathon, you can position yourself along various points of the route, with popular viewing spots including First Avenue in Manhattan, Fourth Avenue in Brooklyn, and Central Park, where the marathon finishes near Tavern on the Green. To get to these locations, you can take the 4, 5, 6 subway lines to 86th Street (Manhattan), the R line to 4th Avenue-9th Street (Brooklyn), or the A, C, B, D lines to 59th Street-Columbus Circle (Central Park). The New York City Marathon is not just a sporting event but a citywide celebration that brings together people from all walks of life to support the runners and enjoy the festive atmosphere.

For those who want to actively participate in local festivities, many of New York City's festivals and events offer opportunities to get involved. For example, during the West Indian Day Parade in Brooklyn, visitors can join the lively celebration of Caribbean culture by dancing along with the parade, sampling Caribbean food from street vendors, and enjoying live music performances. The parade takes place on Labor Day in September and travels along Eastern Parkway in Crown Heights, a neighborhood known for its large Caribbean community. To get to the parade, you can take the 2, 3, 4 subway lines to Franklin Avenue, or the 4 line to Utica Avenue. The West Indian Day Parade is a vibrant and energetic event that offers a taste of the Caribbean in the heart of Brooklyn.

Another way to participate in local festivities is by attending one of New York City's many street fairs and food festivals, which take place throughout the year in various neighborhoods. For example, the Feast of San Gennaro in Little Italy is an annual event that celebrates Italian-American culture with food, music, and religious processions. The feast, which takes place in September, features a wide array of Italian dishes, including cannoli, sausage and peppers, and zeppole, as well as live entertainment and games. To get to the Feast of San Gennaro, you can take the 6 subway line to Spring Street, or the N, Q, R, W lines to Canal Street. Visitors can participate by sampling the delicious food, watching the processions, and enjoying the lively atmosphere of Little Italy.

New York City's festivals and celebrations offer a diverse and exciting array of events that reflect the city's rich cultural heritage and vibrant community spirit. Whether you're watching the Macy's Thanksgiving Day Parade, celebrating LGBTQ+ pride at the Pride March, or enjoying a summer fireworks display, these events provide unforgettable experiences that capture the essence of New York City. By participating in these local festivities, you'll gain a deeper appreciation for the city's traditions and create lasting memories of your visit. From annual parades to seasonal celebrations, there's always something happening in New York City, making it a dynamic and ever-evolving destination for visitors from around the world.

Local Festivals Calendar

New York City is a year-round destination for cultural and community festivals, with each month bringing a unique array of events that showcase the city's diversity and vibrancy. Whether you're interested in music, food, art, or history, there's always something happening in the city to capture your interest. From large-scale parades that draw millions of spectators to intimate neighborhood fairs, the city's festival calendar is packed with events that celebrate both local traditions and global cultures. By planning your visit around these festivals, you can experience the city's cultural richness and participate in celebrations that make New York City such a dynamic place to visit.

January in New York City kicks off the year with the Three Kings Day Parade in East Harlem, a vibrant celebration of the Epiphany that honors the tradition of the Three Wise Men. This event is particularly popular within the city's Hispanic community and features a lively procession with floats, costumed performers, and live music. The parade starts at 106th Street and Lexington Avenue and winds through the streets of East Harlem. To get there, you can take the 6 subway line to 103rd Street. The event is free and open to the public, offering a wonderful opportunity to experience the cultural traditions of the city's Puerto Rican and Latino communities.

February is marked by the Lunar New Year Parade in Chinatown, celebrating the beginning of the lunar calendar year. This colorful parade is one of the most anticipated events in the Chinese community and features traditional lion and dragon dances, martial arts performances, and vibrant floats. The parade route typically runs along Mott Street, Canal Street, and East Broadway. To get to the parade, you can take the 6, N, Q, R, W, or J subway lines to Canal Street, or the B, D lines to Grand Street. The Lunar New Year Parade is free to attend, and it's best to arrive early to secure a good viewing spot. After the parade, visitors can explore Chinatown's many shops and restaurants, offering a full day of cultural immersion.

March brings the St. Patrick's Day Parade, one of the oldest and largest parades in New York City. Held on March 17th, the parade celebrates Irish culture and heritage with bagpipes, marching bands, and a sea of green-clad participants. The parade travels along 5th Avenue, starting at 44th Street and continuing up to 79th Street, passing by iconic landmarks such as St. Patrick's Cathedral and Central Park. To get to the parade, you can take the B, D, F, M, N, Q, R, or W subway lines to 5th Avenue-59th Street. The St. Patrick's Day Parade is a must-see event that draws large crowds, so it's advisable to arrive early and wear comfortable shoes. After the parade, many people continue the celebration in the city's Irish pubs and restaurants, where you can enjoy traditional Irish music, food, and drink.

In April, the Tribeca Film Festival takes center stage, offering a premier platform for filmmakers to showcase their work. Founded in 2002 by Robert De Niro, the festival features a wide range of films, including independent features, documentaries, and shorts, as well as panel discussions, Q&A sessions with filmmakers, and special events. The festival takes place at various venues throughout Lower Manhattan, including the Tribeca Performing Arts Center and the SVA Theatre. To get to the festival, you can take the 1, 2, 3 subway lines to Chambers Street, or the A, C, E lines to Canal Street. Tickets for the Tribeca Film Festival can be purchased online through the festival's official website, and it's recommended to book in advance, as popular screenings often sell out quickly. The festival is a great opportunity to discover new films, engage with filmmakers, and participate in the city's vibrant arts scene.

May is celebrated with the Dance Parade, a colorful and energetic event that celebrates the diversity of dance in New York City. The parade features dancers from a wide range of genres, including salsa, hip-hop, ballet, and traditional folk dances, all showcasing their talents along the parade route. The Dance Parade begins at 21st Street and Broadway and ends at Tompkins Square Park in the East Village, where a dance festival is held with performances and free dance lessons. To get to the parade, you can take the N, R, W subway lines to 23rd Street, or the 6 line to Astor Place. The Dance Parade is free to attend, and it's a fun and lively way to experience the city's diverse dance culture.

June is Pride Month in New York City, and the NYC Pride March is the highlight of the celebrations. The Pride March commemorates the Stonewall Riots of 1969, which were a turning point in the LGBTQ+ rights movement. The march takes place in late June and travels down 5th Avenue, passing by the Stonewall Inn in Greenwich Village, where the riots began. The event is a joyous and colorful celebration of LGBTQ+ identity and equality, featuring floats, performers, and participants from around the world. To get to the Pride March, you can take the A, B, C, D, E, F, M subway lines to West 4th Street-Washington Square, or the 1 line to Christopher Street-Sheridan Square. The Pride March is free to attend, and everyone is welcome to join in the celebration. It's advisable to arrive early to find a good viewing spot, as the event draws large crowds.

July is synonymous with the Fourth of July Fireworks, a spectacular display that lights up the night sky in celebration of Independence Day. The fireworks are launched from barges along the East River, and the best viewing spots are in Midtown Manhattan, Long Island City in Queens, and along the Brooklyn waterfront. To get to these locations, you can take the 4, 5, 6, 7 subway lines to Grand Central-42nd Street, the N, Q, R, W lines to Lexington Avenue-59th Street, or the L, G lines to Long Island City-Court Square. The Fourth of July Fireworks are free to watch, and it's a good idea to arrive early and bring a blanket or chair to sit on. Many people also bring picnics to enjoy while waiting for the fireworks to begin.

August features the Harlem Week Festival, a month-long celebration of the rich cultural heritage of Harlem. Harlem Week includes a variety of events, including concerts, cultural performances, fashion shows, and family activities.

The festival takes place at various locations throughout Harlem, including Marcus Garvey Park, St. Nicholas Park, and the Apollo Theater. To get to Harlem, you can take the 2, 3 subway lines to 125th Street, or the A, B, C, D lines to 125th Street. Harlem Week offers something for everyone, from music lovers to foodies, and it's a great way to experience the vibrant culture of one of New York City's most historic neighborhoods.

September is marked by the West Indian Day Parade, a vibrant celebration of Caribbean culture held on Labor Day. The parade takes place along Eastern Parkway in Brooklyn and features colorful costumes, steel pan bands, and calypso music. The event is a highlight of the city's Caribbean community and draws participants and spectators from around the world. To get to the parade, you can take the 2, 3, 4 subway lines to Franklin Avenue, or the 4 line to Utica Avenue. The West Indian Day Parade is free to attend, and it's a lively and energetic event that offers a taste of the Caribbean in the heart of Brooklyn.

October is celebrated with the Village Halloween Parade, a whimsical and spooky event that takes place in Greenwich Village on Halloween night. The parade features thousands of participants in elaborate costumes, as well as giant puppets, marching bands, and street performers. The parade route travels up 6th Avenue from Spring Street to 16th Street. To get to the parade, you can take the A, B, C, D, E, F, M subway lines to West 4th Street-Washington Square, or the 1, 2, 3 lines to 14th Street. The Village Halloween Parade is free to watch, and everyone is encouraged to dress up and join in the fun. The event is one of the most creative and entertaining celebrations in the city, offering a unique and festive atmosphere.

November brings the Macy's Thanksgiving Day Parade, a holiday tradition that features giant balloons, floats, marching bands, and performances by Broadway casts and musical artists. The parade route starts at 77th Street and Central Park West, continues down to Columbus Circle, and then travels along 6th Avenue before ending at Macy's Herald Square on 34th Street. To get a good spot to watch the parade, it's recommended to arrive early in the morning, as the streets fill up quickly with spectators. The best viewing spots are along Central Park West and 6th Avenue, and you can easily access the route by taking the B, C subway lines to 72nd Street or the 1, 2, 3 lines to 66th Street-Lincoln Center. The Macy's Thanksgiving Day Parade is an iconic New York event that marks the start of the holiday season.

December is filled with holiday celebrations, including the Rockefeller Center Christmas Tree Lighting, a quintessential New York holiday tradition. The tree lighting ceremony usually takes place in late November or early December and features live performances by popular artists, culminating in the illumination of the massive Christmas tree, which is adorned with thousands of twinkling lights. The tree remains lit through early January, and visitors can enjoy ice skating at the Rockefeller Center rink, located just below the tree. To get to Rockefeller Center, you can take the B, D, F, or M subway lines to 47th-50th Streets-Rockefeller Center, or the E, M lines to 5th Avenue-53rd Street.

Finding festival schedules and tickets is easy with the help of online resources and local guides. Websites like NYCgo and Time Out New York provide comprehensive calendars of upcoming events, including detailed information on dates, locations, and ticket availability. Many festivals also have their own official websites where you can purchase tickets and learn more about the event. For free events, it's important to check the schedule in advance and arrive early to secure a good spot, as these events often draw large crowds. For ticketed events, purchasing in advance is recommended, especially for popular festivals that may sell out quickly.

To enjoy festivals like a local, it's important to immerse yourself in the experience and embrace the city's diverse cultures. Dress comfortably, as you may be on your feet for extended periods, and consider bringing a small bag with essentials like water, snacks, and a portable phone charger. Engage with the locals by asking questions, joining in the activities, and sampling the food. Don't be afraid to step outside your comfort zone and try something new, whether it's a traditional dance at a cultural festival or a unique dish at a food fair. Lastly, be respectful of the city's neighborhoods and communities by following any guidelines or rules set by festival organizers, and remember to leave the area as you found it by disposing of trash properly.

New York City's festival calendar offers a rich and diverse array of events that cater to all interests and tastes. By planning your visit around these festivals, you can experience the city's vibrant culture, connect with its communities, and create lasting memories. Whether you're attending a major parade, exploring a local street fair, or enjoying a holiday celebration, New York City's festivals provide an exciting and dynamic way to experience the city throughout the year.

Public Events and Parades

New York City is renowned for its vibrant public events and parades, which draw millions of spectators and participants each year. These events, ranging from grand parades that celebrate cultural heritage to community-driven gatherings that highlight local causes, are integral to the city's identity. They provide an opportunity for residents and visitors alike to experience the energy, diversity, and spirit of New York in a way that is both engaging and memorable.

One of the most famous and widely attended public events in New York City is the Macy's Thanksgiving Day Parade, which takes place annually on Thanksgiving Day in November. This parade, known for its giant helium balloons, elaborate floats, and performances by Broadway casts and musical artists, has been a cherished tradition since 1924. The parade begins at 77th Street and Central Park West, travels down to Columbus Circle, and then continues along 6th Avenue before ending at Macy's Herald Square on 34th Street. The best viewing spots for the parade include the area along Central Park West between 75th and 59th Streets, where the crowds are generally lighter and you can get a closer view of the balloons as they pass by. Another great spot is along 6th Avenue, particularly between 38th and 34th Streets, where you can see the parade as it approaches its final destination. To get to these viewing areas, you can take the B, C subway lines to 72nd Street, or the 1, 2, 3 lines to 66th

Street-Lincoln Center. If you want to secure a prime spot, it's recommended to arrive early in the morning, as spectators often start gathering hours before the parade begins. The Macy's Thanksgiving Day Parade is a must-see event that captures the holiday spirit and is a memorable experience for anyone visiting New York during this time.

Another major event that draws large crowds is the New York City Pride March, which celebrates LGBTQ+ pride and the ongoing fight for equality. Held every June as part of NYC Pride Month, the Pride March is one of the largest LGBTQ+ events in the world, attracting millions of participants and spectators. The march typically begins in Midtown Manhattan, traveling down 5th Avenue, passing by the historic Stonewall Inn in Greenwich Village, and concluding in the West Village. Some of the best viewing spots for the Pride March include the area around Christopher Street and 7th Avenue, where the march passes by the Stonewall Inn, a National Historic Landmark that played a key role in the LGBTQ+ rights movement. Another popular viewing area is along 5th Avenue between 23rd Street and 14th Street, where you can enjoy a lively and festive atmosphere. To get to these locations, you can take the A, B, C, D, E, F, M subway lines to West 4th Street-Washington Square, or the 1 subway line to Christopher Street-Sheridan Square. The Pride March is a joyous and colorful event, and everyone is welcome to join in the celebration, whether by marching, watching, or participating in one of the many Pride-related events and parties that take place throughout the city during June.

For those interested in cultural celebrations, the West Indian Day Parade in Brooklyn is a vibrant and energetic event that celebrates Caribbean culture and heritage. Held on Labor Day in September, the parade takes place along Eastern Parkway in the Crown Heights neighborhood of Brooklyn and features colorful costumes, live music, and performances by steel pan bands and calypso artists. The parade route stretches from Schenectady Avenue to Grand Army Plaza, and the best viewing spots are near the starting point at Schenectady Avenue or along the stretch between Nostrand Avenue and Franklin Avenue. To get to the parade, you can take the 2, 3, 4 subway lines to Franklin Avenue, or the 4 line to Utica Avenue. The West Indian Day Parade is a lively and festive event that offers a taste of the Caribbean in the heart of Brooklyn. In addition to watching the parade, visitors can enjoy Caribbean food from street vendors, listen to live music, and join in the dancing and celebrations that take place along the parade route.

In the winter, the St. Patrick's Day Parade in March is one of New York City's oldest and most iconic parades. Celebrating Irish culture and heritage, the parade features bagpipers, marching bands, and a sea of participants dressed in green. The parade takes place on March 17th and travels along 5th Avenue, starting at 44th Street and continuing up to 79th Street. Some of the best viewing spots for the St. Patrick's Day Parade include the area around St. Patrick's Cathedral between 50th and 51st Streets, where you can watch the parade against the backdrop of the cathedral's stunning Gothic architecture. Another great spot is along 5th Avenue between 59th and 66th Streets, where the crowds are usually less dense, and you can enjoy a more relaxed viewing experience. To get to these locations, you can take the B, D, F, M subway lines to 47th-50th Streets-Rockefeller Center, or the N, Q, R, W lines to 5th Avenue-59th Street. The St. Patrick's Day Parade is a beloved New York tradition that attracts both locals and visitors, offering a lively and festive atmosphere that is perfect for celebrating Irish culture.

For those who prefer a more intimate and community-focused event, the Feast of San Gennaro in Little Italy is a must-attend celebration that takes place in September. This 11-day festival honors San Gennaro, the patron saint of Naples, and features a religious procession, live music, carnival games, and, most notably, a wide array of Italian food. The festival takes place along Mulberry Street, with the main events centered around the area between Canal Street and Houston Street. To get to the Feast of San Gennaro, you can take the 6 subway line to Spring Street, or the N, Q, R, W lines to Canal Street. The best way to experience the Feast of San Gennaro is to wander through the streets, sampling the various Italian delicacies on offer, including cannoli, sausage and peppers, and zeppole. The festival also features live performances and entertainment throughout the day and evening, making it a lively and enjoyable event for people of all ages.

Getting involved in community events and parades in New York City is a great way to connect with locals and experience the city's culture from a different perspective. Many of the city's parades and festivals welcome volunteers and participants, offering a unique opportunity to be part of the action. For example, the Village Halloween Parade in Greenwich Village encourages people to join in the parade by dressing up in creative costumes and marching along with the floats and performers. The parade, which takes place on Halloween night, travels up 6th Avenue from Spring Street to 16th Street and is known for its whimsical and spooky atmosphere. To get to the parade, you can take the A, B, C, D, E, F, M subway lines to West 4th Street-Washington Square, or the 1, 2, 3 lines to 14th Street. To participate in the parade, simply show up in costume and join the lineup at the starting point. The Village Halloween Parade is a fun and interactive way to celebrate Halloween in New York City, and it's open to everyone who wants to participate.

For those interested in supporting a cause, many public events and parades in New York City are organized to raise awareness and funds for various social and environmental issues. The New York City Climate March, for example, is an annual event that brings together thousands of people to advocate for action on climate change. The march typically takes place in September and travels through Midtown Manhattan, with participants carrying signs, banners, and artwork that highlight the importance of environmental sustainability. To get involved in the Climate March, you can check the event's official website for information on how to participate, including details on where to meet and what to bring. The Climate March is a powerful way to show support for environmental causes and connect with like-minded individuals who are passionate about protecting the planet.

New York City's public events and parades offer a wide range of opportunities to experience the city's vibrant culture and community spirit. Whether you're attending a major parade like the Macy's Thanksgiving Day Parade, celebrating

LGBTQ+ pride at the Pride March, or enjoying a local festival like the Feast of San Gennaro, these events provide unforgettable experiences that capture the essence of New York City. By finding the best viewing spots, getting involved in the community, and embracing the festive atmosphere, you'll create lasting memories of your time in the city and gain a deeper appreciation for its diversity and energy. Whether you're a first-time visitor or a seasoned New Yorker, participating in these public events is a must-do experience that will leave you with a greater connection to the city and its people.

Traditional Festivals Celebrating Seasons

New York City is a vibrant cultural hub that celebrates the changing seasons with a diverse array of traditional festivals, each offering a unique experience that reflects the city's rich heritage and community spirit. These festivals are woven into the fabric of New York's identity, marking the transitions from winter to spring, the warmth of summer, the harvest of fall, and the festivities of winter. Whether you're a resident or a visitor, participating in these seasonal celebrations provides a deeper understanding of the city's culture and a chance to enjoy its dynamic atmosphere.

As winter gives way to spring, New York City comes alive with festivals that celebrate renewal and growth. One of the most beloved spring festivals is the Macy's Flower Show, held annually at Macy's Herald Square in late March through early April. This event transforms the iconic department store into a blooming paradise, with elaborate floral displays that showcase thousands of flowers, plants, and trees. Each year, the Flower Show has a different theme, offering visitors a new experience with each visit. To get to Macy's Herald Square, you can take the B, D, F, M, N, Q, R, or W subway lines to 34th Street-Herald Square. The Flower Show is free to visit and is open to the public during store hours. In addition to the stunning floral arrangements, visitors can enjoy special events, including live demonstrations by floral designers, interactive displays, and guided tours. The Macy's Flower Show is a delightful way to welcome spring and enjoy the beauty of nature in the heart of the city.

Spring in New York is also marked by the Sakura Matsuri Cherry Blossom Festival at the Brooklyn Botanic Garden, typically held in late April. This festival celebrates the arrival of cherry blossoms, a symbol of renewal and beauty in Japanese culture. The Brooklyn Botanic Garden, located at 990 Washington Avenue, Brooklyn, is home to one of the largest collections of cherry trees outside Japan, and during the festival, these trees burst into bloom, creating a breathtaking canopy of pink and white blossoms. To get to the Brooklyn Botanic Garden, you can take the 2, 3 subway lines to Eastern Parkway-Brooklyn Museum, or the B, Q lines to Prospect Park. The Sakura Matsuri Festival features traditional Japanese performances, including taiko drumming, tea ceremonies, and martial arts demonstrations, as well as cultural workshops and activities for all ages. Visitors can stroll through the Cherry Esplanade, take photos under the blossoms, and enjoy the serene beauty of the Japanese Hill-and-Pond Garden. The Sakura Matsuri Cherry Blossom Festival is a must-visit for anyone looking to experience the magic of spring in New York City.

As the city transitions into summer, the streets and parks fill with festivals that celebrate the warmth and vibrancy of the season. One of the highlights of the summer festival calendar is the SummerStage series, which runs from June through September in various parks across the five boroughs. SummerStage offers free concerts, dance performances, and theater productions that showcase both local and international talent. The main stage is located in Central Park, at Rumsey Playfield near 72nd Street, but performances are also held in parks throughout the city, including Marcus Garvey Park in Harlem, Coffey Park in Red Hook, and Crotona Park in the Bronx. To get to Central Park's SummerStage, you can take the B, C subway lines to 72nd Street or the 6 line to 68th Street-Hunter College. SummerStage events are free and open to the public, with seating available on a first-come, first-served basis. To enhance your experience, bring a blanket or chair, pack a picnic, and enjoy an evening of live entertainment under the stars. SummerStage is a quintessential New York City experience that brings people together to celebrate the arts in a beautiful outdoor setting.

Another iconic summer festival is the Coney Island Mermaid Parade, held annually in June. This whimsical event is the largest art parade in the nation and celebrates the start of the summer season with a colorful procession of mermaids, sea creatures, and other fantastical characters. The parade takes place along Surf Avenue and the Coney Island Boardwalk, with participants dressed in elaborate costumes inspired by maritime folklore. To get to Coney Island, you can take the D, F, N, or Q subway lines to Coney Island-Stillwell Avenue. The Mermaid Parade is a free event, and visitors are encouraged to dress up and join in the fun. After the parade, you can explore the Coney Island amusement parks, visit the New York Aquarium, or relax on the beach. The Coney Island Mermaid Parade is a unique and lively celebration that embodies the spirit of summer in New York City.

As the leaves begin to turn and the air grows crisp, New York City embraces the beauty of fall with a series of harvest festivals and seasonal celebrations. One of the most popular fall events is the New York City Wine & Food Festival (NYCWFF), held in October. This festival is a food lover's dream, featuring tastings, cooking demonstrations, and events hosted by celebrity chefs and culinary experts. The NYCWFF takes place at various venues across the city, including Pier 94 on the West Side, which is the main location for many of the festival's signature events. To get to Pier 94, you can take the A, C, E subway lines to 50th Street and walk west toward the Hudson River. Tickets for the NYCWFF events can be purchased online through the festival's official website, and it's advisable to book in advance, as popular events often sell out quickly. The New York City Wine & Food Festival is not only a celebration of the city's culinary scene but also supports a good cause, with proceeds benefiting the Food Bank For New York City and No Kid Hungry. Whether you're sampling gourmet dishes, learning from top chefs, or enjoying a wine tasting, the NYCWFF offers a delicious and indulgent way to enjoy the fall season in New York.

October also brings the Village Halloween Parade, one of the city's most iconic fall events. Held on Halloween night, the parade features thousands of participants in elaborate costumes, giant puppets, marching bands, and street performers. The parade route travels up 6th Avenue from Spring Street to 16th Street, and the event is free and open to everyone. To get to the parade, you can take the A, B, C, D, E, F, M subway lines to West 4th Street-Washington Square, or the 1, 2, 3 lines to 14th Street. The Village Halloween Parade is known for its creative and spooky atmosphere, and it's a fantastic way to experience the playful and artistic side of New York City. Whether you're dressing up to join the parade or simply watching from the sidelines, the Village Halloween Parade is a fun and festive way to celebrate Halloween in the city.

As winter approaches, New York City is transformed into a wonderland of lights, decorations, and festive cheer. One of the most beloved winter traditions is the Rockefeller Center Christmas Tree Lighting, which takes place in late November or early December. This event marks the official start of the holiday season in New York, with the lighting of a massive Christmas tree adorned with thousands of twinkling lights. The tree is located at Rockefeller Center, between 49th and 50th Streets and 5th and 6th Avenues. To get to Rockefeller Center, you can take the B, D, F, M subway lines to 47th-50th Streets-Rockefeller Center, or the E, M lines to 5th Avenue-53rd Street. The tree lighting ceremony is free and open to the public, but it's one of the most popular events of the year, so it's important to arrive early to secure a good spot. The tree remains lit through early January, and visitors can also enjoy ice skating at the Rockefeller Center rink, located just below the tree. The Rockefeller Center Christmas Tree Lighting is a magical event that captures the holiday spirit and is a must-see for anyone visiting New York during the winter season.

Winter in New York is also celebrated with the Lunar New Year Parade in Chinatown, which typically takes place in January or February, depending on the lunar calendar. The Lunar New Year Parade is a vibrant and colorful event that celebrates the beginning of the lunar calendar year with dragon and lion dances, traditional music, and elaborate costumes. The parade route winds through the streets of Chinatown, with the main festivities centered around Mott Street, Canal Street, and East Broadway. To get to Chinatown, you can take the 6, J, N, Q, R, W, or Z subway lines to Canal Street, or the B, D lines to Grand Street. In addition to the parade, visitors can enjoy traditional Chinese food, cultural performances, and shopping for New Year decorations and gifts. The Lunar New Year Parade is a lively and festive way to experience one of New York's most vibrant communities and to welcome the new year with joy and celebration.

New York City also has unique seasonal traditions that are celebrated year after year. One such tradition is the Winter Solstice Concerts at the Cathedral of St. John the Divine, held in late December. These concerts, led by musician Paul Winter, celebrate the winter solstice with a mix of world music, dance, and storytelling. The Cathedral of St. John the Divine, located at 1047 Amsterdam Avenue, is one of the largest cathedrals in the world and provides a stunning backdrop for these atmospheric performances. To get to the cathedral, you can take the 1 subway line to 110th Street-Cathedral Parkway. Tickets for the Winter Solstice Concerts can be purchased online through the cathedral's official website, and it's recommended to book in advance, as these concerts are a popular holiday tradition. The Winter Solstice Concerts offer a peaceful and reflective way to mark the longest night of the year and to celebrate the return of the light.

New York City's traditional festivals celebrating the seasons offer a rich and diverse array of experiences that reflect the city's cultural heritage and community spirit. From the blooming beauty of the Macy's Flower Show in spring to the festive cheer of the Rockefeller Center Christmas Tree Lighting in winter, these seasonal celebrations provide opportunities to connect with the city's traditions, enjoy its vibrant atmosphere, and create lasting memories. Whether you're a first-time visitor or a longtime resident, participating in these festivals is a wonderful way to experience the changing seasons in New York City and to appreciate the unique character of this dynamic and ever-evolving metropolis.

Cultural Performances and Theater

New York City is renowned as one of the world's premier cultural capitals, with a rich tapestry of performances and theater that cater to every taste and interest. The city's vibrant arts scene is anchored by its legendary Broadway shows, but it also includes an array of Off-Broadway productions, independent theaters, and live music venues that offer a diverse and dynamic range of entertainment. Whether you're a theater aficionado, a music lover, or simply looking to experience the city's cultural offerings, New York provides an abundance of opportunities to immerse yourself in the performing arts.

Broadway is undoubtedly the crown jewel of New York City's theater scene. Located in the heart of Manhattan, the Broadway Theater District is home to some of the most famous and iconic theaters in the world. The area is centered around Times Square, with theaters lining both sides of Broadway from 41st Street to 53rd Street. Broadway shows are known for their high production values, featuring elaborate sets, stunning costumes, and world-class performances by top actors, singers, and dancers. Some of the most celebrated and long-running Broadway shows include classics like "The Phantom of the Opera," "Les Misérables," "Chicago," and more recent hits like "Hamilton," "The Lion King," and "Wicked."

To experience a Broadway show, you can purchase tickets from a variety of sources. The most reliable option is to buy tickets directly from the theater's box office or through official ticketing websites like Telecharge and Ticketmaster. Prices for Broadway shows can vary widely, depending on the popularity of the show, the day of the week, and the seating location. Premium seats for popular shows can cost several hundred dollars, while more affordable options, such as balcony or mezzanine seats, are often available for under $100. If you're looking to save money on tickets, you can also try the TKTS booths in Times Square, Lincoln Center, and South Street Seaport, where you can purchase same-day discounted tickets for many Broadway and Off-Broadway shows. To get to the TKTS booth in Times Square, you can take the N, Q, R, W, 1, 2, 3, 7, or S subway lines to 42nd Street-Times Square. The booth opens in the afternoon, and it's advisable to arrive early, as popular shows can sell out quickly.

Off-Broadway productions offer an alternative to the glitz and glamour of Broadway, often featuring more experimental and intimate performances. Off-Broadway theaters are generally smaller, with seating capacities ranging from 100 to 499, and they are located outside the main Broadway Theater District, often in neighborhoods like the West Village, the East Village, and Chelsea. These productions tend to be more innovative, exploring new themes, unconventional storytelling techniques, and emerging talent. Some Off-Broadway shows have gained critical acclaim and later transferred to Broadway, such as "Rent," "Dear Evan Hansen," and "The Play That Goes Wrong."

Tickets for Off-Broadway shows are typically more affordable than those for Broadway, with prices ranging from $20 to $100. You can purchase tickets directly from the theater's box office or through websites like TodayTix, which often offers discounts and last-minute deals on Off-Broadway shows. If you're interested in exploring Off-Broadway, some notable theaters to consider include the Public Theater (located at 425 Lafayette Street, accessible via the 6 subway line to Astor Place), the Atlantic Theater Company (located at 336 West 20th Street, accessible via the C, E subway lines to 23rd Street), and the New York Theatre Workshop (located at 79 East 4th Street, accessible via the F, M subway lines to 2nd Avenue). Attending an Off-Broadway production is a great way to experience the cutting edge of New York's theater scene and to discover new and exciting works that push the boundaries of traditional theater.

In addition to Broadway and Off-Broadway, New York City is home to a thriving independent theater scene that offers a wide range of performances, from avant-garde and experimental works to community-based productions and immersive theater experiences. Independent theaters are scattered throughout the city, often in neighborhoods like the Lower East Side, Williamsburg, and Bushwick. These venues tend to be smaller and more intimate, providing a unique and personal connection between the performers and the audience.

One of the most well-known independent theaters in New York is The Flea Theater, located at 20 Thomas Street in Tribeca. The Flea is dedicated to producing bold and innovative works by emerging and established artists, and it offers a diverse lineup of performances throughout the year. To get to The Flea, you can take the A, C, E, or 1 subway lines to Canal Street. Another notable venue is La MaMa Experimental Theatre Club, located at 66 East 4th Street in the East Village, which has a long history of supporting experimental theater and performance art. La MaMa is accessible via the F, M subway lines to 2nd Avenue. These independent theaters provide a platform for artists to explore new ideas and challenge traditional theater conventions, making them an essential part of New York's cultural landscape.

Live music is another integral aspect of New York City's cultural scene, with a vast array of venues catering to every genre and taste. From iconic concert halls to intimate clubs, the city offers endless opportunities to experience live music in a variety of settings. One of the most famous live music venues in New York is Carnegie Hall, located at 881 7th Avenue, between 56th and 57th Streets. Carnegie Hall is renowned for its exceptional acoustics and has hosted some of the world's greatest musicians and orchestras since it opened in 1891. The venue features three distinct performance spaces: the Stern Auditorium/Perelman Stage, Zankel Hall, and Weill Recital Hall. To get to Carnegie Hall, you can take the N, Q, R, W subway lines to 57th Street-7th Avenue, or the F line to 57th Street.

For jazz enthusiasts, The Village Vanguard is a must-visit destination. Located at 178 7th Avenue South in Greenwich Village, The Village Vanguard is one of the oldest and most prestigious jazz clubs in the world, known for its intimate atmosphere and legendary performances by jazz greats like John Coltrane, Miles Davis, and Bill Evans. To get to The Village Vanguard, you can take the 1 subway line to Christopher Street-Sheridan Square. The club offers nightly performances, and it's advisable to book tickets in advance, as shows often sell out quickly.

For a more contemporary music experience, Brooklyn Steel in Williamsburg is a popular venue for indie rock, electronic, and alternative music. Located at 319 Frost Street, Brooklyn Steel is a converted warehouse that has been transformed into a state-of-the-art concert venue with a capacity of 1,800. The venue features a standing-room floor and balcony, as well as a spacious bar area. To get to Brooklyn Steel, you can take the L subway line to Graham Avenue. The venue hosts a wide range of artists and bands, and tickets can be purchased online through the venue's official website or through ticketing platforms like Ticketmaster.

New York City's cultural performances and theater scene offer a wealth of opportunities to experience world-class entertainment in a variety of settings. Whether you're attending a Broadway show in the heart of Times Square, exploring an Off-Broadway production in the West Village, or enjoying live music at an iconic venue like Carnegie Hall, the city provides a rich and diverse cultural landscape that caters to every taste and interest.

Local Myths, Legends, and Folklore

New York City, with its rich history and vibrant culture, is a place where myths, legends, and folklore have been woven into the fabric of its identity. The stories passed down through generations capture the imagination, and the tales of haunted places, mysterious figures, and legendary events shape the way people view this iconic metropolis. Whether you're a visitor or a local, exploring these myths and legends can provide a deeper understanding of the city's culture and history.

One of the most enduring legends in New York City is that of The Ghosts of Washington Square Park. Washington Square Park, located in the heart of Greenwich Village, is one of the city's most famous public spaces, known for its iconic arch and bustling atmosphere. However, beneath the park lies a dark history that has given rise to numerous ghost stories.

In the late 18th and early 19th centuries, the area was used as a potter's field, where thousands of indigent and unknown people were buried. Later, during the Yellow Fever epidemic, mass graves were dug in the area to bury the victims of the disease. Today, it's said that the spirits of those buried beneath the park still linger, and many people have reported strange occurrences, such as cold spots, eerie sounds, and ghostly apparitions. To experience this haunting history, you can visit Washington Square Park by taking the A, B, C, D, E, F, M subway lines to West 4th Street-Washington Square or the 1 subway line to Christopher Street-Sheridan Square. Walking through the park, especially at night, can be a chilling experience as you contemplate the countless souls that rest beneath your feet.

Another famous legend from New York's past is that of The Headless Horseman, a tale made famous by Washington Irving's short story "The Legend of Sleepy Hollow." While the story is set in the village of Sleepy Hollow in Westchester County, just north of the city, the legend has become an integral part of New York folklore. The tale tells of Ichabod Crane, a schoolteacher who encounters a ghostly figure known as the Headless Horseman, a Hessian soldier who lost his head to a cannonball during the Revolutionary War. The Horseman is said to ride through the night in search of his missing head, and the story has captivated readers and inspired countless adaptations in literature, film, and theater. To explore the origins of this legend, you can visit Sleepy Hollow, which is accessible from New York City by taking the Metro-North Hudson Line from Grand Central Terminal to Tarrytown. From there, it's a short bus ride or walk to Sleepy Hollow. The town embraces its haunted history with events and attractions like the Sleepy Hollow Cemetery tours and the Great Jack O'Lantern Blaze, making it a perfect day trip for those interested in New York's spooky folklore.

In addition to these famous tales, New York City is also home to a wealth of lesser-known legends and folklore that have shaped the local culture. One such story is that of The Mole People, a mythical community said to live in the abandoned subway tunnels beneath the city. According to urban legend, these people are homeless individuals who have retreated from society and created a subterranean world of their own, complete with makeshift homes, electricity, and even farms. While the existence of such a community has never been proven, the legend has captured the public's imagination and has been the subject of books, documentaries, and articles. The idea of a hidden world beneath the city streets taps into the fascination with New York's vast and mysterious underground, where miles of tunnels, sewers, and forgotten spaces exist just out of sight. While exploring these areas is not advisable due to safety concerns and legal restrictions, the story of the Mole People continues to be a part of New York's urban mythology.

Another intriguing piece of folklore is the story of The Bermuda Triangle of New York, a mysterious area in the East River where ships and planes have allegedly disappeared under unexplained circumstances. The area is roughly defined by the points of Roosevelt Island, the United Nations Headquarters, and the Queensboro Bridge. While the legend is likely exaggerated, it has been fueled by incidents such as the disappearance of a Navy training plane in 1952 and the sinking of several ships in the area during the 19th and early

20th centuries. The idea of a Bermuda Triangle in the heart of New York City adds an element of intrigue to the city's waters and serves as a reminder of the unknown forces that sometimes seem to defy explanation. Visitors interested in this legend can view the East River and its surrounding landmarks from various vantage points, such as Roosevelt Island, which is accessible via the Roosevelt Island Tramway from Manhattan's East 59th Street.

For those looking to experience New York City's haunted history firsthand, there are several ghost tours and haunted sites that offer a spine-tingling glimpse into the city's past. One of the most popular ghost tours is the Greenwich Village Ghost Tour, which takes participants through the narrow, winding streets of one of New York's oldest and most historic neighborhoods. The tour includes stops at haunted locations like the Merchant's House Museum, an impeccably preserved 19th-century townhouse that is said to be haunted by the ghost of Gertrude Tredwell, the last member of the Tredwell family to live in the house. The Merchant's House Museum is located at 29 East 4th Street, and you can get there by taking the 6 subway line to Astor Place or the N, R, W lines to 8th Street-NYU. The Greenwich Village Ghost Tour is a popular activity during the Halloween season but is offered year-round for those interested in the city's ghostly lore.

Another haunted site worth visiting is The Dakota, a historic apartment building on the Upper West Side of Manhattan. Built in 1884, The Dakota is best known as the home of John Lennon, who was tragically assassinated outside the building in 1980. However, The Dakota has long been associated with paranormal activity, with reports of ghostly figures, strange sounds, and unexplained events dating back to the early 20th century. The building's Gothic architecture and storied history add to its eerie atmosphere, making it a popular destination for those interested in New York's haunted past. The Dakota is located at 1 West 72nd Street, across from Central Park, and you can get there by taking the B, C subway lines to 72nd Street. While the building is private and not open to the public, you can view it from the outside and reflect on the legends and stories that have made it a focal point of New York City's ghostly folklore.

For a more immersive ghostly experience, consider visiting The Morris-Jumel Mansion, the oldest house in Manhattan, located in the Washington Heights neighborhood. Built in 1765, the mansion served as a headquarters for George Washington during the Revolutionary War and has a long and storied history. Over the years, many visitors and staff have reported ghostly encounters, including sightings of the mansion's former owner, Eliza Jumel, who is said to haunt the house. The Morris-Jumel Mansion is located at 65 Jumel Terrace, and you can get there by taking the C subway line to 163rd Street-Amsterdam Avenue. The mansion offers guided tours that explore its history and hauntings, providing a fascinating and eerie look at one of New York's most historic homes.

New York City's myths, legends, and folklore are an integral part of its cultural heritage, offering a glimpse into the city's mysterious and haunted past. From the ghostly spirits of Washington Square Park to the legend of the Headless Horseman, these stories continue to captivate and intrigue both locals and visitors alike. By exploring these tales and visiting the haunted sites associated with them, you can experience a different side of New York City that goes beyond the usual tourist attractions. Whether you're walking through a haunted park, visiting a legendary building, or taking a ghost tour, you'll gain a deeper appreciation for the stories that have shaped New York's identity and continue to resonate with those who seek out the city's hidden and eerie history.

Religious Sites and Pilgrimages

New York City, known for its diversity and cultural richness, is home to an extraordinary array of religious sites that reflect the spiritual heritage of its inhabitants. These places of worship not only serve as religious centers for their respective communities but also as landmarks of historical and architectural significance. Visitors to the city can explore a wide range of churches, synagogues, mosques, and other spiritual sites that offer a glimpse into the diverse faiths practiced in New York.

One of the most iconic religious sites in New York City is St. Patrick's Cathedral, located on Fifth Avenue between 50th and 51st Streets in Midtown Manhattan. This magnificent cathedral is the largest Catholic church in the United States and serves as the seat of the Archbishop of New York. Completed in 1879, St. Patrick's Cathedral is an architectural masterpiece, featuring a neo-Gothic design with twin spires that rise 330 feet above the bustling streets of Manhattan. The interior of the cathedral is equally impressive, with its grand nave, intricately carved altars, and stunning stained glass windows. Visitors to St. Patrick's Cathedral can attend Mass, light a candle, or simply take in the serene beauty of the space. To get to the cathedral, you can take the B, D, F, M subway lines to 47th-50th Streets-Rockefeller Center, or the E, M lines to 5th Avenue-53rd Street. When visiting, it's important to dress modestly and maintain a quiet demeanor, especially during religious services, to show respect for those in prayer.

Another significant religious site in New York City is the Cathedral of St. John the Divine, located at 1047 Amsterdam Avenue in the Morningside Heights neighborhood of Manhattan. This Episcopal cathedral is the largest Anglican cathedral in the world and one of the largest Christian churches globally. The cathedral's construction began in 1892, and although it remains technically unfinished, it stands as a testament to the city's architectural and spiritual aspirations. The Cathedral of St. John the Divine is renowned for its eclectic architectural style, which blends Romanesque, Gothic, and modern elements. The interior of the cathedral is equally impressive, with its soaring vaults, massive stained glass windows, and the celebrated Peace Fountain, which symbolizes the triumph of good over evil. The cathedral also hosts various cultural events, including concerts, art exhibitions, and the annual Blessing of the Animals. To visit the Cathedral of St. John the Divine, you can take the 1 subway line to 110th Street-Cathedral Parkway. Visitors are welcome to explore the cathedral, attend services, or simply enjoy the tranquil gardens that surround the building. As with all places of worship, it's important to be respectful, particularly during services or other religious activities.

New York City is also home to a number of historic synagogues that reflect the rich heritage of the Jewish community. One of the most notable is the Eldridge Street Synagogue, located at 12 Eldridge Street in the Lower East Side. Built in 1887, this synagogue was the first great house of worship built by Eastern European Jews in the United States. The synagogue's architecture is a stunning blend of Moorish, Gothic, and Romanesque styles, with a striking rose window that is a focal point of the building's facade. After decades of decline, the Eldridge Street Synagogue underwent a meticulous restoration and now serves as both a place of worship and a museum, known as the Museum at Eldridge Street. The museum offers guided tours that provide insight into the history of the synagogue, the Jewish immigrant experience in New York, and the architectural significance of the building. To get to the Eldridge Street Synagogue, you can take the B, D subway lines to Grand Street, or the F line to East Broadway. When visiting, it's important to dress modestly, particularly when entering the main sanctuary, and to be mindful of the sacred nature of the space.

Another important synagogue in New York City is Congregation Shearith Israel, also known as the Spanish and Portuguese Synagogue, located at 2 West 70th Street on the Upper West Side. Established in 1654, Shearith Israel is the oldest Jewish congregation in the United States. The current synagogue building, completed in 1897, is a striking example of classical architecture, featuring a grand sanctuary with Corinthian columns, a domed ceiling, and intricate woodwork. The congregation follows the Sephardic liturgical tradition, and its services are conducted in Hebrew, with elements of Spanish and Portuguese. Visitors to Shearith

Israel can attend services or arrange a guided tour to learn about the congregation's rich history and its role in the development of Jewish life in America. To get to the synagogue, you can take the 1, 2, 3 subway lines to 72nd Street. As with all places of worship, visitors should dress modestly and observe the customs of the congregation, particularly during services.

For those interested in exploring Islamic architecture and culture, the Islamic Cultural Center of New York is a must-visit site. Located at 1711 3rd Avenue on the Upper East Side, the Islamic Cultural Center is one of the most prominent mosques in New York City. Completed in 1991, the mosque's design reflects traditional Islamic architectural elements, with a striking minaret, a large dome, and an intricately decorated prayer hall. The mosque serves as both a place of worship and a cultural center for the city's Muslim community, offering educational programs, lectures, and community events. Visitors to the Islamic Cultural Center are welcome to attend Friday prayers (Jumu'ah) or visit the mosque outside of prayer times to learn more about Islam and the local Muslim community. To get to the Islamic Cultural Center, you can take the 4, 5, 6 subway lines to 86th Street. When visiting, it's important to dress modestly (long sleeves and pants or skirts) and remove your shoes before entering the prayer hall. Women may also be required to cover their heads with a scarf.

New York City is also home to several spiritual sites that are significant to a variety of religious and philosophical traditions. One such site is the Theosophical Society of America, located at 242 East 53rd Street in Midtown

Manhattan. The Theosophical Society is dedicated to the study of comparative religion, philosophy, and science, with the goal of promoting universal brotherhood and spiritual growth. The society's New York headquarters offers lectures, workshops, and study groups on a wide range of spiritual topics, including meditation, esoteric teachings, and the wisdom traditions of various cultures. Visitors are welcome to attend events or explore the society's extensive library, which houses a vast collection of books and resources on spiritual and philosophical topics. To get to the Theosophical Society, you can take the E, M subway lines to Lexington Avenue-53rd Street. When visiting, it's important to approach the space with an open mind and a respectful attitude toward the diverse spiritual practices and beliefs represented there.

When visiting religious sites and participating in pilgrimages in New York City, it's essential to be mindful of local customs and practices. Each faith tradition has its own set of guidelines regarding dress, behavior, and rituals, and observing these practices is a way to show respect for the sacred nature of these spaces. In general, modest clothing is recommended when visiting churches, synagogues, mosques, and other places of worship. It's also important to maintain a quiet and respectful demeanor, particularly during religious services or prayer times. If you're unsure about the appropriate behavior or dress code, it's always a good idea to ask someone at the site for guidance or look for posted signs with instructions.

New York City's religious sites and pilgrimages offer a unique opportunity to explore the city's diverse spiritual heritage and to connect with the faith traditions that have shaped its cultural landscape. Whether you're visiting a grand cathedral, a historic synagogue, or a peaceful mosque, these sacred spaces provide a window into the spiritual life of the city and its inhabitants. By approaching these sites with respect and reverence, you'll be able to experience the deep sense of history, community, and faith that permeates these places of worship. Whether you're attending a service, participating in a pilgrimage, or simply seeking a moment of reflection, New York City's religious sites offer a rich and meaningful experience for all who visit.

CHAPTER 10

FOOD AND DINING IN NEW YORK CITY

Dining (for different travelers)

New York City is a culinary paradise, offering a diverse and dynamic dining scene that caters to every palate and occasion. Whether you're traveling with your family, seeking a romantic meal for two, exploring the city on a budget, or simply looking to savor the best street food, New York has something to offer. The city's restaurants and eateries reflect its rich cultural tapestry, with options ranging from fine dining establishments to humble food trucks.

For families traveling to New York City, finding a restaurant that accommodates both adults and children while offering a memorable dining experience is key. One of the best family-friendly restaurants in the city is Ellen's Stardust Diner, located at 1650 Broadway in the Theater District. Ellen's Stardust Diner is famous for its singing waitstaff, who are aspiring Broadway performers. As you enjoy classic American diner fare, including burgers, milkshakes, and breakfast all day, you'll be entertained by live performances of show tunes and pop hits. The lively atmosphere and interactive experience make it a hit with kids and adults alike. To get to Ellen's Stardust Diner, you can take the N, Q, R, W, 1, 2, 3 subway lines to 49th Street or the B, D, F, M lines to 47th-50th Streets-Rockefeller Center. Be prepared for a bit of a wait, especially during peak hours, but the experience is well worth it.

Another great option for families is Serendipity 3, located at 225 East 60th Street on the Upper East Side. Serendipity 3 is a whimsical restaurant known for its over-the-top desserts, including the famous Frrrozen Hot Chocolate. The menu also features a variety of comfort foods like foot-long hot dogs, chicken pot pie, and pasta dishes. The restaurant's playful decor, with its eclectic mix of vintage items, Tiffany lamps, and quirky artwork, adds to the fun and family-friendly vibe. To get to Serendipity 3, you can take the N, Q, R, W, 4, 5, 6 subway lines to Lexington Avenue-59th Street. Reservations are recommended, as the restaurant is a popular spot for both locals and tourists.

For families looking to experience something a bit different, Alice's Tea Cup is a charming tea house with three locations in Manhattan. Inspired by Lewis Carroll's "Alice in Wonderland," Alice's Tea Cup offers a magical experience with whimsical decor, a wide selection of teas, and a menu that includes scones, sandwiches, salads, and other light fare. The restaurant is especially popular for afternoon tea, which comes with tiered trays of sandwiches, scones with clotted cream and jam, and assorted sweets. Children are provided with fairy wings and glitter as part of the experience, making it a delightful outing for families. The original location, Chapter I, is located at 102 West 73rd Street, near Central Park. To get there, you can take the B, C subway lines to 72nd Street. It's recommended to make a reservation, especially for afternoon tea, as the tea house is a favorite among locals and visitors alike.

When it comes to romantic dining spots, New York City offers a wealth of options that provide the perfect setting for an intimate meal. One if by Land, Two if by Sea is one of the most romantic restaurants in the city, housed in a historic carriage house at 17 Barrow Street in the West Village. The restaurant's candlelit dining rooms, with their exposed brick walls, chandeliers, and roaring fireplaces, create a warm and elegant atmosphere that's ideal for a special occasion. The menu features classic American and French-inspired cuisine, with dishes like beef Wellington, lobster, and duck à l'orange. To get to One if by Land, Two if by Sea, you can take the 1 subway line to Christopher Street-Sheridan Square or the A, C, E, B, D, F, M lines to West 4th Street-Washington Square. Reservations are essential, especially for weekend evenings, as the restaurant is a popular choice for anniversaries, proposals, and other romantic celebrations.

Another excellent choice for couples is The River Café, located at 1 Water Street in Brooklyn, under the Brooklyn Bridge. The River Café offers breathtaking views of the Manhattan skyline and the Statue of Liberty, making it one of the most scenic dining spots in the city. The restaurant's romantic setting is complemented by a menu that features New American cuisine, with an emphasis on fresh, seasonal ingredients. Dishes like foie gras, rack of lamb, and chocolate marquise are beautifully presented, and the extensive wine list ensures a perfect pairing for every course. To get to The River Café, you can take the A, C subway lines to High Street-Brooklyn Bridge or the F line to York Street. Due to its popularity and limited seating, reservations are highly recommended, particularly for window tables with the best views.

For a more casual yet equally romantic dining experience, Buvette in the West Village offers a cozy and intimate setting that's perfect for a date night. Located at 42 Grove Street, Buvette is a French-inspired gastroteque that serves small plates and dishes meant for sharing. The menu includes classics like croque monsieur, ratatouille, and coq au vin, along with a carefully curated selection of wines and cocktails. The rustic decor, with its marble bar, wooden tables, and vintage accents, adds to the charm of the place. To get to Buvette, you can take the 1 subway line to Christopher Street-Sheridan Square or the A, C, E, B, D, F, M lines to West 4th Street-Washington Square. The restaurant operates on a first-come, first-served basis, so it's best to arrive early to secure a table.

For travelers on a budget, New York City offers plenty of affordable dining options that don't skimp on flavor or quality. One of the city's most famous budget-friendly eateries is Joe's Pizza, located at 7 Carmine Street in Greenwich Village. Joe's Pizza has been serving up classic New York-style slices since 1975, and it's a favorite among locals and tourists alike. The no-frills pizzeria is known for its thin, crispy crust, tangy tomato sauce, and just the right amount of cheese. A slice costs only a few dollars, making it an excellent choice for a quick and satisfying meal. To get to Joe's Pizza, you can take the A, B, C, D, E, F, M subway lines to West 4th Street-Washington Square. The pizzeria is open late, making it a popular spot for a late-night snack.

Another great budget-friendly option is Mamouns Falafel, with its original location at 119 MacDougal Street in Greenwich Village. Mamouns has been serving authentic

Middle Eastern food since 1971, and it's known for its delicious falafel, shawarma, and hummus. The falafel sandwich, made with freshly fried falafel balls, tahini sauce, lettuce, tomatoes, and pickles, is a favorite among vegetarians and meat-eaters alike, and it's priced at just a few dollars. The casual, counter-service setup makes it easy to grab a quick bite to eat, whether you're dining in or taking it to go. To get to Mamouns, you can take the A, B, C, D, E, F, M subway lines to West 4th Street-Washington Square. The restaurant is open late, making it a popular spot for a budget-friendly meal any time of day.

For those looking to experience New York's diverse culinary scene on a budget, The Halal Guys is a must-visit. What started as a food cart on the corner of 53rd Street and 6th Avenue has grown into a beloved institution, known for its flavorful halal platters and sandwiches. The menu is simple, with options like chicken and beef gyro platters served over rice with lettuce, tomatoes, and pita, topped with the famous white sauce and hot sauce. The portions are generous, and the prices are affordable, making it a popular choice for both locals and tourists. To get to The Halal Guys, you can take the B, D, F, M subway lines to 47th-50th Streets-Rockefeller Center or the N, Q, R, W, 1, 2, 3 lines to 49th Street. The food cart is open late, making it a great option for a late-night meal.

For those who enjoy the casual and vibrant atmosphere of street food, New York City's food trucks offer a wide variety of delicious and affordable options. Wafels & Dinges is a popular food truck that serves authentic Belgian waffles with a variety of toppings, known as "dinges." The menu includes classic waffles topped with whipped cream, strawberries, and chocolate sauce, as well as savory options like the pulled pork waffle. The truck operates at various locations throughout the city, so it's best to check their website or social media for their current location. Popular spots include Bryant Park, Union Square, and Central Park. To get to these locations, you can take the B, D, F, M subway lines to 42nd Street-Bryant Park, the N, R, W, Q, 4, 5, 6 lines to Union Square, or the A, B, C, D, 1 lines to Columbus Circle for Central Park. Enjoying a freshly made waffle from Wafels & Dinges while exploring the city's parks and public spaces is a quintessential New York experience.

Another beloved food truck is The Cinnamon Snail, which specializes in vegan and organic food. The menu features creative dishes like the "Beastmode Burger Deluxe," made with a grilled ancho chili seitan burger, jalapeño mac and cheese, arugula, and chipotle mayo, all served on a pretzel bun. The Cinnamon Snail also offers a variety of pastries, including donuts, cookies, and cinnamon rolls. The truck operates at different locations throughout the city, including Midtown Manhattan, the Financial District, and Brooklyn. To find out where the truck will be, you can check their website or social media. Whether you're vegan or simply looking to try something new, The Cinnamon Snail offers a unique and delicious street food experience that's both budget-friendly and satisfying.

New York City's dining scene is as diverse and dynamic as the city itself, offering a wide range of options to suit every taste, budget, and occasion. Whether you're dining with family, enjoying a romantic meal, exploring budget-friendly eateries, or sampling the city's street food, there's no shortage of culinary experiences to discover. By knowing where to go, how to get there, and what to expect, you can make the most of your dining adventures in New York City, creating memories that will last long after your meal is over. Whether you're savoring a slice of pizza, enjoying a candlelit dinner, or indulging in a late-night falafel, the city's culinary offerings provide a delicious and unforgettable way to experience the heart and soul of New York.

Local Cuisine and Must-Try Dishes

New York City is a culinary melting pot where cultures from around the world converge to create a vibrant and diverse food scene. The city's cuisine reflects its rich history and cultural diversity, offering a wide range of flavors and dishes that have become iconic over the years. For first-time visitors, exploring the local cuisine is an essential part of experiencing the city's unique character. From classic New York-style pizza to bagels with lox, the city's food is as much a part of its identity as its skyline.

When it comes to iconic New York City foods, few items are as synonymous with the city as New York-style pizza. Characterized by its thin, foldable crust, generous layer of tomato sauce, and just the right amount of melted mozzarella cheese, New York-style pizza is a must-try for anyone visiting the city. The pizza is typically sold by the slice, making it a quick and convenient meal or snack. One of the best places to experience authentic New York-style pizza is Di Fara Pizza, located at 1424 Avenue J in the Midwood neighborhood of Brooklyn. Di Fara has been serving some of the city's most beloved pizza since 1965, with each pie made by hand by the legendary pizzaiolo Domenico DeMarco. The quality of the ingredients, including imported Italian tomatoes, fresh mozzarella, and a drizzle of extra virgin olive oil, sets Di Fara's pizza apart from the rest. To get to Di Fara Pizza, you can take the Q subway line to Avenue J. Be prepared to wait in line, as the pizzeria is a popular destination for both locals and tourists, but the wait is well worth it for a taste of what many consider the best pizza in New York.

Another quintessential New York food is the bagel with lox and cream cheese. New York City is famous for its bagels, which are known for their dense, chewy texture and perfectly crisp crust. The combination of a freshly baked bagel with a generous spread of cream cheese, topped with silky slices of smoked salmon (lox), capers, onions, and sometimes tomato, is a classic New York breakfast. To experience this iconic dish, head to Russ & Daughters, located at 179 East Houston Street on the Lower East Side. Russ & Daughters has been serving high-quality smoked fish and bagels since 1914, and it remains a beloved institution in the city. The shop offers a wide variety of bagels and toppings, but the classic lox and cream cheese on an everything bagel is a must-try. To get to Russ & Daughters, you can take the F subway line to 2nd Avenue. The shop can get crowded, especially on weekends, so consider visiting early in the morning to avoid the rush.

For those with a sweet tooth, no visit to New York City would be complete without trying a slice of New York cheesecake. This rich and creamy dessert, made with cream cheese, eggs, sugar, and a graham cracker crust, is a staple of New York's dessert scene. While many restaurants and bakeries offer their own versions of cheesecake, one of the most famous is found at Junior's Restaurant, located at 386 Flatbush Avenue Extension in Downtown Brooklyn. Junior's has been serving its legendary cheesecake since 1950, and it's known for its dense yet fluffy texture and perfectly balanced flavor. The original plain cheesecake is a classic, but Junior's also offers a variety of flavors, including strawberry, chocolate swirl, and raspberry. To get to Junior's, you can take the B, D, N, Q, R, 2, 3, 4, 5 subway lines to Atlantic Avenue-Barclays Center or the A, C, G lines to Hoyt-Schermerhorn Streets. Enjoy a slice of cheesecake after a meal, or take one to go to savor later.

One of New York City's most famous street foods is the hot dog, and while you can find hot dog carts on nearly every corner, certain spots have become legendary for their franks. Gray's Papaya, located at 2090 Broadway at 72nd Street, is one such spot. Known for its inexpensive and delicious hot dogs, Gray's Papaya is a no-frills joint where you can grab a classic New York dog topped with mustard, sauerkraut, or onions. The "Recession Special" (two hot dogs and a drink) is a popular choice, and the papaya juice, for which the shop is named, is a refreshing complement to the savory franks. To get to Gray's Papaya, you can take the 1, 2, 3 subway lines to 72nd Street. The stand is open 24 hours, making it a great option for a quick bite at any time of day or night.

Another iconic New York dish is the Pastrami on Rye, a classic deli sandwich that has become a symbol of the city's Jewish culinary heritage. The sandwich is typically made with thick slices of pastrami (cured and smoked beef) piled high on rye bread, with mustard as the traditional condiment. One of the best places to experience this classic sandwich is Katz's Delicatessen, located at 205 East Houston Street on the Lower East Side. Katz's has been serving up its famous pastrami sandwiches since 1888, and it's a must-visit for any food lover. The sandwiches are enormous, so consider sharing if you're not too hungry, or take half home for later. To get to Katz's, you can take the F subway line to 2nd Avenue or the J, Z lines to Delancey Street. The deli is a popular spot, especially around lunchtime, so be prepared for a bit of a wait. While there, don't forget to check out the wall of celebrity photos and the famous "Send a Salami to Your Boy in the Army" sign, which dates back to World War II.

For those looking to explore the city's culinary diversity, Chinatown is a must-visit destination. Located in Lower Manhattan, Chinatown is home to a wide variety of Chinese restaurants, bakeries, and food markets. One of the must-try dishes in Chinatown is soup dumplings (xiaolongbao), which are delicate dumplings filled with seasoned pork and hot broth. The key to eating soup dumplings is to carefully bite into the dumpling to release the broth, then enjoy the tender filling. One of the best places to try soup dumplings is Joe's Shanghai, located at 46 Bowery. Joe's Shanghai is famous for its soup dumplings, which come in both pork and crab varieties. To get to Joe's Shanghai, you can take the B, D subway lines to Grand Street or the J, Z lines to Canal Street. Be prepared to wait during peak dining hours, as the restaurant is a popular destination for both locals and tourists.

For a taste of New York's Italian-American heritage, head to Little Italy, located in Lower Manhattan near Chinatown. Little Italy is known for its Italian restaurants, bakeries, and specialty shops, and it's a great place to sample classic dishes like spaghetti and meatballs, lasagna, and cannoli. One of the most famous bakeries in Little Italy is Ferrara Bakery & Cafe, located at 195 Grand Street. Ferrara has been serving traditional Italian pastries and desserts since 1892, and it's a must-visit for anyone with a sweet tooth. The cannoli, with its crisp shell and creamy ricotta filling, is a particular favorite. To get to Little Italy, you can take the N, R, W subway lines to Prince Street or the 6 line to Spring Street. After indulging in some delicious Italian fare, take a stroll through the neighborhood to soak in the old-world charm and vibrant atmosphere.

New York City's local cuisine is as diverse and dynamic as the city itself, offering a wide range of iconic foods and must-try dishes that reflect its rich cultural heritage. From the classic New York-style pizza and bagels with lox to the indulgent cheesecake and hearty pastrami on rye, the city's food scene is a delicious journey through its history and culture. By knowing where to find these authentic local dishes and how to get there, you can fully immerse yourself in the culinary traditions that make New York City a global food capital. Whether you're grabbing a slice of pizza in Brooklyn, enjoying a bagel in the Lower East Side, or savoring a hot dog on the streets of Manhattan, the city's cuisine offers a taste of its unique character and spirit. So, come hungry and be prepared to eat your way through the Big Apple, one iconic dish at a time.

Street Food Guide

New York City's street food scene is a vibrant and integral part of the city's culinary culture. From the bustling avenues of Manhattan to the quieter streets of the outer boroughs, food trucks and street vendors offer an array of delicious, affordable, and convenient meals that capture the essence of the city's diverse culinary traditions. Whether you're in the mood for a quick snack, a hearty meal, or something sweet, New York's street food vendors provide endless options that cater to every taste and preference.

One of the most iconic street food vendors in New York City is The Halal Guys, which started as a simple food cart on the corner of 53rd Street and 6th Avenue in Midtown Manhattan. The Halal Guys have since become a culinary institution, famous for their generous portions of chicken and beef gyro served over rice, accompanied by lettuce, tomatoes, pita bread, and their signature white and hot sauces. The combination of tender meat, flavorful rice, and the perfect blend of sauces has made The Halal Guys a must-visit for anyone looking to experience New York's street food at its finest. To get to The Halal Guys, you can take the B, D, F, M subway lines to 47th-50th Streets-Rockefeller Center or the N, Q, R, W, 1, 2, 3 lines to 49th Street. The cart is open late, making it a popular spot for both lunch and a late-night bite. The long lines, especially during peak hours, are a testament to the quality and popularity of the food, but the wait is well worth it for the delicious and satisfying meal that awaits.

Another popular food truck that has gained a devoted following is The Cinnamon Snail, known for its inventive vegan and organic cuisine. The Cinnamon Snail offers a wide variety of creative dishes, from sandwiches and burgers to pastries and donuts, all made with high-quality, plant-based ingredients. One of the truck's most popular items is the "Beastmode Burger Deluxe," a seitan burger topped with jalapeño mac and cheese, arugula, and chipotle mayo, all served on a pretzel bun. The Cinnamon Snail also offers a variety of sweet treats, including the famous crème brûlée donut and the peanut butter chocolate ganache donut. The truck operates at various locations throughout the city, including Midtown Manhattan and the Financial District, so it's best to check their website or social media for their current location. To get to The Cinnamon Snail, you can take the 1, 2, 3, A, C, E subway lines to Times Square-42nd Street for Midtown or the 4, 5, J, Z lines to Wall Street for the Financial District. The Cinnamon Snail is a great option for those looking to experience innovative and delicious vegan food on the go.

For those craving something sweet, Wafels & Dinges is a must-visit food truck that serves authentic Belgian waffles with a variety of toppings, known as "dinges." The truck offers both sweet and savory waffle options, with toppings ranging from fresh strawberries and whipped cream to bacon and maple syrup. One of the most popular combinations is the "Throwdown Wafel," a Liege waffle topped with speculoos spread (a spiced cookie butter) and whipped cream. The Liege waffle, with its caramelized sugar coating and chewy texture, is a particular favorite and a must-try for anyone visiting the truck. Wafels & Dinges operates at various locations throughout the city, including Bryant Park, Union Square, and Central Park. To get to these locations, you can take the B, D, F, M subway lines to 42nd Street-Bryant Park, the N, R, W, Q, 4, 5, 6 lines to Union Square, or the A, B, C, D, 1 lines to Columbus Circle for Central Park. Enjoying a freshly made waffle from Wafels & Dinges while exploring one of the city's parks is a quintessential New York experience that combines the best of street food with the city's vibrant outdoor spaces.

New York City's street food scene also includes a wide variety of international cuisines, reflecting the city's diverse population. King of Falafel & Shawarma, located in Astoria, Queens, is a beloved food truck that offers some of the best Middle Eastern street food in the city. The menu includes classic dishes like falafel, shawarma, and chicken kebabs, all served with pita bread, hummus, and a variety of sauces. The falafel, made from ground chickpeas and spices, is crispy on the outside and tender on the inside, making it a favorite among vegetarians and meat-eaters alike. The truck's shawarma, made from marinated meat that is cooked on a vertical rotisserie and sliced thin, is equally popular. To get to King of Falafel & Shawarma, you can take the N, W subway lines to Broadway in Astoria, Queens. The truck is located at the corner of Broadway and 31st Street, and it's a great spot to grab a quick and flavorful meal while exploring the vibrant neighborhood of Astoria.

For those looking to experience classic American street food, Nathan's Famous in Coney Island is a must-visit destination. Nathan's Famous is known for its hot dogs, which have been a staple of New York's street food scene since 1916. The hot dogs are served with a variety of toppings, including mustard, sauerkraut, and onions, and are best enjoyed with a side of crinkle-cut fries. Nathan's Famous also offers other classic American fare, such as burgers, chicken sandwiches, and cheese fries. To get to Nathan's Famous, you can take the D, F, N, Q subway lines to Coney Island-Stillwell Avenue. The restaurant is located at 1310 Surf Avenue, just a short walk from the famous Coney Island boardwalk and beach. A visit to Nathan's Famous is not only a chance to enjoy some delicious street food but also an opportunity to experience a piece of New York's culinary history.

One of the best ways to eat like a local on the go in New York City is to take advantage of the city's many food carts and street vendors, which can be found on nearly every corner. These vendors offer a wide variety of quick and affordable meals, from hot dogs and pretzels to falafel and tacos. One of the most popular street food items in New York is the dirty water dog, a hot dog that is boiled in seasoned water and served with a variety of toppings, including mustard, ketchup, sauerkraut, and onions. These hot dogs are sold by vendors throughout the city and are a quick and satisfying option for those looking for a classic New York snack. Another popular street food item is the pretzel, a large, soft pretzel that is often topped with coarse salt and served with mustard. Pretzels can be found at many street carts throughout the city, and they are a great option for a quick and portable snack.

In addition to hot dogs and pretzels, New York's street food scene includes a wide variety of international cuisines, such as Mexican tacos, Indian samosas, and Chinese dumplings. Tacos El Bronco, located in Sunset Park, Brooklyn, is a popular taco truck that offers some of the best Mexican street food in the city. The menu includes a variety of tacos, including carne asada (grilled steak), al pastor (marinated pork), and lengua (beef tongue), all served on soft corn tortillas and topped with cilantro, onions, and salsa. The truck also offers other Mexican specialties, such as burritos, quesadillas, and tamales. To get to Tacos El Bronco, you can take the D, N, R subway lines to 36th Street in Brooklyn. The truck is located at the corner of 4th Avenue and 43rd Street, and it's a great spot to grab a quick and delicious meal while exploring the diverse neighborhood of Sunset Park.

Another great option for those looking to experience international street food is the Red Hook Ball Fields in Red Hook, Brooklyn. Every weekend from late spring to early fall, the ball fields are home to a variety of food vendors who offer a wide range of Latin American street food, including pupusas, arepas, and empanadas. The pupusas, which are thick corn tortillas filled with cheese, beans, or meat, are a particular favorite, and they are often served with a side of curtido, a tangy cabbage slaw. The arepas, which are made from cornmeal and filled with cheese, meat, or avocado, are another popular option. To get to the Red Hook Ball Fields, you can take the F, G subway lines to Smith-9th Streets, and then transfer to the B61 bus to Red Hook. The ball fields are located at the corner of Bay Street and Clinton Street, and they offer a unique and delicious way to experience the flavors of Latin America in New York City.

In conclusion, New York City's Street food scene offers a wide range of delicious and affordable options that cater to every taste and preference. From iconic vendors like The Halal Guys and Nathan's Famous to hidden gems like Tacos El Bronco and the Red Hook Ball Fields, the city's food trucks and street vendors provide a unique and flavorful way to experience the diverse culinary traditions that make New York one of the world's great food capitals. Whether you're grabbing a quick bite on the go or indulging in a late-night snack, eating like a local means taking advantage of the city's vibrant street food culture. So, be sure to explore the many food trucks, carts, and vendors that line the streets of New York City, and savor the flavors that make this city a true culinary destination.

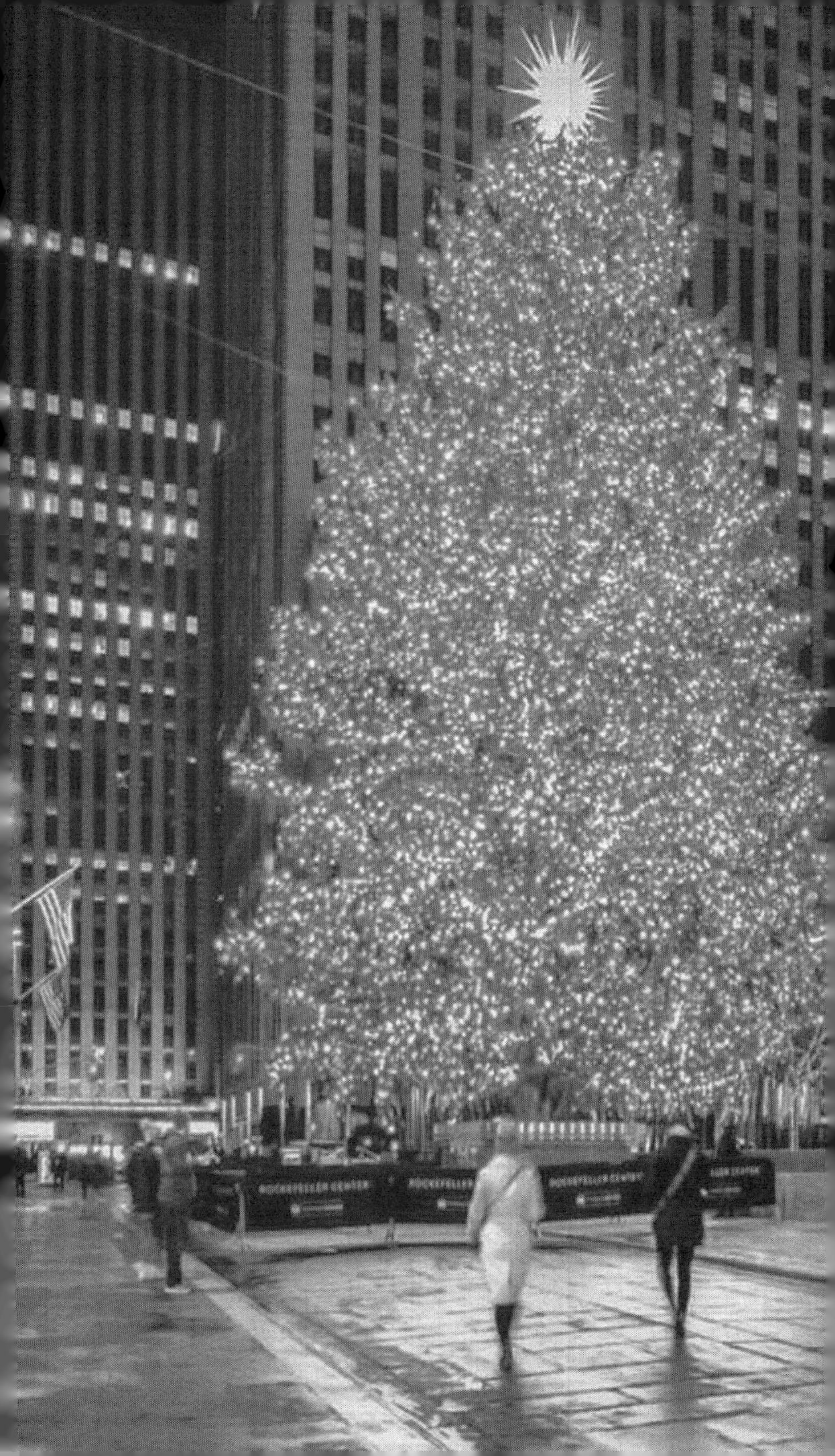

CHAPTER 11

SHOPPING AND ARTS

Shopping Guide

When visiting New York City, finding the perfect souvenir to bring back home is an important part of the travel experience. Souvenirs are not just keepsakes; they are a way to bring a piece of the city's culture, history, and spirit back with you. The key to selecting a memorable and meaningful souvenir is to look beyond the typical trinkets and explore items that truly capture the essence of New York City. From handcrafted goods and local art to food products and vintage finds, there are countless unique souvenirs that reflect the city's diversity and creativity.

One of the most iconic and unique souvenirs to bring back from New York City is a piece of local art. The city is home to countless talented artists who create everything from paintings and prints to sculptures and jewelry. A visit to the Union Square Greenmarket, located at 17th Street and Broadway, offers a great opportunity to purchase original works from local artists. The market, which operates year-round on Mondays, Wednesdays, Fridays, and Saturdays, features a wide variety of vendors selling everything from handmade crafts to fresh produce. Many of the artists at the market sell prints and small paintings that capture the city's iconic skyline, neighborhoods, and landmarks. Purchasing a piece of local art not only supports the artist but also allows you to bring a unique and personal piece of New York back home with you. To get to Union Square Greenmarket, you can take the L, N, Q, R, W, 4, 5, 6 subway lines to Union Square-14th Street.

Another great place to find unique souvenirs is the Artists & Fleas market in Chelsea, located at 88 Tenth Avenue. Artists & Fleas is a curated market that features a rotating selection of local artists, designers, and vintage collectors. The market is open on weekends and offers a wide variety of goods, including handmade jewelry, clothing, vintage items, and art. One of the best things about Artists & Fleas is the chance to meet the makers behind the products and learn more about their creative process. Whether you're looking for a one-of-a-kind piece of jewelry, a vintage poster, or a hand-sewn leather bag, you're sure to find something special at Artists & Fleas. To get to the market, you can take the A, C, E, L subway lines to 14th Street-Eighth Avenue or the 1, 2, 3 lines to 14th Street-Seventh Avenue.

If you're looking for food-related souvenirs, New York City has plenty to offer. One of the most popular food souvenirs is New York bagels. While it's not possible to bring fresh bagels back home, you can purchase bagel chips, which are made from sliced and toasted bagels and come in a variety of flavors. Zabar's, located at 2245 Broadway on the Upper West Side, is a famous gourmet food store that sells bagel chips, along with other New York food staples like smoked salmon, deli meats, and specialty cheeses. Zabar's also offers a wide selection of coffee, teas, and baked goods that make for great gifts or personal treats. To get to Zabar's, you can take the 1, 2, 3 subway lines to 79th Street. While you're there, be sure to explore the store's extensive selection of kitchenware, as well as its famous deli counter.

For those who enjoy cooking, spices and seasonings from New York's international food markets make for excellent souvenirs. Kalustyan's, located at 123 Lexington Avenue in the Murray Hill neighborhood, is a specialty food store that offers an incredible selection of spices, herbs, and international ingredients. Kalustyan's has been serving New York's diverse communities since 1944, and it's a favorite destination for both professional chefs and home cooks. The store's shelves are lined with spices from around the world, including hard-to-find varieties like sumac, za'atar, and harissa. In addition to spices, Kalustyan's also sells dried fruits, nuts, teas, and sauces, making it a great place to pick up unique and flavorful souvenirs. To get to Kalustyan's, you can take the 6 subway line to 28th Street or the N, R, W lines to 23rd Street.

Vintage lovers will appreciate the Chelsea Flea Market, located at 29 West 25th Street, between Sixth Avenue and Broadway. The market is open on weekends and features a wide variety of vendors selling everything from vintage clothing and accessories to antique furniture and collectibles. Whether you're searching for a vintage leather jacket, a mid-century modern lamp, or a rare vinyl record, the Chelsea Flea Market offers a treasure trove of unique finds. One of the best things about shopping at the flea market is the opportunity to haggle with vendors and score a great deal on a one-of-a-kind item. To get to the Chelsea Flea Market, you can take the F, M, N, R, W subway lines to 23rd Street or the 1 subway line to 28th Street.

When shopping for souvenirs in New York City, it's important to keep a few tips in mind to ensure that you get the best value for your money. First, always be open to bargaining when shopping at markets, flea markets, and street vendors. While haggling may not be appropriate in a traditional retail store, it's often expected at markets, and vendors are usually willing to negotiate on price. Start by offering a price that's slightly lower than what you're willing to pay, and be prepared to meet the vendor somewhere in the middle. Remember to be polite and respectful when bargaining, and don't be afraid to walk away if you can't agree on a price.

Another tip for shopping smart in New York City is to shop around before making a purchase. Many markets and stores carry similar items, so it's worth taking the time to compare prices and quality before committing to a purchase. If you're shopping for vintage or antique items, it's also a good idea to do a little research beforehand so that you have an idea of what the item is worth and what to look for in terms of condition and authenticity.

Finally, when shopping for souvenirs, consider purchasing items that are locally made or produced. Not only do these items often have a higher level of craftsmanship and quality, but they also support local artisans and businesses. Look for items that are labeled as "Made in New York" or "Locally Sourced," and ask vendors about the origin of the products they're selling. Whether you're purchasing a piece of jewelry, a jar of honey, or a bottle of hot sauce, choosing locally made items ensures that your souvenir is truly a reflection of New York City.

Shopping for souvenirs in New York City is an exciting and rewarding experience that allows you to bring a piece of the city's culture and creativity back home with you. From local art and vintage finds to food products and handcrafted goods, there are countless unique souvenirs that capture the essence of the city. By visiting markets like Union Square Greenmarket, Artists & Fleas, and Chelsea Flea Market, you'll discover a wide variety of items that reflect the diversity and energy of New York. Remember to bargain, shop around, and choose locally made products to ensure that you bring back souvenirs that are not only beautiful but also meaningful. Whether you're purchasing a piece of art, a bag of spices, or a vintage treasure, the souvenirs you bring back from New York City will serve as a lasting reminder of your time in this vibrant and dynamic city.

Shopping Districts and Malls

Shopping in New York City is an experience like no other. The city is a global shopping destination, offering everything from high-end luxury boutiques to quirky independent shops and sprawling malls. Whether you're looking to splurge on designer labels, discover unique local artisans, or find the best deals on name-brand goods, New York City's shopping districts and malls have something for everyone.

One of the most iconic shopping destinations in New York City is Fifth Avenue, often referred to as "Millionaire's Row." Fifth Avenue is synonymous with luxury shopping, and it's home to some of the world's most famous and prestigious stores. Stretching from 49th Street to 60th Street in Midtown

Manhattan, Fifth Avenue is lined with flagship stores from high-end brands like Tiffany & Co., Gucci, Louis Vuitton, and Prada. Whether you're window shopping or looking to make a significant purchase, strolling down Fifth Avenue is an experience in itself, with its grand storefronts and the hustle and bustle of shoppers from around the world. One must-visit spot is the Apple Store, located at 767 Fifth Avenue near Central Park. The store's iconic glass cube entrance leads you down to a massive underground retail space where you can explore the latest tech gadgets. To get to Fifth Avenue, you can take the E, M subway lines to Fifth Avenue-53rd Street or the N, Q, R, W, 4, 5, 6 lines to 59th Street.

Another famous shopping district is SoHo (South of Houston Street), known for its trendy boutiques, art galleries, and designer stores. SoHo's cobblestone streets and cast-iron buildings create a charming backdrop for shopping, and the neighborhood is a favorite among both locals and tourists. SoHo offers a mix of high-end brands and independent boutiques, making it a great place to find unique fashion items, accessories, and home goods. Popular stores in SoHo include Uniqlo, Zara, Adidas, and Supreme, as well as luxury brands like Chanel and Dior. In addition to fashion, SoHo is also home to a number of art galleries and specialty shops, where you can find everything from contemporary art to artisanal chocolates. To get to SoHo, you can take the N, R, W subway lines to Prince Street or the C, E lines to Spring Street.

For a more eclectic shopping experience, head to Greenwich Village and The West Village. These neighborhoods are known for their bohemian vibe and are home to a variety of independent boutiques, vintage shops, and specialty stores. Greenwich Village, located around Washington Square Park, is a great place to find unique clothing, books, and records. One popular destination is Strand Bookstore, located at 828 Broadway near Union Square. Strand is a New York City institution, boasting 18 miles of new, used, and rare books. Whether you're a literature lover or just looking for a unique souvenir, Strand is a must-visit. The nearby West Village is known for its charming, tree-lined streets and a more laid-back shopping experience. Specialty shops in the West Village include The Meadow, a boutique that specializes in gourmet salts, chocolates, and bitters, and McNally Jackson Books, an independent bookstore with a carefully curated selection of titles. To get to Greenwich Village and The West Village, you can take the A, B, C, D, E, F, M subway lines to West 4th Street-Washington Square.

When it comes to malls and shopping centers, New York City offers a variety of options that cater to different shopping preferences. The Shops at Columbus Circle, located at 10 Columbus Circle in the Time Warner Center, is an upscale shopping destination with a stunning view of Central Park. The mall features a mix of luxury brands and high-end retailers, including Michael Kors, Hugo Boss, and Coach. The Shops at Columbus Circle is also home to Bouchon Bakery and Per Se, two eateries by famed chef Thomas Keller. The shopping center's central location makes it a convenient stop for visitors exploring Central Park, and the views from the mall's upper levels provide a great photo opportunity. To get to The Shops at Columbus Circle, you can take the A, C, B, D, 1 subway lines to 59th Street-Columbus Circle.

Another popular shopping center is Brookfield Place, located at 230 Vesey Street in Lower Manhattan. Brookfield Place is a luxury shopping and dining destination with a modern, sophisticated atmosphere. The mall features high-end retailers like Gucci, Saks Fifth Avenue, Burberry, and Hermès, as well as a variety of upscale restaurants and cafes. One of the highlights of Brookfield Place is its stunning views of the Hudson River and the Statue of Liberty, making it a great place to shop and dine while taking in the sights. The shopping center is also home to the Winter Garden Atrium, a glass-enclosed indoor garden with towering palm trees, which provides a serene escape from the busy streets outside. To get to Brookfield Place, you can take the 1, R, W subway lines to Rector Street or the E subway line to World Trade Center.

For those looking for a more traditional mall experience, Queens Center Mall in Elmhurst, Queens, is a great option. Located at 90-15 Queens Boulevard, Queens Center Mall is one of the largest shopping malls in New York City, featuring a wide range of stores, including Macy's, JCPenney, H&M, Forever 21, and Sephora. The mall also has a large food court with a variety of dining options, making it a convenient place to spend a few hours shopping and grabbing a bite to eat. Queens Center Mall is easily accessible by public transportation, and you can get there by taking the M, R subway lines to Woodhaven Boulevard or the Q60 bus to Queens Boulevard. The mall's central location in Queens makes it a popular shopping destination for both locals and visitors.

For a more unique shopping experience, consider visiting Chelsea Market, located at 75 Ninth Avenue in the Meatpacking District. Chelsea Market is a food and retail marketplace housed in a former factory building, offering a wide variety of specialty shops, food vendors, and artisanal products. The market is a great place to find unique gifts and souvenirs, as well as sample some of the best food in the city. Popular shops in Chelsea Market include Posman Books, a local bookstore with a curated selection of titles, Artists & Fleas, a marketplace featuring local artists and designers, and Anthropologie, a lifestyle brand offering clothing, accessories, and home goods. The market also features a number of food vendors, where you can grab a bite to eat while shopping, including Los Tacos No. 1, The Lobster Place, and Fat Witch Bakery. To get to Chelsea Market, you can take the A, C, E, L subway lines to 14th Street-Eighth Avenue or the 1, 2, 3 lines to 14th Street-Seventh Avenue.

Finally, for those interested in specialty shops and boutiques, NoLIta (North of Little Italy) is a neighborhood worth exploring. Located just north of Little Italy in Lower Manhattan, NoLIta is known for its independent boutiques, vintage stores, and trendy cafes. The neighborhood has a laid-back, bohemian vibe, making it a great place to wander and discover hidden gems. Some popular shops in NoLIta include Clic, a boutique offering photography books, home decor, and unique gifts, Warm, a clothing and lifestyle store with a curated selection of fashion and accessories, and Love Adorned, a jewelry and home goods store with an eclectic mix of handmade and vintage items. To get to NoLIta, you can take the 6 subway line to Spring Street or the N, R, W subway lines to Prince Street.

In conclusion, New York City offers an unparalleled shopping experience, with a wide range of shopping districts, malls, and specialty shops to explore. Whether you're looking to indulge in luxury shopping on Fifth Avenue, discover trendy boutiques in SoHo, or find unique gifts at Chelsea Market, there's something for everyone in the city's diverse shopping landscape. By visiting these iconic shopping destinations and exploring the city's neighborhoods, you'll be able to find the perfect items to bring home, whether they're designer clothes, handmade jewelry, or delicious food products. Shopping in New York City is not just about the purchases you make; it's about the experience of discovering the city's vibrant culture, creativity, and style through its many shops and markets. So, take your time, explore the city's shopping districts, and enjoy the thrill of finding something special in the heart of the Big Apple.

Local Art and Music Scene

New York City's art and music scene is a vibrant and integral part of the city's cultural fabric. With a rich history as a hub for artists, musicians, and performers, the city offers an endless array of opportunities to experience and engage with creative expressions across various mediums. From world-renowned galleries and intimate art spaces to legendary music venues and emerging local talent, New York's art and music scene is as diverse and dynamic as the city itself. Whether you're a passionate art lover, a music enthusiast, or simply curious about the city's creative pulse, exploring New York's local art and music scene is a must.

One of the most iconic neighborhoods for experiencing New York's art scene is Chelsea, located on the west side of Manhattan. Chelsea is home to a high concentration of art galleries, with many clustered between 10th and 11th Avenues, from 18th to 28th Streets. The neighborhood is known for its contemporary art spaces that showcase works from both established and emerging artists. Gagosian Gallery, located at 555 West 24th Street, is one of the most prominent galleries in Chelsea, featuring exhibitions by some of the most influential artists of our time. Another notable gallery is David Zwirner, located at 525 West 19th Street, which is known for its innovative exhibitions and commitment to representing a diverse range of artists. Visiting these galleries is a great way to experience contemporary art in a setting that encourages exploration and discovery. To get to Chelsea, you can take the A, C, E subway lines to 23rd Street and walk west toward the Hudson River.

For those interested in experiencing more experimental and avant-garde art, The Lower East Side is a neighborhood worth exploring. The Lower East Side has long been a haven for artists and creatives, and its galleries often feature cutting-edge works that push the boundaries of traditional art forms. New Museum, located at 235 Bowery, is a contemporary art museum that focuses on new and emerging artists. The museum's exhibitions often challenge conventional notions of art and provide a platform for artists whose work addresses social, political, and cultural issues. In addition to the New Museum, the Lower East Side is home to a number of smaller galleries and art spaces, such as Jeffrey Deitch Gallery and Canada Gallery, which showcase a diverse range of artistic practices. To get to the Lower East Side, you can take the F subway line to 2nd Avenue or the J, Z lines to Bowery.

Brooklyn's DUMBO (Down Under the Manhattan Bridge Overpass) neighborhood is another thriving arts district, known for its stunning views of the Manhattan skyline and its vibrant creative community. DUMBO is home to a variety of art galleries, studios, and performance spaces, making it a great place to experience both visual and performing arts. Smack Mellon, located at 92 Plymouth Street, is a nonprofit art space that supports emerging artists through exhibitions, studio programs, and artist residencies. The space often features experimental and interdisciplinary works that challenge traditional artistic practices. Another must-visit spot in DUMBO is St. Ann's Warehouse, located at 45 Water Street, which is known for its innovative theater productions and live performances. St. Ann's Warehouse hosts a wide range of events, from experimental theater to live music, and is a key player in Brooklyn's cultural scene. To get to DUMBO, you can take the F subway line to York Street or the A, C lines to High Street.

New York City is also home to a rich and diverse music scene, with live music venues that cater to every genre and taste. Greenwich Village has long been associated with the city's folk and jazz music scenes, and it remains a vibrant area for live music today. The Village Vanguard, located at 178 Seventh Avenue South, is one of the most famous jazz clubs in the world. Established in 1935, the club has hosted legendary musicians like John Coltrane, Miles Davis, and Bill Evans, and it continues to be a premier destination for jazz lovers. Another iconic venue in Greenwich Village is The Bitter End, located at 147 Bleecker Street, which has been a staple of the city's live music scene since 1961. The Bitter End has hosted performances by artists like Bob Dylan, Joni Mitchell, and Lady Gaga, and it remains a popular spot for both established and up-and-coming musicians. To get to Greenwich Village, you can take the A, B, C, D, E, F, M subway lines to West 4th Street-Washington Square.

For those interested in exploring Brooklyn's music scene, Williamsburg is a neighborhood that offers a wide variety of live music venues and performance spaces. Music Hall of Williamsburg, located at 66 North 6th Street, is a popular venue that hosts indie rock, electronic, and alternative music acts. The venue has a capacity of 650 people, making it an intimate setting for live performances. Another notable venue in Williamsburg is Brooklyn Bowl, located at 61 Wythe Avenue, which combines live music with bowling, food, and drinks. Brooklyn Bowl hosts a diverse range of musical acts, from rock and hip-hop to funk and soul, and it's a great place to experience the energy and creativity of Brooklyn's music scene. To get to Williamsburg, you can take the L subway line to Bedford Avenue or the G subway line to Metropolitan Avenue.

Supporting local artists and musicians is an important way to contribute to New York City's vibrant creative community. One of the best ways to support local artists is by attending gallery openings, art shows, and performances. Many galleries and art spaces in the city offer free or low-cost admission to exhibitions, making it accessible for everyone to experience and appreciate art. Purchasing works from local artists, whether it's a painting, a print, or a piece of jewelry, is another way to support the creative community while also acquiring a unique and meaningful souvenir. Many artists in New York also sell their work online through platforms like Etsy or their own websites, so it's worth exploring these options if you're unable to visit the city in person.

Supporting local musicians can be as simple as attending a live show or purchasing music directly from the artist. Many of the city's live music venues, especially smaller, independent ones, rely on ticket sales and bar revenue to stay afloat, so attending shows is a direct way to support both the venue and the musicians performing. Additionally, many local musicians sell merchandise like vinyl records, t-shirts, and posters at their shows, so purchasing these items is another way to show support. If you're unable to attend a live show, consider streaming or purchasing music from local artists through platforms like Bandcamp, which allows musicians to earn a higher percentage of revenue compared to other streaming services.

New York City's art and music scene offers endless opportunities to experience and engage with creative expression across a wide range of mediums. From the contemporary art galleries of Chelsea to the experimental art spaces of the Lower East Side and the vibrant music venues of Greenwich Village and Williamsburg, the city is a hub for artistic innovation and cultural diversity. By visiting galleries, attending live performances, and supporting local artists and musicians, you'll not only enrich your own experience but also contribute to the thriving creative community that makes New York City a global cultural capital. Whether you're a longtime art lover or a casual music fan, exploring the city's local art and music scene is an essential part of any visit to New York, offering a deeper connection to the city's unique and dynamic cultural landscape.

Local Artisans and Crafts

New York City is a vibrant hub for artisans and craftspeople, offering a rich array of handmade goods that reflect the city's diverse cultural fabric and innovative spirit. From meticulously crafted jewelry and ceramics to artisanal textiles and unique home decor, the city is home to a thriving community of makers who bring creativity and skill to every piece they create. Whether you're looking to purchase one-of-a-kind items, learn a new craft, or support the local artisan community, New York City provides numerous opportunities to immerse yourself in the world of handmade goods.

One of the best places to find handmade goods in New York City is Brooklyn Flea, a beloved market that showcases the work of local artisans alongside vintage vendors and food stalls. Located at various locations throughout Brooklyn, including Williamsburg and Dumbo, Brooklyn Flea operates on weekends and has become a go-to destination for those seeking unique, handcrafted items. Here, you can find everything from hand-poured candles and handmade leather goods to intricately designed jewelry and original artworks. The market is also known for its friendly atmosphere, where you can meet the artisans, learn about their creative processes, and purchase items directly from the makers themselves. To get to Brooklyn Flea, you can take the L subway line to Bedford Avenue or the F subway line to York Street, depending on the market location.

Another great spot for discovering handmade goods is Artists & Fleas, which has multiple locations in New York City, including Chelsea Market in Manhattan and Williamsburg in Brooklyn. Artists & Fleas is a curated marketplace that brings together local artists, designers, and makers in a lively and creative environment. Each market features a rotating selection of vendors, ensuring that there's always something new and exciting to discover. Whether you're looking for handcrafted jewelry, artisanal soaps, or hand-dyed textiles, Artists & Fleas offers a wide range of unique products that you won't find anywhere else. The market is also a great place to find gifts and souvenirs that capture the spirit of New York City's creative community. To visit Artists & Fleas, you can take the A, C, E, L subway lines to 14th Street-Eighth Avenue for the Chelsea Market location or the L subway line to Bedford Avenue for the Williamsburg location.

For those interested in learning more about the crafts themselves, New York City offers a variety of workshops and classes where you can explore your creative side and learn new skills. 3rd Ward, located in Brooklyn, is a creative hub that offers a wide range of classes in everything from woodworking and metalworking to photography and graphic design. The workshops are designed for all skill levels, so whether you're a beginner looking to try something new or an experienced maker looking to hone your craft, you'll find a class that suits your needs. The hands-on nature of the workshops allows you to work with tools and materials under the guidance of skilled instructors, giving you the confidence to create your own handcrafted items. To get to 3rd Ward, you can take the L subway line to Morgan Avenue.

Another popular venue for craft workshops is Makeville Studio, located in the Gowanus neighborhood of Brooklyn. Makeville Studio specializes in woodworking and offers classes that cover a wide range of techniques, from basic woodworking to advanced furniture making. The studio is fully equipped with tools and materials, and the small class sizes ensure that you receive personalized instruction and guidance. Whether you're interested in building your own furniture, creating custom home decor, or simply learning the basics of woodworking, Makeville Studio provides a supportive and creative environment where you can bring your ideas to life. To get to Makeville Studio, you can take the F, G subway lines to Carroll Street.

Supporting local craft communities is an important way to contribute to the sustainability of New York City's artisan culture. One way to do this is by purchasing directly from local artisans at markets, pop-up shops, and online platforms like Etsy. By buying handmade goods, you're not only acquiring unique and high-quality items, but you're also supporting the livelihoods of the makers who pour their time, energy, and passion into their work. Many artisans in New York City also sell their products through their own websites or social media platforms, allowing you to connect with them directly and learn more about their creative processes.

Another way to support the local craft community is by attending craft fairs and artisan markets. Events like the

Renegade Craft Fair, which takes place in various locations across the city, bring together hundreds of independent makers and offer a wide range of handmade goods, from clothing and accessories to home decor and artwork. These events provide a platform for artisans to showcase their work, connect with customers, and build their businesses. By attending craft fairs, you're not only supporting local makers but also helping to foster a sense of community and appreciation for handmade goods.

Volunteering or participating in community programs that support artisans and craftspeople is another way to give back to the local craft community. Organizations like Made in NYC, a nonprofit that promotes locally made products and supports small manufacturers and artisans, offer various opportunities to get involved, from attending events and workshops to volunteering your time or skills. By supporting organizations that advocate for and empower local makers, you're helping to ensure that New York City's craft community continues to thrive and evolve.

New York City is a treasure trove of handmade goods, with countless opportunities to discover, create, and support the work of local artisans and craftspeople. Whether you're shopping for unique gifts at Brooklyn Flea, taking a woodworking class at Makeville Studio, or attending a craft fair, you'll find that the city's craft community is vibrant, diverse, and deeply rooted in creativity. By engaging with this community, you'll not only acquire beautiful and meaningful items but also gain a deeper appreciation for the artistry and craftsmanship that goes into creating them. Supporting local artisans is not just about making a purchase;

it's about celebrating the creative spirit that makes New York City such a special place. So, take the time to explore the city's markets, workshops, and events, and experience the joy of handmade goods in the heart of the Big Apple.

Local Crafts Workshops

New York City is a bustling metropolis, not only known for its towering skyscrapers, diverse culinary scene, and vibrant arts culture but also for its rich tradition of craftsmanship. The city is home to a thriving community of artisans and craftspeople who are eager to share their skills and knowledge through various workshops and classes. These hands-on experiences provide a unique opportunity for both locals and tourists to learn traditional crafts and modern techniques, create their own handmade items, and gain a deeper appreciation for the art of making.

One of the most popular destinations for craft workshops in New York City is Brooklyn Craft Company, located in the Greenpoint neighborhood of Brooklyn. This bright and welcoming studio offers a wide range of hands-on workshops, from sewing and knitting to jewelry making and block printing. The classes are designed for all skill levels, so whether you're a complete beginner or an experienced crafter looking to learn a new technique, you'll find something that suits your interests. The instructors at Brooklyn Craft Company are passionate about their crafts and provide step-by-step guidance to help you create something beautiful. In addition to scheduled classes, the studio also hosts private events and parties, making it a great place for a fun and creative outing with friends. To get to Brooklyn Craft Company, you can take the G subway line to Nassau Avenue or the L line to Bedford Avenue.

For those interested in learning traditional crafts, Textile Arts Center in Brooklyn's Gowanus neighborhood is a must-visit. The Textile Arts Center is dedicated to preserving and promoting the art of textile making, offering workshops in weaving, dyeing, printing, and other textile techniques. The center's mission is to provide a space for learning, experimentation, and creativity, with classes taught by experienced artisans who are deeply knowledgeable about their craft. One of the center's most popular offerings is the Weaving Basics workshop, where participants learn to set up and operate a loom, create their own woven fabric, and explore different patterns and textures. The Textile Arts Center also offers longer-term programs, such as the Artist in Residence program, which provides emerging textile artists with the resources and studio space to develop their work. To get to the Textile Arts Center, you can take the F, G subway lines to Carroll Street.

Another excellent option for hands-on craft workshops is CraftJam, which operates out of various locations across Manhattan. CraftJam offers a diverse range of workshops, including embroidery, calligraphy, macrame, and more. What sets CraftJam apart is its focus on making crafting accessible and fun for everyone. The workshops are casual and social, often held in trendy venues where participants can enjoy drinks and snacks while they work on their projects. The instructors are friendly and approachable, ensuring that everyone feels comfortable and confident as they learn new skills. CraftJam also offers corporate events and private parties, making it a popular choice for team-building activities and celebrations. To find a CraftJam workshop near you, check their website for the latest schedule and locations, which can include places like cafes, co-working spaces, and event venues in neighborhoods like SoHo, NoMad, and the East Village.

For those who prefer a more immersive learning experience, Mugi Studio in the Upper West Side of Manhattan offers pottery and ceramics classes in a cozy, community-oriented setting. Mugi Studio is known for its small class sizes, which allow for personalized instruction and plenty of hands-on practice. The studio offers classes for all skill levels, from introductory courses for beginners to advanced workshops for those looking to refine their techniques. One of the studio's most popular classes is the Wheel Throwing workshop, where participants learn to shape clay on a potter's wheel and create functional and decorative pieces. The relaxed and supportive environment at Mugi Studio makes it a great place to unwind and get creative, whether you're working on a one-time project or developing your skills over a series of classes. To get to Mugi Studio, you can take the 1, 2, 3 subway lines to 72nd Street.

For those interested in finding craft classes throughout the city, there are several online platforms and resources that can help you discover workshops and connect with local artisans. Websites like CourseHorse and Eventbrite list a wide range of classes and events, including craft workshops in various disciplines. These platforms allow you to search for classes by date, location, and skill level, making it easy to find a workshop that fits your schedule and interests. Many of the workshops listed on these platforms are hosted by local studios, galleries, and community centers, so you'll have the opportunity to explore different neighborhoods and meet new people as you learn.

Supporting local craft communities is an essential part of keeping New York City's artisan culture alive and thriving. By attending workshops and classes, you're not only learning new skills and creating your own handmade items, but you're also contributing to the livelihood of local artisans and helping to sustain the city's creative economy. Many of the studios and craft spaces in New York City rely on community support to continue offering their programs, so your participation in workshops can have a meaningful impact.

New York City offers a wealth of opportunities to engage with local crafts through hands-on workshops and classes. Whether you're interested in learning traditional textile techniques at the Textile Arts Center, exploring the world of pottery at Mugi Studio, or trying your hand at modern crafts with CraftJam, there's something for everyone in the city's vibrant craft scene. By participating in these workshops, you'll not only gain new skills and create beautiful, handmade items, but you'll also connect with the city's rich tradition of craftsmanship and support the artisans who make it all possible. Whether you're a resident of New York City or a visitor looking to experience something unique, exploring the city's craft workshops is a rewarding and memorable way to engage with the local culture. So, roll up your sleeves, unleash your creativity, and discover the joy of making in the heart of New York City.

Local Street Art and Graffiti

New York City is often hailed as one of the world's great cultural capitals, and its street art and graffiti scene plays a crucial role in this reputation. The city's walls, buildings, and public spaces are canvases for artists to express their creativity, share their messages, and challenge viewers to see the world from different perspectives. Street art in New York City is not just about colorful murals and graffiti tags; it's a form of public art that tells stories, reflects the city's diverse cultures, and often serves as a voice for those who may not have a platform elsewhere.

One of the most famous neighborhoods for street art in New York City is Bushwick in Brooklyn. Over the past decade, Bushwick has transformed from an industrial area to a vibrant artistic hub, largely thanks to the rise of street art in the neighborhood. The Bushwick Collective is at the heart of this transformation. Founded by local resident Joe Ficalora in 2012, the Bushwick Collective is a curated outdoor gallery featuring murals by artists from around the world. Walking through the streets of Bushwick, particularly around Troutman Street and Saint Nicholas Avenue, you'll encounter an ever-changing array of large-scale murals that showcase a wide range of styles, themes, and techniques. Each piece is unique, often reflecting the cultural background or social commentary of the artist. To get to Bushwick, you can take the L subway line to Jefferson Street or the M subway line to Central Avenue.

Another iconic location for street art is Wynwood Walls in Miami, which has its counterpart in New York City known as The Graffiti Hall of Fame. Located at East 106th Street and Park Avenue in East Harlem, the Graffiti Hall of Fame has been a sanctuary for graffiti artists since 1980. Originally founded by community activist Ray Rodriguez, the space was created as a safe and legal place for artists to practice their craft. Today, it remains a historic site where both seasoned graffiti legends and up-and-coming artists showcase their skills. The walls of the Graffiti Hall of Fame are covered in vibrant murals and intricate tags, each telling a story about the artist's journey, the community, or a larger societal issue. The site is a testament to the evolution of graffiti from a form of rebellion to an accepted and celebrated art form. To visit the Graffiti Hall of Fame, you can take the 6 subway line to 103rd Street.

In Manhattan's Lower East Side, street art is woven into the fabric of the neighborhood. This area has a long history of being a breeding ground for creativity and counter-culture, and its walls reflect this legacy. One of the most famous street art spots in the Lower East Side is Freeman Alley, located off Rivington Street between Bowery and Chrystie Street. The narrow alley is lined with ever-changing street art, from murals to paste-ups to stencils. Artists from all over the world come to Freeman Alley to leave their mark, making it a dynamic and constantly evolving gallery of street art. Another notable spot in the Lower East Side is 100 Gates Project, an initiative that began in 2014 to transform the metal roll-down gates of local businesses into canvases for artists. As you walk through the neighborhood, you'll see an array of colorful gates, each telling its own story and adding to the vibrant atmosphere of the area. To get to the Lower East Side, you can take the F subway line to Delancey Street or the J, Z lines to Bowery.

No exploration of New York City's street art scene would be complete without a visit to 5 Pointz—or at least, the memory of it. Located in Long Island City, Queens, 5 Pointz was once known as the "Graffiti Mecca" of the world. This sprawling industrial complex was covered in graffiti and murals by artists from around the globe, serving as a community space where artists could collaborate, learn from each other, and showcase their work. Unfortunately, 5 Pointz was demolished in 2014 to make way for luxury condos, but its legacy lives on in the hearts of street art enthusiasts and in the work of artists who continue to draw inspiration from it. The area around MoMA PS1 in Long Island City, which is an extension of the Museum of Modern Art dedicated to contemporary art, continues to be a vibrant area for street art. The walls surrounding MoMA PS1 are often adorned with large-scale murals that echo the spirit of 5 Pointz. To visit Long Island City, you can take the 7 subway line to Court Square.

The stories behind the murals in these neighborhoods are as diverse as the city itself. Some murals are deeply personal, reflecting the artist's own experiences, struggles, and triumphs. Others are political, using art as a means to comment on social issues such as inequality, immigration, and climate change. For example, in Bushwick, you might come across a mural that pays homage to the neighborhood's Puerto Rican heritage, while in the Lower East Side, you could find a piece that addresses the gentrification of the area.

Many murals also celebrate cultural icons, with portraits of musicians, activists, and historical figures who have left their mark on the city and beyond. The stories behind these murals add layers of meaning to the artwork, making it more than just something to look at, but something to engage with on a deeper level.

To fully appreciate the street art in New York City, taking a street art tour is highly recommended. Several companies and organizations offer guided tours that take you through the city's most famous street art neighborhoods, providing insights into the history, culture, and stories behind the art. Graff Tours is one such company that offers street art tours in Bushwick, the Lower East Side, and other neighborhoods. Their tours are led by knowledgeable guides who are often artists themselves, providing a unique perspective on the art and the community. Another option is Street Art Walk, which offers walking tours of Williamsburg, Brooklyn—a neighborhood known for its vibrant street art scene. These tours allow you to see the art up close, learn about the artists and their work, and even meet some of the artists themselves. If you prefer to explore on your own, there are also self-guided street art maps available online, which you can use to plan your own route and discover the city's street art at your own pace.

New York City's street art and graffiti scene is a dynamic and integral part of the city's cultural landscape. From the colorful murals of Bushwick to the historic walls of the Graffiti Hall of Fame, the city is home to a rich tapestry of public art that reflects its diverse communities, histories, and voices. By exploring these famous street art locations, learning the stories behind the murals, and taking a street art tour, you'll gain a deeper understanding of the city's creative spirit and the role that street art plays in shaping New York's identity. Whether you're a longtime resident or a first-time visitor, immersing yourself in the city's street art scene is an experience that will leave you inspired and with a new appreciation for the art that surrounds you.

Local Architecture and Building Styles

New York City's architectural landscape is a fascinating blend of old and new, where centuries of history and modern innovation coexist side by side. The city is home to some of the world's most iconic buildings, renowned architectural landmarks, and a diversity of building styles that reflect its rich cultural heritage. Exploring New York City's architecture offers a unique window into its past, present, and future, providing a deeper understanding of the forces that have shaped this dynamic metropolis.

One of the most famous architectural landmarks in New York City is the Empire State Building, located in Midtown Manhattan at 350 Fifth Avenue. Completed in 1931, this Art Deco skyscraper was the tallest building in the world until 1971 and remains one of the most recognizable structures in the city. Designed by William F. Lamb of the architectural firm Shreve, Lamb & Harmon, the Empire State Building embodies the spirit of early 20th-century New York, with its soaring height, symmetrical lines, and decorative spire. Visitors can take an elevator to the 86th-floor observation deck for panoramic views of the city, making it a must-see destination for anyone interested in New York's architectural history. To get to the Empire State Building, you can take the B, D, F, M, N, Q, R, or W subway lines to 34th Street-Herald Square, or the 1, 2, 3 lines to 34th Street-Penn Station.

Another iconic building that defines New York City's skyline is the Chrysler Building, located at 405 Lexington Avenue in Midtown Manhattan. Completed in 1930, the Chrysler Building is another masterpiece of the Art Deco style, designed by architect William Van Alen. The building's most distinctive features are its terraced crown, adorned with stainless steel arches and triangular windows, and its spire, which was a closely guarded secret during construction and allowed the Chrysler Building to briefly claim the title of the world's tallest building. The Chrysler Building is often regarded as one of the most beautiful skyscrapers in the world, and while the interior is not open to the public, the lobby, with its elaborate Art Deco decorations, is worth a visit. To visit the Chrysler Building, you can take the 4, 5, 6, or 7 subway lines to Grand Central-42nd Street.

New York City is also home to the Flatiron Building, one of the city's earliest skyscrapers and a symbol of its early 20th-century architectural boom. Located at 175 Fifth Avenue, where Broadway and Fifth Avenue intersect, the Flatiron Building was completed in 1902 and designed by architect Daniel Burnham. The building's distinctive triangular shape, which resembles a flat iron, makes it one of the most photographed buildings in the city. The Flatiron Building's Beaux-Arts style, with its limestone facade and decorative details, represents a departure from the more ornate styles of previous decades and is a precursor to the modern skyscraper.

Although the Flatiron Building is primarily an office building, its exterior is a popular subject for photographers and a key stop on any architectural tour of New York City. To visit the Flatiron Building, you can take the N, R, or W subway lines to 23rd Street.

The Woolworth Building, located at 233 Broadway in Lower Manhattan, is another architectural gem that showcases New York City's rich history. Completed in 1913, the Woolworth Building was designed by architect Cass Gilbert and was the tallest building in the world at the time. The building's Gothic Revival style, with its ornate terra cotta facade, intricate detailing, and soaring tower, earned it the nickname "The Cathedral of Commerce." The Woolworth Building was commissioned by retail magnate Frank W. Woolworth as the headquarters for his five-and-dime store empire, and its design reflects both the opulence of the Gilded Age and the aspirations of early 20th-century New York. While the upper floors of the Woolworth Building are not open to the public, guided tours are available that provide access to the stunning lobby, with its mosaics, stained glass, and marble finishes. To get to the Woolworth Building, you can take the 2, 3, A, C, J, or Z subway lines to Fulton Street.

The Guggenheim Museum, located at 1071 Fifth Avenue on the Upper East Side, is a modern architectural landmark that stands in contrast to the more traditional buildings of the city. Designed by legendary architect Frank Lloyd Wright and completed in 1959, the Guggenheim Museum is famous for its unique spiral design, which challenges conventional ideas of what a museum should look like. The building's white, cylindrical form, which widens as it rises, creates a continuous ramp that allows visitors to view the art collection in a seamless flow. The Guggenheim's design is a testament to Wright's belief in organic architecture, where the structure and its environment are in harmony. The museum is not only a must-visit for art lovers but also for those interested in modern architecture. To visit the Guggenheim Museum, you can take the 4, 5, or 6 subway lines to 86th Street and walk west to Fifth Avenue.

Beyond these iconic landmarks, New York City is a treasure trove of architectural diversity, with each neighborhood offering its own unique character and history. The Greenwich Village neighborhood, for example, is known for its charming brownstones and historic row houses, many of which date back to the 19th century. The narrow, tree-lined streets of Greenwich Village provide a stark contrast to the bustling avenues of Midtown, offering a glimpse into the city's past. Walking through the neighborhood, you'll find Federal-style townhouses, Greek Revival buildings, and Italianate brownstones, each with its own story to tell. To explore Greenwich Village, you can take the A, B, C, D, E, F, M subway lines to West 4th Street-Washington Square.

The Financial District in Lower Manhattan, home to Wall Street and the New York Stock Exchange, is another area rich in architectural history. The district is a mix of old and new, with historic buildings like the New York Stock Exchange Building and Federal Hall standing alongside modern skyscrapers like One World Trade Center. The narrow, winding streets of the Financial District reflect the original Dutch settlement of New Amsterdam, and many of the buildings in the area date back to the 19th and early 20th centuries. Exploring the Financial District offers a fascinating journey through the history of New York City as a center of commerce and finance. To visit the Financial District, you can take the 2, 3, 4, 5, J, Z subway lines to Wall Street.

New York City's architectural diversity also extends to its bridges, with the Brooklyn Bridge being one of the most famous examples. Completed in 1883, the Brooklyn Bridge was the first steel-wire suspension bridge in the world and a marvel of engineering at the time. Designed by John A. Roebling and completed by his son, Washington Roebling, the bridge's Gothic-style towers and sweeping cables have made it an iconic symbol of New York City. Walking or biking across the Brooklyn Bridge offers stunning views of the Manhattan skyline and is a quintessential New York experience. The bridge connects Lower Manhattan to the Brooklyn neighborhood of DUMBO, and to access the pedestrian walkway, you can take the 4, 5, 6 subway lines to Brooklyn Bridge-City Hall in Manhattan or the A, C, F lines to High Street-Brooklyn Bridge in Brooklyn.

To explore New York City's architectural diversity, there are several ways to immerse yourself in the city's built environment. Walking tours are an excellent way to experience the architecture up close and learn about the history and significance of different buildings. Organizations like the Municipal Art Society and New York City Walking Tours offer guided architectural tours that cover various neighborhoods and themes, from Art Deco skyscrapers in Midtown to the brownstones of Brooklyn. These tours are led by knowledgeable guides who provide insights into the architectural styles, historical context, and cultural significance of the buildings you'll encounter.

For those who prefer a more independent approach, self-guided architectural tours are also an option. There are numerous books, apps, and online resources that provide detailed information on New York City's architecture, allowing you to create your own itinerary and explore at your own pace. Some popular self-guided tour routes include a walk along Fifth Avenue, where you can see landmarks like St. Patrick's Cathedral, the New York Public Library, and the Empire State Building, or a tour of the Flatiron District, which includes the Flatiron Building, the Met Life Tower, and the historic Madison Square Park.

New York City's architectural landscape is a rich tapestry of styles, periods, and influences that tell the story of the city's growth and evolution. From the grandeur of the Empire State Building and the Chrysler Building to the historic charm of Greenwich Village and the innovative design of the Guggenheim Museum, the city's buildings are as diverse as its people. Exploring New York's architecture offers a unique way to connect with the city's history, culture, and creativity, whether you're visiting famous landmarks, discovering hidden gems, or simply wandering through its streets. Whether you're a seasoned architecture enthusiast or a curious traveler, New York City's architectural wonders are sure to leave a lasting impression.

CHAPTER 12

NATURE AND OUTDOOR ACTIVITIES

Local Wildlife and Nature Reserves

New York City, known for its bustling urban landscape, is also home to a surprising array of parks, natural areas, and wildlife reserves that offer a breath of fresh air and a connection to nature amidst the city's skyscrapers. These green spaces are not only vital for the well-being of the city's residents but also serve as important habitats for a variety of wildlife. Whether you're interested in a quiet walk through a park, bird watching, or a day trip to a nearby nature reserve, New York City provides numerous opportunities to experience the natural world.

One of the most famous green spaces in the city is Central Park, located in the heart of Manhattan. Spanning 843 acres, Central Park is a sanctuary for both people and wildlife. Designed by Frederick Law Olmsted and Calvert Vaux in the mid-19th century, the park features a mix of landscapes, including woodlands, meadows, and water bodies, making it an ideal habitat for a wide variety of species. Bird watching is particularly popular in Central Park, especially during migration seasons when you can spot warblers, hawks, and other birds passing through the city. The Ramble, a densely wooded area in the park, is a hotspot for birdwatchers and nature lovers. In addition to bird watching, visitors to Central Park can enjoy a leisurely rowboat ride on the Central Park

Lake, explore the peaceful paths of the North Woods, or relax by the Great Lawn. To get to Central Park, you can take the A, B, C, D, 1, 2, 3 subway lines to various stations along the park's west side, or the N, Q, R, W lines to Fifth Avenue/59th Street on the east side.

Another significant natural area in New York City is Prospect Park in Brooklyn. Also designed by Olmsted and Vaux, Prospect Park offers 526 acres of green space and is home to a diverse range of wildlife. The park's Lullwater and Lake areas are particularly rich in birdlife, attracting species such as herons, egrets, and woodpeckers. The park also features the Ravine, a wooded area with streams and waterfalls that provide a tranquil escape from the city's hustle and bustle. For those interested in learning more about the park's flora and fauna, the Audubon Center at the Boathouse offers educational programs and guided tours. The center is also a great starting point for exploring the park's many trails and wildlife habitats. To visit Prospect Park, you can take the B, Q subway lines to Prospect Park station, or the 2, 3 lines to Grand Army Plaza.

For a more coastal experience, Jamaica Bay Wildlife Refuge in Queens is one of the most important urban wildlife refuges in the United States. Part of the Gateway National Recreation Area, Jamaica Bay encompasses over 9,000 acres of salt marshes, islands, and water, providing critical habitat for more than 330 species of birds, as well as fish, shellfish, and other wildlife. The refuge is a paradise for birdwatchers, especially during the spring and fall migrations when thousands of birds stop here on their journey along the Atlantic Flyway. Visitors can explore the refuge's trails, which offer stunning views of the bay and opportunities to observe wildlife in their natural habitat. The refuge also has an Environmental Education Center, where you can learn about the area's ecology and the efforts to preserve it. To get to Jamaica Bay Wildlife Refuge, you can take the A subway line to Broad Channel, and then it's a short walk to the refuge entrance.

If you're looking for a more rugged outdoor experience, Inwood Hill Park at the northern tip of Manhattan offers a rare glimpse of the city's natural history. This park is unique in that it contains the last natural forest and salt marsh in Manhattan, providing a habitat for a variety of wildlife, including red-tailed hawks, raccoons, and even the occasional coyote. Inwood Hill Park is also home to ancient glacial potholes, Native American caves, and historic sites, making it a fascinating place to explore. The park's Cloisters Lawn offers beautiful views of the Hudson River and the New Jersey Palisades, while the Salt Marsh is a great spot for bird watching. To reach Inwood Hill Park, you can take the A subway line to 207th Street, or the 1 line to 215th Street.

For those interested in venturing beyond the city, several nearby nature reserves offer a chance to escape into the wilderness without traveling too far. Bear Mountain State Park, located about 50 miles north of New York City, is a popular destination for hiking, picnicking, and wildlife watching. The park is home to a variety of habitats, including forests, wetlands, and the Hudson River shoreline, which support species such as black bears, white-tailed deer, and bald eagles. The park's Appalachian Trail section offers some of the best hiking in the region, with scenic vistas and challenging terrain. To get to Bear Mountain State Park, you can take a Metro-North train from Grand Central Terminal to Peekskill, and then a short taxi or bus ride to the park.

Another excellent day trip option is the Palisades Interstate Park, located across the Hudson River in New Jersey. The park features 2,500 acres of cliffs, woodlands, and riverfront, with numerous trails for hiking, biking, and nature walks. The Palisades Cliffs offer breathtaking views of the Hudson River and Manhattan skyline, and the park is a haven for birdwatchers, with species such as peregrine falcons and great blue herons frequently spotted along the cliffs. The park also has several historic sites, picnic areas, and a visitor center with exhibits on the area's natural and cultural history. To get to the Palisades Interstate Park, you can take a New Jersey Transit bus from Port Authority Bus Terminal to the park entrance, or drive across the George Washington Bridge.

New York City's parks and natural areas provide ample opportunities for wildlife watching, whether you're looking to spot birds, observe marine life, or simply enjoy the beauty of nature. In addition to the locations mentioned above, other notable wildlife-watching spots include the New York Botanical Garden in the Bronx, Pelham Bay Park in the Bronx, and Marine Park in Brooklyn. Each of these sites offers its own unique ecosystem and species, making them ideal destinations for nature lovers.

While New York City is often associated with its iconic skyline and urban hustle, it is also a city rich in natural beauty and wildlife. From the expansive green spaces of Central Park and Prospect Park to the coastal habitats of Jamaica Bay and the rugged terrain of Inwood Hill, the city's parks and natural areas provide a refuge for both people and wildlife. Whether you're a resident or a visitor, taking the time to explore these green spaces and nearby nature reserves offers a rewarding and refreshing escape from the urban environment. Whether you're bird watching, hiking, or simply enjoying the serenity of nature, New York City's parks and reserves are sure to provide memorable experiences and a deeper appreciation for the natural world in an urban setting.

Guided Nature Walks

New York City, known for its bustling streets and towering skyscrapers, also offers a surprising variety of opportunities for nature enthusiasts to explore the natural world. Guided nature walks in and around the city provide a chance to step away from the urban environment and immerse yourself in the beauty of New York's parks, wetlands, and natural reserves. These walks, led by knowledgeable guides, allow participants to learn about the city's diverse ecosystems, native wildlife, and plant species, all while enjoying the tranquility of the great outdoors.

One of the best places to start your exploration is Central Park, located in the heart of Manhattan. Central Park is not just a green oasis amidst the city's concrete jungle; it's also home to a rich variety of flora and fauna. Guided nature walks through Central Park often focus on the park's birdlife, especially during migration seasons when the park becomes a crucial stopover for many bird species. The Ramble, a 36-acre woodland area within the park, is a prime spot for birdwatching, where you might spot species like the American woodcock, warblers, and even red-tailed hawks. These walks usually start at the Belvedere Castle, which offers stunning views of the park and is an excellent meeting point. To get to Central Park, you can take the A, B, C, D, 1, 2, 3 subway lines to various stations along the park's west side, or the N, Q, R, W lines to Fifth Avenue/59th Street on the east side.

Another fantastic location for a guided nature walk is Prospect Park in Brooklyn. Designed by the same architects who created Central Park, Prospect Park offers a different experience with its diverse habitats, including woodlands, wetlands, and open meadows. The Audubon Center at the Boathouse is a hub for nature-related activities and guided tours. These walks often focus on the park's ecology, highlighting the different bird species, native plants, and even the history of the park's design. The Lullwater area and Lake are particularly rich in birdlife, making them focal points for many nature walks. These guided walks not only provide educational insights but also allow participants to connect with nature in a serene setting. To visit Prospect Park, you can take the B, Q subway lines to Prospect Park station, or the 2, 3 lines to Grand Army Plaza.

For those interested in exploring coastal ecosystems, the Jamaica Bay Wildlife Refuge in Queens is an exceptional destination. This area is part of the larger Gateway National Recreation Area and is known for its vast salt marshes, islands, and rich birdlife. Guided nature walks at Jamaica Bay often focus on birdwatching, especially during the spring and fall migrations when thousands of birds stop here on their journey along the Atlantic Flyway. The refuge is home to over 330 species of birds, as well as various fish, shellfish, and other wildlife. These tours typically start at the Visitor Center, where participants can learn about the refuge's ecology and the conservation efforts that protect this vital habitat. Walks may take you along trails that offer stunning views of the bay and the surrounding wetlands, providing a unique perspective on New York City's natural environment. To get to Jamaica Bay Wildlife Refuge, you can take the A subway line to Broad Channel, and then it's a short walk to the refuge entrance.

If you're looking for a more rugged nature experience, Inwood Hill Park at the northern tip of Manhattan offers guided walks that take you through the last natural forest on the island. This park is unique in its combination of natural and historical features, including glacial potholes, Native American caves, and remnants of the original salt marsh. Guided walks in Inwood Hill Park often explore the park's rich history, as well as its diverse plant and animal life. The park is a haven for birdwatchers, with species like red-tailed hawks, woodpeckers, and owls frequently spotted in the area. Walks may take you along the park's wooded trails, with stops at scenic overlooks that provide views of the Hudson River and the New Jersey Palisades. To reach Inwood Hill Park, you can take the A subway line to 207th Street, or the 1 line to 215th Street.

For those willing to venture a bit further from the city, Pelham Bay Park in the Bronx offers guided nature walks in New York City's largest park. Covering more than 2,700 acres, Pelham Bay Park features a mix of forest, marsh, and coastline, providing diverse habitats for wildlife. Guided walks in this park often focus on the park's unique ecology, including its salt marshes, oak forests, and birdlife. The park is also home to the historic Bartow-Pell Mansion, where some tours may begin or end. Walks may take you through areas like the Orchard Beach and the Hunter Island Marine Sanctuary, where you can explore tidal pools, spot wading birds, and learn about the park's natural history. To visit Pelham Bay Park, you can take the 6 subway line to Pelham Bay Park station, the last stop on the line.

Guided nature walks in New York City are often led by experienced naturalists, park rangers, or volunteers from organizations like the New York City Audubon Society, the Urban Park Rangers, and the New York Botanical Garden. These walks provide not only an opportunity to see wildlife and natural beauty up close but also to learn about the ecological challenges facing the city and the efforts being made to preserve its natural areas. Participants can expect to gain insights into the flora and fauna of New York City, learn how to identify different species, and understand the importance of conservation in an urban environment.

What can you expect on a nature walk? Most guided nature walks last between one to two hours and cover a moderate distance, making them suitable for participants of all ages and fitness levels. Walks typically begin with an introduction to the area, where the guide will explain the natural and historical significance of the site. As you walk, the guide will point out various species of plants and animals, explain their roles in the ecosystem, and answer any questions you might have. You'll also learn how to observe wildlife responsibly, minimizing your impact on the environment while maximizing your enjoyment of the experience.

To make the most of your guided nature walk, it's a good idea to wear comfortable walking shoes, dress appropriately for the weather, and bring a water bottle. Binoculars and a camera can also enhance your experience, especially if you're interested in birdwatching or photography. Some walks may require advance registration, so it's a good idea to check with the organization or park offering the tour to ensure your spot.

Guided nature walks in New York City offer a wonderful opportunity to connect with the natural world, learn about the city's diverse ecosystems, and enjoy the beauty of its parks and reserves. Whether you're exploring the woodlands of Central Park, the wetlands of Jamaica Bay, or the rugged terrain of Inwood Hill Park, these walks provide a unique and enriching experience that highlights the often-overlooked natural side of New York City. Whether you're a seasoned nature lover or a curious beginner, guided nature walks are a great way to discover the hidden green spaces of the city and gain a deeper appreciation for its environmental diversity.

Local Adventure Sports

New York City is not only a hub for culture, entertainment, and dining; it also offers a surprising array of opportunities for adventure sports enthusiasts. Whether you're a thrill-seeker looking for your next adrenaline rush or someone who simply wants to try something new, the city and its surrounding areas have plenty to offer. From kayaking on the Hudson River to rock climbing in Central Park, there are numerous activities that allow you to experience the city from a different perspective.

One of the most popular outdoor adventure activities in New York City is kayaking. The city's waterways provide a unique setting for this sport, allowing paddlers to glide past iconic landmarks while enjoying the tranquility of being on the water. One of the best places to go kayaking is the Hudson River, where several organizations offer free and low-cost kayaking programs during the warmer months. For example, the Downtown Boathouse at Pier 26 offers free walk-up kayaking, making it accessible even for beginners. Another popular spot is Brooklyn Bridge Park, where you can paddle along the East River with stunning views of the Manhattan skyline. The Brooklyn Bridge Park Boathouse offers free kayaking sessions from Pier 2, providing a great way to explore the waterfront. Both locations are easily accessible by public transportation: you can take the 1, A, C, E subway lines to reach the Downtown Boathouse or the 2, 3 lines to Clark Street for Brooklyn Bridge Park.

For those who prefer land-based adventure, rock climbing in Central Park offers a thrilling challenge right in the middle of Manhattan. While Central Park is better known for its peaceful landscapes, it also features several natural rock formations that are popular with climbers. Rat Rock near the Heckscher Playground is a favorite spot for bouldering, offering a variety of routes suitable for different skill levels. Bouldering here is an exciting way to test your strength and technique without the need for ropes or harnesses. Another popular spot is Cat Rock, located near the southern end of the park, which offers slightly more challenging routes. Rock climbing in Central Park is generally free and accessible, but it's recommended to bring your own climbing shoes and chalk for the best experience. To reach Central Park, you can take the A, B, C, D, 1, 2, 3 subway lines to various stations along the park's perimeter.

For a more exhilarating experience, skydiving is an adventure sport that can be done just outside of New York City. Skydive Long Island in Calverton offers tandem skydiving experiences that allow you to jump from 13,500 feet with an experienced instructor. The freefall provides an unparalleled adrenaline rush, followed by a peaceful parachute descent with views of Long Island and the Atlantic Ocean. Although skydiving isn't located directly in the city, it's a popular activity for those looking to experience something truly unforgettable. To get to Skydive Long Island, you can take the Long Island Rail Road (LIRR) from Penn Station to Riverhead, and then a short taxi ride to the drop zone.

For water enthusiasts, surfing at Rockaway Beach in Queens is another exciting option. Rockaway Beach is the only legal surfing beach in New York City, offering consistent waves that attract surfers of all levels. The beach has designated surfing areas, with the best spots located between 67th and 92nd Streets. Local surf schools like Locals Surf School offer lessons for beginners, as well as board rentals for more experienced surfers. Surfing at Rockaway Beach is a great way to experience the thrill of riding waves while enjoying the beach atmosphere. To get to Rockaway Beach, you can take the A subway line to Rockaway Boulevard and transfer to the S shuttle to Beach 90th Street.

For those interested in exploring the city from a different angle, cycling is a fantastic way to combine adventure with sightseeing. New York City has an extensive network of bike lanes and paths that allow cyclists to explore the city's neighborhoods and parks. One of the most popular routes is the Hudson River Greenway, a dedicated bike path that runs along the west side of Manhattan from Battery Park to the George Washington Bridge. The Greenway offers stunning views of the Hudson River, the Statue of Liberty, and the New Jersey skyline. Another great option is the Brooklyn Waterfront Greenway, which takes cyclists along the East River, past landmarks like the Brooklyn Navy Yard and Brooklyn Bridge Park. For a more challenging ride, you can cycle across the George Washington Bridge and into the Palisades Interstate Park, where you'll find scenic roads and steep climbs. Bikes can be rented from various locations around the city, including Citi Bike stations and local bike shops. The Hudson River Greenway is accessible from multiple points along the west side, while the Brooklyn Waterfront Greenway can be reached via the A, C subway lines to High Street.

When participating in adventure sports, safety should always be a top priority. Here are some tips to ensure a safe and enjoyable experience:

1. Know your limits: Choose activities that match your skill level and physical fitness. It's important to challenge yourself, but not at the expense of your safety.

2. Use proper gear: Whether you're kayaking, climbing, or surfing, make sure you have the right equipment. This includes wearing a life jacket when kayaking, using climbing shoes and chalk for bouldering, or wearing a helmet when cycling.

3. Follow local regulations: Each sport may have specific rules and guidelines, such as designated surfing areas or bike lane usage. Respect these regulations to ensure a safe experience for yourself and others.

4. Stay aware of your surroundings: In an urban environment like New York City, it's essential to be aware of other people, vehicles, and potential hazards. Always keep an eye out for pedestrians, traffic, and other participants.

5. Take lessons if you're a beginner: If you're new to an activity, consider taking lessons from a certified instructor. This can help you learn the basics, improve your technique, and reduce the risk of injury.

6. Stay hydrated and take breaks: Adventure sports can be physically demanding, especially in hot or cold weather. Make sure to drink plenty of water and take breaks as needed to avoid exhaustion.

New York City offers a wealth of opportunities for adventure sports enthusiasts. Whether you're paddling along the Hudson River, scaling a rock face in Central Park, or riding the waves at Rockaway Beach, the city provides a unique and thrilling environment for outdoor activities. With proper preparation and safety precautions, these adventures can be both exciting and rewarding, allowing you to experience the city in a whole new way.

Popular Walking and Hiking Trails

New York City, with its iconic skyline and bustling streets, might not be the first place that comes to mind when thinking of walking and hiking trails. However, the city offers a surprising array of scenic walks and trails that cater to all levels of hikers, from leisurely strollers to those seeking a more challenging experience. Whether you're looking to escape the urban hustle for a while or simply explore the city from a different perspective, these trails provide a perfect opportunity to connect with nature and enjoy the outdoors.

One of the most popular trails for hikers in New York City is the Central Park Reservoir Loop. This 1.58-mile loop around the Jacqueline Kennedy Onassis Reservoir offers stunning views of the water and the city skyline. The trail is relatively flat and well-maintained, making it suitable for all levels of hikers, including families with children and those looking for a relaxing walk. Along the way, you'll encounter beautiful cherry blossoms in the spring, colorful foliage in the fall, and a peaceful atmosphere year-round. The trail is also a favorite spot for joggers, so expect some company during your walk. To reach the Central Park Reservoir, you can take the A, B, C, D, 1, 2, 3 subway lines to various stations along the park's west side, or the N, Q, R, W lines to Fifth Avenue/59th Street on the east side.

For those seeking a more immersive nature experience, the Inwood Hill Park Trail in Upper Manhattan offers a taste of the city's wild side. This park is home to the last natural forest on Manhattan Island and provides a network of trails that wind through its wooded hills and along the Hudson River. The trails vary in difficulty, with some steep sections that can be challenging for beginners, but the rewards are worth it. Along the way, you'll encounter ancient trees, rock formations, and stunning views of the river and the New Jersey Palisades. The park is also rich in history, with Native American caves and remnants of old estates adding to the experience. The Inwood Hill Park Trail is a great choice for hikers looking to escape the city without leaving Manhattan. To get there, you can take the A subway line to 207th Street, or the 1 line to 215th Street.

Another excellent option for hikers is the Bronx River Greenway, which offers a more extended and varied experience. This trail stretches for several miles along the Bronx River, passing through several parks and natural areas, including the New York Botanical Garden and the Bronx Zoo. The greenway is perfect for those looking to combine their hike with some sightseeing, as it provides access to some of the Bronx's most famous attractions. The trail is relatively flat and well-marked, making it suitable for all levels of hikers. As you walk along the greenway, you'll enjoy views of the river, shaded pathways, and the chance to spot wildlife such as birds and turtles. The Bronx River Greenway can be accessed from various points along the river, with the easiest access via the 2, 5 subway lines to Bronx Park East.

For a unique hiking experience that combines nature with history, the High Bridge Trail offers a chance to walk across New York City's oldest standing bridge. The High Bridge, which connects the Bronx and Manhattan, was originally built in 1848 as part of the Croton Aqueduct system. Today, it has been restored and converted into a pedestrian walkway, offering stunning views of the Harlem River and the surrounding neighborhoods. The trail itself is short, just over a mile long, but it can be combined with a walk through nearby parks such as Highbridge Park and Fort George Hill for a longer hike. The High Bridge Trail is a great choice for those interested in the city's history and architecture, as well as for anyone looking for a scenic and accessible walk. To reach the High Bridge, you can take the 1 subway line to 168th Street, or the C line to 155th Street.

For those looking for a more challenging hike, the Alley Pond Park Trails in Queens offer a variety of options. Alley Pond Park is one of the city's largest parks and features several miles of trails that wind through wetlands, forests, and meadows. The trails vary in difficulty, with some sections being more rugged and hilly, making them suitable for more experienced hikers. One of the park's highlights is the Tulip Tree Trail, which leads to the city's oldest and tallest tree, a tulip poplar that is over 400 years old. The park is also home to a wide variety of wildlife, including birds, frogs, and even the occasional deer. Alley Pond Park is a great destination for those looking to explore a more natural and less crowded side of New York City. To get there, you can take the E, F subway lines to Kew Gardens-Union Turnpike, followed by a bus ride on the Q46 to the park's entrance.

Before setting out on a hike in New York City, it's essential to be well-prepared to ensure a safe and enjoyable experience. Here are some tips to help you get ready:

1. **Wear appropriate footwear:** Even if you're walking on paved trails, wearing comfortable, sturdy shoes is essential. For more rugged trails, consider wearing hiking boots to provide additional support and protection.

2. **Dress in layers:** New York City's weather can be unpredictable, so it's a good idea to dress in layers that you can add or remove as needed. In cooler weather, bring a jacket or sweater, and in warmer weather, wear lightweight, breathable clothing.

3. **Bring water and snacks:** Staying hydrated is crucial, especially during longer hikes. Bring a water bottle and some snacks to keep your energy up, especially if you're planning to be out for several hours.

4. **Check the weather forecast:** Before heading out, check the weather forecast to ensure you're prepared for any changes in conditions. If heavy rain or extreme weather is expected, it may be best to postpone your hike.

5. **Carry a map or use a GPS:** While many trails in New York City are well-marked, it's always a good idea to carry a map or use a GPS app on your phone to help you navigate. This is especially important if you're exploring less familiar areas or more extensive parks.

6. **Respect the environment:** Stay on designated trails to protect the natural environment and avoid disturbing

wildlife. If you bring snacks or drinks, be sure to pack out all trash and leave the area as you found it.

7. Be mindful of your surroundings: While New York City is generally safe, it's important to be aware of your surroundings, especially if you're hiking alone. Stick to well-populated trails and consider going with a group if you're unfamiliar with the area.

New York City offers a diverse range of walking and hiking trails that cater to all levels of experience. Whether you're looking for a leisurely stroll through Central Park, a challenging hike in Inwood Hill Park, or a scenic walk along the Bronx River, there's something for everyone. These trails provide a unique way to experience the city's natural beauty, escape the hustle and bustle, and connect with the outdoors. By preparing properly and following safety guidelines, you can enjoy a memorable and rewarding hiking experience in the heart of one of the world's most vibrant cities.

Fishing Spots and Regulations

Fishing in New York City is a rewarding experience that many might not initially consider when thinking of this bustling metropolis. However, the city's diverse waterways offer numerous opportunities for both seasoned anglers and beginners alike. From freshwater lakes to saltwater bays, New York City provides various fishing spots that allow you to connect with nature and experience the thrill of the catch while surrounded by the urban landscape.

One of the most popular fishing spots in New York City is Central Park's Harlem Meer. Located in the northeastern corner of Central Park, the Harlem Meer is a picturesque lake surrounded by trees and wildlife, creating a serene setting for fishing. The lake is stocked with various fish species, including largemouth bass, bluegill, and carp, making it an ideal spot for anglers of all skill levels. The best times to fish at the Harlem Meer are early morning and late afternoon, especially during the warmer months when the fish are more active. To reach the Harlem Meer, you can take the 2, 3 subway lines to 110th Street and walk into the park. Remember, catch-and-release fishing is encouraged here to preserve the fish population.

Another excellent location for fishing within the city is Prospect Park Lake in Brooklyn. This 55-acre lake is the largest body of water in Brooklyn and is home to species such as largemouth bass, pumpkinseed sunfish, and catfish. The lake's varied shoreline provides ample space for fishing, and there are also designated fishing piers that make it easy to cast your line. Fishing at Prospect Park Lake is a peaceful experience, with the surrounding parkland offering a tranquil escape from the city's noise. The lake is accessible by the Q, B subway lines to Prospect Park, or the F, G lines to 15th Street-Prospect Park. Like Harlem Meer, catch-and-release is the practice here, so anglers are encouraged to handle fish with care and return them to the water.

For those interested in saltwater fishing, Jamaica Bay in Queens is a prime destination. This expansive bay is part of the Gateway National Recreation Area and is known for its diverse marine life, including striped bass, bluefish, flounder, and weakfish. Jamaica Bay offers various fishing spots, from piers and jetties to sandy beaches, giving anglers multiple options depending on their preferences. The bay's proximity to the Atlantic Ocean means that it's best to fish here during the spring and fall when migratory species are abundant. To get to Jamaica Bay, you can take the A subway line to Broad Channel or the Q52/Q53 buses to Rockaway Boulevard. If you're fishing from a boat, there are several marinas in the area where you can rent a vessel or book a guided fishing trip.

For a more remote fishing experience, Orchard Beach Lagoon in the Bronx offers a mix of saltwater and brackish fishing. The lagoon is located within Pelham Bay Park, New York City's largest park, and is a well-known spot for catching species like striped bass, bluefish, and flounder. The lagoon's calm waters and abundant fish population make it a favorite among local anglers. The surrounding parkland provides plenty of opportunities for picnicking and relaxing after a day of fishing. To reach Orchard Beach Lagoon, you can take the 6 subway line to Pelham Bay Park and then catch the Bx12 bus to Orchard Beach. The best times to fish here are during the early morning or late evening, particularly in the spring and fall when the fish are most active.

In addition to these popular spots, fishing enthusiasts can also explore Sheepshead Bay in Brooklyn. This bay is known for its charter fishing boats that offer day trips into the deeper waters of the Atlantic Ocean. From Sheepshead Bay, you can catch species such as fluke, porgy, and black sea bass, making it a great option for those looking to experience deep-sea fishing without leaving the city. The fishing boats usually depart early in the morning and return by late afternoon, providing a full day of fishing and adventure. Sheepshead Bay is accessible by the B, Q subway lines to Sheepshead Bay station, and the marina is just a short walk from the station.

When it comes to fishing in New York City, it's essential to be aware of the permits and regulations that apply. All anglers aged 16 and older are required to have a New York State fishing license when fishing in freshwater. This license can be obtained online through the New York State Department of Environmental Conservation (DEC) website or at various sporting goods stores throughout the city. The license is valid for a year from the date of purchase and allows you to fish in any freshwater body within the state. For saltwater fishing, New York State does not require a license, but anglers must register with the state's Marine and Coastal District registry, which is free and can be done online.

Regulations for fishing in New York City also include size and bag limits for certain species to help maintain healthy fish populations. For example, there are specific limits on the size and number of striped bass that can be kept each day. It's crucial to familiarize yourself with these regulations before heading out to fish to ensure that you're complying with local laws and contributing to the conservation of fish species. The DEC website provides up-to-date information on fishing regulations, including seasonal closures and protected species.

The best seasons for fishing in New York City vary depending on the species and location. Generally, the spring and fall months are considered the prime fishing seasons, particularly for saltwater species like striped bass and bluefish, which migrate through the city's waters during these times. Freshwater fishing can be productive year-round, but the warmer months of late spring through early fall are often the most rewarding, as fish are more active and easier to catch.

Fishing in New York City offers a unique way to experience the city's natural beauty and connect with its diverse aquatic ecosystems. Whether you prefer the calm waters of Central Park's Harlem Meer, the expansive bays of Jamaica Bay, or the remote lagoon at Orchard Beach, there's a fishing spot in the city that's perfect for you. By following local regulations, obtaining the necessary permits, and choosing the right time of year, you can enjoy a successful and enjoyable fishing experience in one of the world's most vibrant cities.

Local Boat Tours and Cruises

New York City, with its stunning skyline, iconic landmarks, and expansive waterways, offers visitors a unique perspective from the water. Local boat tours and cruises provide an exceptional opportunity to see the city in a way that walking or driving simply cannot match. Whether you're interested in sightseeing, experiencing the city's history, or enjoying a romantic evening, New York's waterways offer something for everyone.

One of the most popular ways to explore the city by water is through sightseeing cruises. These tours typically last between one to three hours and take passengers on a journey around Manhattan, providing close-up views of some of the city's most famous landmarks. One of the most iconic sightseeing cruises is the Circle Line Sightseeing Cruise, which offers several options, including the Full Island Cruise, Harbor Lights Cruise, and Landmark Cruise. The Full Island Cruise is particularly popular, as it circumnavigates the entire island of Manhattan, offering views of the Statue of Liberty, Ellis Island, the Brooklyn Bridge, and the Empire State Building, among others. Departing from Pier 83 on the Hudson River, this cruise gives passengers a comprehensive view of the city's diverse neighborhoods and architectural wonders.

Another fantastic sightseeing option is the Statue of Liberty and Ellis Island Ferry. Departing from Battery Park at the southern tip of Manhattan, this ferry takes visitors to two of the most significant historical sites in the United States. The Statue of Liberty, standing proudly on Liberty Island, is a symbol of freedom and democracy, while Ellis Island served as the gateway for millions of immigrants coming to America. The ferry ride itself provides stunning views of the New York Harbor, the Lower Manhattan skyline, and the Brooklyn Bridge. Once on the islands, visitors can explore the Statue of Liberty Museum and the Ellis Island National Museum of Immigration, which offer deep insights into the history and significance of these iconic sites.

For those looking for a more luxurious experience, dinner cruises are an excellent choice. These cruises combine gourmet dining with breathtaking views of the city at night. One of the most popular options is the Bateaux New York Dinner Cruise, which departs from Chelsea Piers. The cruise features a glass-enclosed dining room, allowing for unobstructed views of the city's landmarks as you enjoy a multi-course meal. The experience is enhanced with live music and a dance floor, making it a perfect choice for special occasions. As the boat glides along the Hudson and East Rivers, you'll see the Statue of Liberty, the Brooklyn Bridge, and the Manhattan skyline illuminated against the night sky, creating an unforgettable experience.

In addition to the classic sightseeing and dinner cruises, New York City also offers a variety of specialty boat tours that cater to different interests. For history enthusiasts, the New York Historical Harbor Tour offers a deep dive into the city's maritime history. Departing from Pier 16 at the South Street Seaport, this tour explores the city's role as a major port and its rich nautical heritage. The tour includes commentary from knowledgeable guides, who provide insights into the history of the harbor, the ships that once docked there, and the people who worked in the maritime industry.

For nature lovers, the Audubon Winter NYC Seals and Wildlife Tour is a unique experience. Departing from Pier 17, this tour takes passengers around New York Harbor and the surrounding areas to spot harbor seals, migratory birds, and other wildlife. The tour is led by naturalists from the New York City Audubon Society, who provide information about the animals and their habitats. This tour is particularly popular during the winter months when the seals are most active.

When planning a boat tour in New York City, there are a few tips to keep in mind to ensure you have the best possible experience. First, book your tickets in advance, especially during peak tourist seasons. Many of the popular cruises sell out quickly, and booking ahead ensures you get a spot on the tour of your choice. You can book tickets directly through the cruise operators' websites, at the departure piers, or through third-party vendors.

Next, consider the time of day you want to take the cruise. Daytime cruises offer clear views of the city's landmarks and are perfect for taking photos, while evening cruises provide a more romantic atmosphere with the city lights reflecting off the water. If you're interested in photography, a sunset or twilight cruise might offer the best of both worlds, with the city transitioning from day to night.

Dress appropriately for the weather, as the temperature on the water can be cooler than on land, especially during the evening or in the colder months. It's a good idea to bring a jacket or sweater, even in the summer, as the breeze on the water can be chilly.

For those prone to seasickness, consider taking a motion sickness remedy before boarding. While most cruises are relatively smooth, the motion of the boat can cause discomfort for some passengers.

When it comes to getting to the departure points, most of the major cruises leave from Manhattan's west side, particularly from Pier 83 (Circle Line), Chelsea Piers (dinner cruises), and Battery Park (Statue of Liberty Ferry). These locations are easily accessible by subway, bus, or taxi. For Pier 83 and Chelsea Piers, you can take the C, E subway lines to 50th Street or the 1 line to 28th Street and walk west. For Battery

Park, the 1, R, W subway lines to South Ferry or the 4, 5 lines to Bowling Green will get you close to the departure point.

Finally, make the most of your boat tour by taking advantage of any onboard amenities. Many cruises offer snacks and drinks for purchase, and some have audio guides or live commentary that provide interesting facts about the sights you're seeing. Listening to these can greatly enhance your understanding and appreciation of the landmarks you're passing by.

New York City's boat tours and cruises offer a unique and memorable way to experience the city. Whether you're interested in sightseeing, history, or just enjoying a beautiful evening on the water, there's a cruise that will fit your interests. By planning ahead, choosing the right tour, and preparing for the weather, you can ensure that your time on the water is one of the highlights of your visit to New York City.

Scenic Lookout Points

New York City is renowned for its iconic skyline and breathtaking views, making it a paradise for those who appreciate stunning vistas and love to capture memorable photographs. The city offers a variety of scenic lookout points, each providing a unique perspective of the metropolis, from towering skyscrapers to expansive parks. Whether you're a seasoned photographer or simply someone who enjoys taking in the beauty of the city, these spots are sure to leave a lasting impression.

One of the most famous and sought-after viewpoints in New York City is the Top of the Rock Observation Deck at Rockefeller Center. Located in Midtown Manhattan, this observation deck offers panoramic views of the city, including an unobstructed view of the Empire State Building, Central Park, and the surrounding boroughs. The Top of the Rock is situated on the 70th floor of Rockefeller Center, and its open-air deck allows visitors to enjoy the cityscape without the interference of glass. To reach the Top of the Rock, you can take the B, D, F, M subway lines to 47-50th Streets-Rockefeller Center station. From there, it's just a short walk to the entrance on West 50th Street. Visiting in the late afternoon allows you to see the city transition from day to night, offering the chance to capture both daylight and twilight shots. To avoid crowds and have more space to take photos, it's advisable to book your tickets online in advance and aim for a weekday visit.

Another must-visit location for stunning views is the Empire State Building. This iconic skyscraper has two observation decks: one on the 86th floor and another on the 102nd floor. The 86th-floor deck, which is open-air, provides a 360-degree view of the city, allowing you to see landmarks such as Times Square, the Statue of Liberty, and the Brooklyn Bridge. The 102nd-floor deck, enclosed by glass, offers an even higher vantage point, giving you a bird's-eye view of the city. The Empire State Building is located at 350 Fifth Avenue, and you can reach it by taking the B, D, F, M, N, Q, R, or W subway lines to 34th Street-Herald Square station. For the best photos, visit early in the morning or late at night when the city lights are on full display. Be prepared for long lines, especially during peak tourist seasons, so consider purchasing skip-the-line tickets to maximize your time on the observation decks.

For those who prefer outdoor views with a more natural setting, Central Park's Belvedere Castle is an excellent choice. Located in the heart of Central Park, this miniature castle offers a picturesque view of the park's landscapes, including Turtle Pond, the Great Lawn, and the surrounding city skyline. The castle itself is a charming structure, adding a fairytale-like quality to your photos. To reach Belvedere Castle, take the B, C subway lines to 81st Street-Museum of Natural History station and walk east into the park. The castle is situated on a hill, providing an elevated view that is particularly beautiful during the fall when the park's foliage turns vibrant shades of red, orange, and yellow. For photographers, the best time to visit is during the golden hour, either at sunrise or sunset, when the soft light enhances the colors and contrasts in your shots.

Another fantastic spot for panoramic views is the One World Observatory at One World Trade Center. As the tallest building in the Western Hemisphere, the observatory offers unparalleled views from the 100th, 101st, and 102nd floors. The elevator ride to the top is an experience in itself, featuring a time-lapse video of New York City's skyline evolving over centuries. Once at the top, you'll have a 360-degree view of the entire city, including the Hudson River, the East River, and beyond. The observatory also features interactive displays that provide historical and cultural context to the landmarks you're viewing. One World Trade Center is located at 285 Fulton Street in Lower Manhattan, and you can get there by taking the A, C, J, Z, 2, 3, 4, or 5 subway lines to Fulton Street station. For the best experience, visit on a clear day when visibility is highest, allowing you to see as far as 50 miles in every direction.

For a more tranquil and lesser-known scenic spot, head to Brooklyn Heights Promenade. This pedestrian walkway offers one of the best views of the Manhattan skyline, the Brooklyn Bridge, and the Statue of Liberty. The promenade is particularly popular with locals and provides a peaceful setting to enjoy the city's beauty away from the hustle and bustle of tourist crowds. It's an excellent location for taking photos at sunset, as the sun sets behind the skyline, casting a warm glow over the buildings and the East River. To reach Brooklyn Heights Promenade, take the 2, 3 subway lines to Clark Street station or the A, C subway lines to High Street-Brooklyn Bridge station. From either station, it's a short walk to the promenade. Bring a tripod if you're planning to take night shots, as the steady surface will help you capture the lights of the city with clarity.

When visiting these scenic lookout points, it's essential to keep a few photography tips in mind to capture the best possible shots. First, consider the time of day you're visiting. Early morning and late afternoon are generally the best times for photography, as the light is softer and creates less harsh shadows. These times also offer the opportunity to capture the golden hour, when the sunlight gives the city a warm, glowing appearance.

Next, be mindful of your camera settings. For cityscape shots, use a smaller aperture (higher f-stop number) to ensure a greater depth of field, keeping both the foreground and background in focus. If you're shooting at night, use a slower shutter speed to allow more light into the camera, but be sure to stabilize your camera with a tripod to avoid blurry images.

Another tip is to experiment with different angles. While it's tempting to take photos from the most obvious vantage points, try moving around and finding unique perspectives that showcase the city in a different light. For example, framing the Empire State Building between two trees in Central Park or capturing the reflection of the skyline in the Hudson River can add a creative touch to your photos.

Finally, don't forget to enjoy the moment. While capturing the perfect shot is important, take some time to simply take in the view and appreciate the beauty of New York City. These scenic lookout points offer more than just photo opportunities; they provide a chance to connect with the city's essence and create lasting memories of your visit.

New York City's scenic lookout points offer some of the most spectacular views in the world. Whether you're gazing out from the Top of the Rock, taking in the city's history from Belvedere Castle, or watching the sunset from Brooklyn Heights Promenade, each location provides a unique perspective on the city that never sleeps. By planning your visit, considering the best times for photography, and experimenting with different angles, you'll be able to capture stunning images that truly reflect the grandeur and vibrancy of New York City.

CHAPTER 13

TRAVELING WITH SPECIAL NEEDS

Accessible Travel Tips

Traveling in New York City offers an incredible experience, but for those with mobility issues or disabilities, careful planning can make the journey smoother and more enjoyable. The city has made significant strides in accessibility over the years, but it's essential to know what to expect and how to navigate the city effectively. With thoughtful preparation, travelers with mobility concerns can fully enjoy the many attractions, cultural experiences, and diverse neighborhoods New York City has to offer.

Navigating the city with mobility issues requires awareness of the challenges and resources available. The city's extensive subway system, while convenient, can present difficulties. Not all stations are equipped with elevators or ramps, and some that do have elevators may experience service interruptions. To plan your travel efficiently, the MTA (Metropolitan Transportation Authority) provides an online map that highlights accessible stations. It's advisable to plan your routes ahead of time, using accessible stations as your entry and exit points. Additionally, when using the subway, you can request assistance from MTA staff, who are available to help passengers with disabilities. Most subway stations are accessible by taking the A, B, C, D, and E lines, as these have a higher percentage of accessible stations. However, always check the status of the elevators in advance, as they can occasionally be out of service.

For those who prefer to avoid the subway, New York City's bus system is a great alternative. Every city bus is equipped with a lift or ramp, making them fully accessible for wheelchair users. The bus stops are also generally close to many major attractions, making it easier to travel across the city without the need for subway transfers. The MTA Bus Time app allows you to track buses in real-time, which can be particularly useful when planning your journey. Buses generally cover all five boroughs, and they operate 24/7, although frequency may vary, especially late at night.

Another option for getting around is using the city's accessible taxis, known as Accessible Dispatch. These taxis are specially equipped to accommodate wheelchairs and can be hailed on the street, booked via phone, or through the Accessible Dispatch app. This service covers all five boroughs and operates at the same cost as a standard yellow taxi, ensuring that people with disabilities have the same convenience and affordability. If you're planning to travel by taxi, the app allows you to see the estimated wait time and book a taxi in advance, which can be particularly helpful during peak hours or in less busy areas of the city.

When it comes to accessible attractions and facilities, New York City offers a wide range of options. Major landmarks such as the Empire State Building, the Statue of Liberty, and the Metropolitan Museum of Art have made significant efforts to accommodate visitors with disabilities. The Empire State Building, for example, offers accessible entrances, ramps, and restrooms. There are also tactile exhibits for the visually impaired, and wheelchairs are available for rent on-site. The observatory decks are fully accessible, allowing all visitors to enjoy the breathtaking views of the city. The Empire State Building is located at 350 Fifth Avenue, and the nearest accessible subway station is Herald Square-34th Street.

The Statue of Liberty and Ellis Island are also accessible, with ramps and elevators available at both locations. Visitors can use accessible ferries from Battery Park to reach the islands. These ferries are equipped with ramps and are spacious enough to accommodate wheelchairs. Once on the islands, accessible pathways and elevators ensure that everyone can enjoy the exhibits and take in the stunning views of New York Harbor. The ferries depart from Battery Park in Lower Manhattan, and the nearest accessible subway station is South Ferry on the 1 line.

Central Park is another must-visit destination, and it has numerous accessible paths and restrooms. The Central Park Conservancy offers free mobility tours using an accessible cart, allowing visitors with disabilities to explore the park's iconic sites, such as Bethesda Terrace, the Great Lawn, and the Conservatory Garden. These tours provide a unique way to experience the park without the need for extensive walking. The park is easily accessible from multiple subway lines, with the 72nd Street stations on the B and C lines being particularly convenient.

If you're interested in arts and culture, the Metropolitan Museum of Art is fully accessible, with ramps, elevators, and accessible restrooms available throughout the museum. The museum offers assistive listening devices, large print guides, and verbal description tours for visitors with visual or hearing impairments. The museum is located at 1000 Fifth Avenue, and the nearest accessible subway station is 86th Street on the 4, 5, and 6 lines.

Planning an accessible trip to New York City involves more than just considering transportation and attractions. It's also important to choose accommodations that cater to your needs. Many hotels in the city offer accessible rooms equipped with features such as roll-in showers, grab bars, and lowered beds. It's advisable to contact the hotel directly before booking to confirm that the room meets your specific requirements. The Americans with Disabilities Act (ADA) requires that all public spaces, including hotels, are accessible, but the level of accessibility can vary, so it's best to verify in advance.

Dining out in New York City is another aspect where accessibility should be considered. Many restaurants in the city have made efforts to comply with ADA regulations, offering accessible entrances, seating, and restrooms. However, due to the city's older infrastructure, some restaurants may still have steps at the entrance or narrow spaces that can be challenging to navigate. When choosing a restaurant, it's a good idea to call ahead and ask about accessibility or use apps like OpenTable, which often include information about accessibility features.

If you're planning to visit theaters, Broadway shows, or concert venues, most major locations are equipped with accessibility features, including wheelchair seating, assistive listening devices, and captioning services. When purchasing tickets, be sure to inform the box office of your accessibility needs, so they can provide the appropriate accommodations. Popular venues like the Lincoln Center and Radio City Music Hall have comprehensive accessibility services, ensuring that all guests can enjoy their performances comfortably.

New York City has made significant strides in making the city accessible to all visitors, but it still requires some planning to navigate effectively. By researching in advance, using available resources, and choosing accessible transportation and accommodations, you can enjoy a memorable trip to New York City. From its world-class attractions to its vibrant cultural scene, the city offers endless possibilities for exploration, regardless of your mobility level.

Transportation for Remote Areas

Exploring remote areas around New York City offers a unique opportunity to experience natural landscapes, historical sites, and small-town charm that contrasts with the city's urban environment. However, for individuals with special needs, accessing these less-visited areas can present challenges. Proper planning and understanding the available transportation options are crucial for ensuring a smooth and enjoyable journey. Whether you're looking to venture into the scenic Hudson Valley, the beaches of Long Island, or the mountains of the Catskills, this guide will help you navigate the logistics and make the most of your travels beyond the city.

Getting to hard-to-reach places around New York City often requires a combination of transportation methods, as public transit options may be limited in these areas. For individuals with special needs, it's essential to choose routes and services that offer the necessary accommodations. One of the most reliable ways to travel to remote areas is by using the Metro-North Railroad, which connects the city with various destinations in the Hudson Valley and Connecticut. The Metro-North Railroad is generally accessible, with many stations equipped with elevators or ramps, as well as accessible restrooms and seating. However, it's advisable to check the accessibility of specific stations in advance, as some smaller stops may have limited facilities. For those looking to visit destinations like Cold Spring, Beacon, or Poughkeepsie, the Metro-North Railroad provides a convenient and scenic route, offering stunning views of the Hudson River along the way. Trains depart from Grand Central Terminal, which is fully accessible and provides additional services for travelers with disabilities, such as assistance with boarding and disembarking.

For travelers interested in exploring Long Island, the Long Island Rail Road (LIRR) is the primary mode of transportation. The LIRR connects New York City to various destinations across Long Island, including the North Fork, South Fork, and popular beach towns like Montauk and Fire Island. The LIRR is also accessible, with many stations offering elevators, ramps, and accessible restrooms. However, similar to the Metro-North Railroad, it's important to verify the accessibility of specific stations before traveling. Some of the more remote stations may have fewer amenities, and assistance may be required for boarding and disembarking.

For example, if you're planning a trip to Montauk, known for its picturesque beaches and historic lighthouse, you can take the LIRR from Penn Station, which is fully accessible. Once in Montauk, you may need to arrange for accessible local transportation, such as taxis or shuttle services, to reach specific attractions.

When traveling to the Catskills or other mountainous regions, access can be more challenging due to the terrain and limited public transportation options. In these cases, renting an accessible vehicle may be the best option, as it allows for greater flexibility and control over your travel itinerary. Several car rental companies in New York City offer accessible vehicles, including vans with ramps or lifts, ensuring that travelers with mobility issues can comfortably reach their destinations. When planning your route, be sure to research the accessibility of rest areas, gas stations, and lodging along the way, as some rural areas may have limited facilities. For those interested in outdoor activities such as hiking, fishing, or exploring nature reserves, the Catskills offer a range of accessible trails and parks, including the Ashokan Rail Trail, a 12-mile accessible path with stunning views of the Catskill Mountains and the Ashokan Reservoir. The trail is located about 2 hours north of the city, and renting an accessible vehicle from New York City would be the most convenient way to get there.

If you're looking to visit more isolated areas that are not easily accessible by public transportation, consider using specialized transportation services designed for individuals with disabilities. These services, such as Access-A-Ride, provide door-to-door transportation within the city and to some surrounding areas. While Access-A-Ride is primarily intended for travel within New York City, it may be possible to arrange transportation to nearby destinations, depending on availability and scheduling. Another option is to use ride-sharing apps like Uber or Lyft, which offer accessible vehicle options in some areas. However, availability may be limited in remote regions, so it's advisable to check the app in advance and consider booking your ride ahead of time.

When exploring beyond the city, it's also important to consider the challenges posed by the terrain and infrastructure in remote areas. Some attractions may not be fully accessible, particularly in older or more rural locations where modern accessibility standards may not be in place. It's a good idea to contact the destination in advance to inquire about specific accommodations, such as accessible parking, restrooms, and paths. For example, if you're planning to visit the historic town of Sleepy Hollow, known for its connection to Washington Irving's "The Legend of Sleepy Hollow," you can drive from New York City, which takes about an hour. The town offers several accessible attractions, including the Sleepy Hollow Cemetery, where Irving is buried. However, the terrain may be uneven in some areas, so it's recommended to plan your visit carefully and bring any necessary mobility aids.

Traveling to remote areas also requires careful planning regarding lodging. While many hotels and inns in rural areas offer accessible rooms, the level of accessibility can vary, especially in older buildings. It's important to book your accommodations in advance and confirm that the room meets your specific needs. Look for lodging that offers accessible entrances, roll-in showers, and other features that make your stay comfortable. If you're staying in a more secluded area, consider bringing additional supplies, such as portable ramps or shower chairs, to ensure that your accommodations are fully equipped for your needs.

Exploring remote areas around New York City can be a rewarding experience, offering a chance to connect with nature, discover historical sites, and enjoy a slower pace of life. With thoughtful planning and consideration of the available transportation options, individuals with special needs can navigate these regions with confidence and enjoy all that the surrounding areas have to offer. Whether you're hiking in the Catskills, relaxing on the beaches of Long Island, or exploring the charming towns of the Hudson Valley, New York's remote areas provide a diverse and enriching experience that complements the excitement of the city itself.

Bike Rentals and Cycling Routes

Cycling in New York City offers an incredible way to explore the city's neighborhoods, parks, and waterfronts while enjoying the freedom of movement and fresh air. For people with special needs, cycling can be an empowering and accessible activity, provided that the right resources and safety precautions are in place.

When it comes to renting bikes in New York City, several options are available that cater to different needs and preferences. One of the most popular and accessible options is

Citi Bike, New York's bike-sharing program. Citi Bike offers a fleet of bicycles stationed at docking points throughout the city, making it easy to pick up and drop off a bike at various locations. While Citi Bike does not specifically offer adaptive bicycles for those with special needs, some of their stations are wheelchair accessible, and the program is expanding to provide more inclusive options. You can find Citi Bike stations near major subway stops, parks, and tourist attractions, making it convenient to start your ride from almost anywhere in the city. To use Citi Bike, you can purchase a single ride, day pass, or membership through their app, which also provides information on bike availability and docking locations. Citi Bike is an excellent option for short rides and exploring urban areas where docking stations are plentiful.

For those who require adaptive bicycles, such as handcycles, recumbent bikes, or tandem bikes, several specialized bike rental shops in New York City cater to these needs. One such place is Bike and Roll NYC, which offers a variety of adaptive bicycles for rent, including options for riders with mobility issues. Located at Pier 84 in Hudson River Park, Bike and Roll NYC is easily accessible and provides a scenic starting point for rides along the Hudson River Greenway. The shop staff is knowledgeable and can assist in selecting the right bike for your needs, as well as provide tips on accessible cycling routes. To get to Bike and Roll NYC, you can take the A, C, or E subway lines to 42nd Street-Port Authority Bus Terminal and walk west towards the Hudson River. Alternatively, taxis and ride-sharing services can drop you off directly at the pier.

Another option for adaptive bike rentals is Unlimited Biking, which has multiple locations throughout the city, including Central Park, Brooklyn Bridge, and Harlem. Unlimited Biking offers a range of adaptive bikes, including tricycles, tandem bikes, and bikes with trailers for children or adults with special needs. The Central Park location is particularly popular, as it provides direct access to the park's extensive network of cycling paths, allowing for a leisurely and safe ride away from city traffic. To reach Unlimited Biking's Central Park location, you can take the B or C subway lines to 72nd Street and walk a short distance to the park's entrance. For those planning a longer ride, Unlimited Biking offers guided tours that can be tailored to accommodate special needs, ensuring that everyone can enjoy the experience.

Once you have secured a bike, New York City offers a variety of cycling routes that cater to different abilities and preferences. The Hudson River Greenway is one of the city's most popular cycling routes, stretching over 13 miles along the western edge of Manhattan. This paved path is flat and separated from vehicular traffic, making it an ideal choice for cyclists of all skill levels, including those with special needs. The Greenway offers stunning views of the Hudson River, the Statue of Liberty, and the New Jersey skyline, with plenty of opportunities to stop and enjoy the scenery at parks and piers along the way. For those who want to explore further, the Greenway connects to other bike paths, such as the East River Esplanade and the Harlem River Drive Greenway, allowing for a longer and more varied ride. The Greenway can be accessed from multiple points, including Battery Park at the southern tip of Manhattan, and Riverside Park near 72nd Street. Public transportation options, such as the 1, 2, or 3 subway lines, can bring you close to these entry points, and taxis or ride-sharing services are also convenient for reaching the Greenway.

Central Park is another excellent location for cycling, offering a car-free environment and a network of scenic paths that wind through the park's greenery. The park's main loop road is about 6 miles long and is shared with pedestrians, joggers, and horse-drawn carriages, creating a lively but manageable atmosphere. The loop is mostly flat, with a few gentle hills, making it suitable for adaptive bicycles and riders of varying abilities. In addition to the loop, Central Park has several smaller paths and trails that lead to iconic landmarks such as Bethesda Terrace, the Conservatory Garden, and the Jacqueline Kennedy Onassis Reservoir. The park's central location makes it easily accessible from various parts of the city, with multiple subway lines, including the A, B, C, D, 1, 2, 3, and 4, 5, 6 lines, stopping nearby. Central Park's bike rentals are available at various points, including the Columbus Circle and 72nd Street entrances.

For those looking to explore beyond Manhattan, the Brooklyn Waterfront Greenway offers a scenic ride along the Brooklyn shoreline, passing through neighborhoods such as Brooklyn Heights, DUMBO, and Red Hook. This 26-mile route is mostly flat and separated from traffic, providing a safe and enjoyable ride with views of the Manhattan skyline, Brooklyn Bridge, and the Statue of Liberty. The Greenway also passes through several parks, including Brooklyn Bridge Park and the Brooklyn Navy Yard, where you can stop to rest and take in the sights. To reach the Brooklyn Waterfront Greenway, you can take the 2 or 3 subway lines to Clark

Street or the A or C lines to High Street-Brooklyn Bridge and start your ride from the Brooklyn Heights area. The Greenway is well-marked with signs, making it easy to navigate, and several bike rental shops in the area offer adaptive bikes for those with special needs.

While cycling in New York City can be a fun and accessible activity, it's important to follow safety guidelines to ensure a safe and enjoyable experience. Always wear a helmet, regardless of your cycling experience, as it significantly reduces the risk of head injuries in the event of an accident. New York City law requires children under 14 to wear helmets, but it's strongly recommended for all cyclists. Make sure your bike is in good working condition, with properly inflated tires, functioning brakes, and visible lights or reflectors for riding at night or in low-light conditions.

When cycling on city streets, be aware of traffic laws and ride in designated bike lanes whenever possible. Many of the city's major streets, including 1st Avenue, 2nd Avenue, and 8th Avenue, have protected bike lanes that provide a safer environment for cyclists. However, always be vigilant for turning vehicles, pedestrians, and obstacles in the road. Use hand signals to indicate your intentions to drivers and other cyclists, and avoid weaving between parked cars or riding on sidewalks, which is illegal in most parts of the city.

If you're planning to ride on shared paths, such as those in Central Park or along the Hudson River Greenway, be mindful of other users, including pedestrians, joggers, and skaters. Keep to the right side of the path, pass others on the left, and use a bell or call out to alert others when passing. It's also important to be aware of your surroundings and avoid distractions, such as using your phone while riding. If you need to check directions or take a break, find a safe place to stop off the path.

For those with special needs, it's essential to plan your route in advance and choose paths that match your abilities. Consider the terrain, distance, and availability of accessible rest stops or facilities along the way. If you're unsure about your route, many bike rental shops and cycling organizations in the city offer maps and advice on accessible routes, as well as guided tours that can be customized to your needs.

New York City offers a wealth of cycling opportunities for people with special needs, from accessible bike rentals to scenic and safe cycling routes. Whether you're exploring the Hudson River Greenway, Central Park, or the Brooklyn Waterfront Greenway, cycling is a wonderful way to experience the city's sights, sounds, and culture at your own pace. By following safety guidelines and choosing the right routes, you can enjoy a memorable and fulfilling cycling adventure in the heart of New York City.

OPERATOR GUIDE

When planning a trip to New York City, choosing the right tour operator can make all the difference in how you experience the city. With so many tour companies offering a wide range of services, it's crucial to find one that fits your needs, interests, and budget. Whether you're interested in sightseeing, cultural experiences, or something more off the beaten path, the right tour operator can enhance your visit and ensure you make the most of your time in the city.

One of the most well-known and widely recommended tour operators in New York City is Gray Line New York. They offer a variety of tours, including the iconic hop-on-hop-off bus tours that allow you to explore the city at your own pace. These buses have multiple routes covering major attractions such as Times Square, Central Park, the Empire State Building, and the Statue of Liberty. The hop-on-hop-off option gives you the flexibility to spend as much or as little time as you like at each stop, making it a great choice for first-time visitors. Gray Line New York also offers guided tours, such as the Night Tour, which provides a unique view of the city's landmarks illuminated against the night sky. To access Gray Line services, you can purchase tickets online through their website or at various locations throughout the city, including Times Square and near major attractions.

Another reputable tour operator is Big Bus Tours, known for its comprehensive city tours that cover both Manhattan and Brooklyn. Big Bus Tours is a fantastic option for those who want a broad overview of New York City's neighborhoods and landmarks. Their open-top buses provide an excellent vantage point for taking in the city's skyline, and the tour includes audio commentary available in multiple languages, providing historical insights and interesting facts as you ride. The tour routes include popular sites like the Brooklyn Bridge, the Flatiron Building, and Wall Street, making it ideal for visitors who want to see a lot in a short amount of time. Big Bus Tours also offers a variety of ticket options, including multi-day passes that can be purchased online or at their main stops in the city.

For those interested in walking tours, Free Tours by Foot is a highly recommended option. As the name suggests, these tours operate on a pay-what-you-wish basis, making them accessible to travelers on any budget. The company offers a wide range of themed tours, including food tours, history tours, and neighborhood tours that focus on areas like the Lower East Side, Harlem, and Greenwich Village. Free Tours by Foot is known for its knowledgeable guides who provide engaging and informative commentary, making the experience both educational and enjoyable. To join a tour, you simply need to book a spot through their website, and you'll receive details on where to meet your guide. The tours typically begin at central locations easily accessible by public transportation, such as subway stops or well-known landmarks.

If you're interested in something more specialized, Inside Out Tours offers unique and immersive experiences that go beyond the typical tourist attractions. This company focuses on the cultural and historical aspects of New York City, offering tours that highlight the city's diverse neighborhoods, immigrant history, and artistic heritage. Some of their popular tours include the Gospel Tour of Harlem, which takes you to a live gospel service, and the Underground Railroad Tour, which explores the history of slavery and abolitionism in the city. Inside Out Tours is ideal for travelers who want to delve deeper into the stories and cultures that have shaped New York. Tours can be booked online, and meeting points are usually in easily accessible locations such as subway stations or prominent neighborhood landmarks.

For those seeking a luxurious and personalized experience, New York City Private Tours provides custom-tailored tours that cater to your specific interests and preferences. This company offers private tours for individuals, couples, and small groups, with itineraries that can be customized to include everything from iconic landmarks to hidden gems. Whether you want a full-day tour of Manhattan, a specialized art and museum tour, or a private culinary tour, New York City Private Tours can create an experience that suits your needs. The guides are experienced professionals who are well-versed in the city's history, culture, and attractions, ensuring a high-quality and personalized experience. You can book these tours through their website or by contacting the company directly to discuss your preferences and arrange a tailored itinerary.

When choosing a tour operator in New York City, reliability and reputation are key factors to consider. Start by researching the company's reviews on platforms like TripAdvisor, Yelp, and Google Reviews to get a sense of other travelers' experiences. Look for consistent positive feedback regarding the quality of the guides, the organization of the tours, and the overall value for money. It's also important to check whether the tour company is licensed and insured, as this ensures that they operate within the city's regulations and prioritize safety.

Another important consideration is the type of tour that best suits your interests and travel style. Some companies specialize in large group tours that cover broad areas and popular attractions, while others focus on small group or private tours that offer a more intimate and personalized experience. Consider whether you prefer a guided tour with in-depth commentary or a more flexible option like a hop-on-hop-off bus tour that allows you to explore at your own pace. Also, think about the length of the tour and whether it fits into your schedule. Some tours last only a couple of hours, while others can take up an entire day.

Price is another factor to take into account, especially if you're traveling on a budget. While some tours may seem expensive, they often include additional perks such as skip-the-line access to popular attractions, meals, or transportation. Make sure to compare the inclusions of different tours to determine which offers the best value. Additionally, many tour operators offer discounts for booking online in advance, so it's worth checking the company's website for any special deals or promotions.

It's also important to consider accessibility when choosing a tour operator, especially if you or someone in your group has mobility issues or other special needs. Some tours may involve a lot of walking, stairs, or crowded spaces, which may not be suitable for everyone. Check with the tour company to see if they offer accessible options, such as wheelchair-friendly routes or tours with minimal walking. Many reputable operators are happy to accommodate special requests and will work with you to ensure that the tour is enjoyable for everyone.

Finally, when selecting a tour company, look for operators that prioritize sustainability and responsible tourism. New York City is a bustling metropolis, and tourism can have a significant impact on the environment and local communities. Choose companies that support local businesses, promote environmentally friendly practices, and give back to the community. This could include using electric or hybrid vehicles for transportation, supporting local guides and artisans, or donating a portion of their profits to local charities.

Finding the right tour operator in New York City can greatly enhance your experience and help you make the most of your visit. Whether you're looking for a classic sightseeing tour, a deep dive into the city's cultural history, or a luxurious private experience, there are many reputable companies to choose from. By considering factors such as reliability, accessibility, price, and sustainability, you can select a tour that aligns with your interests and ensures a memorable and enriching experience in the city that never sleeps.

Public Restrooms and Facilities

Finding clean and accessible restrooms in New York City can be a challenge for tourists, especially in a city as large and bustling as New York. However, with a little planning and the right resources, you can easily locate convenient restroom facilities throughout the city. Knowing where to go, what apps to use, and understanding the basic etiquette will help you avoid any discomfort and ensure a smoother experience as you explore the city.

One of the best places to find clean and well-maintained restrooms in New York City is in the large public parks. Central Park, for instance, has several restroom facilities scattered throughout its 843 acres. Popular spots include the facilities near Bethesda Terrace, the Dairy Visitor Center, and the Heckscher Playground. Central Park's restrooms are generally well-maintained, and you'll often find them located near major attractions within the park. To get to Central Park, you can take the subway to several stops along its perimeter, such as 59th Street–Columbus Circle (A, C, B, D, 1 trains), 72nd Street (B, C trains), or 86th Street (B, C trains). Once you're in the park, you can easily walk to the nearest restroom facility, following the park's clear signage.

Another reliable option for clean public restrooms is the New York Public Library's Stephen A. Schwarzman Building, located on 42nd Street and 5th Avenue. This historic library offers restrooms on several floors, which are clean and easily accessible. The library's location in Midtown Manhattan makes it a convenient stop if you're exploring nearby attractions like Bryant Park, Times Square, or the shopping areas along 5th Avenue. You can reach the library via the 42nd Street–Bryant Park subway station (B, D, F, M trains) or the Grand Central–42nd Street station (4, 5, 6, 7, S trains).

Large department stores and hotels often provide some of the cleanest restroom facilities available to the public, even for non-customers. Stores like Macy's in Herald Square, located at 151 West 34th Street, have restrooms on multiple floors. Macy's is a tourist attraction in itself, being one of the largest department stores in the world. If you're shopping or sightseeing in the area, including Times Square or the Empire State Building, Macy's can be a convenient stop. The store is easily accessible by subway via the 34th Street–Herald Square station (B, D, F, M, N, Q, R, W trains).

If you're near Union Square, consider visiting the restrooms in the Whole Foods Market located at 4 Union Square South. Whole Foods' restrooms are usually well-maintained and clean, and you can easily pop in while exploring the Union Square Greenmarket or nearby shopping areas. Union Square is a major transit hub, so it's easy to get there via the 14th Street–Union Square station (4, 5, 6, L, N, Q, R, W trains).

For those in lower Manhattan, particularly around Wall Street or the World Trade Center, the Brookfield Place shopping center offers modern, clean restrooms. Brookfield Place is located at 230 Vesey Street and offers high-end shopping and dining with excellent restroom facilities. You can reach it via the World Trade Center subway station (A, C, E trains) or the Chambers Street station (1, 2, 3 trains).

In addition to these locations, there are several apps available that can help you find public restrooms throughout New York City. One of the most popular is the "Sit or Squat" app, which allows users to search for nearby restrooms based on their current location. The app includes user reviews and ratings, so you can choose a restroom that's known for being clean and well-maintained. Another useful app is "Flush," which also helps you locate public restrooms in the city. Both apps are free and available on iOS and Android, making them convenient tools to have during your trip.

When using public restrooms in New York City, it's important to be mindful of local restroom etiquette. While it may seem straightforward, understanding and following these unspoken rules can help ensure a pleasant experience for everyone. For instance, restrooms in New York are typically unstaffed, so it's important to clean up after yourself and leave the space as tidy as possible. This includes flushing the toilet, disposing of paper towels properly, and wiping down the sink area if needed. If the restroom has a line, it's customary to move quickly and avoid lingering inside the stall or at the sink. New Yorkers value efficiency, especially in busy places, so being considerate of others waiting will be appreciated.

Another point of etiquette involves the use of restrooms in restaurants, cafes, or stores. If you're not a customer, it's polite to ask for permission before using the facilities, or better yet, make a small purchase as a courtesy. In many establishments, restrooms are reserved for paying customers, and staff may require you to show a receipt or token to access the facilities. However, this varies depending on the business, so it's always best to check.

If you find yourself in a pinch and need to use a restroom in a busy area like Times Square or SoHo, Starbucks locations are often a reliable option. While some may require a code to access the restroom, staff are generally accommodating if you ask politely. Be aware that these restrooms can be very busy, so expect a wait during peak hours.

Finally, it's important to note that many restrooms in New York City are not equipped with baby-changing facilities, so if you're traveling with young children, plan accordingly. Large department stores, museums, and some public parks like Central Park do offer these amenities, but they may not be available everywhere.

While finding clean and accessible restrooms in New York City can be challenging, knowing where to look and using the right resources can make the process much easier. Parks, large stores, shopping centers, and libraries are generally reliable options for well-maintained facilities. Using restroom-finding apps can also help you locate nearby options quickly. By following local restroom etiquette, you'll not only have a more pleasant experience but also contribute to keeping the city's public facilities clean and usable for everyone. Whether you're exploring Central Park, shopping along 5th Avenue, or sightseeing downtown, being prepared with these tips will ensure that you're never far from a convenient and clean restroom in New York City.

Health and Fitness Facilities

New York City, known for its vibrant culture and fast-paced lifestyle, is also home to a wide range of health and fitness facilities that cater to both locals and tourists. Whether you're looking to keep up with your regular workout routine, try something new, or indulge in some relaxation, the city offers plenty of options to meet your needs. From well-equipped gyms and fitness centers to outdoor activities and luxurious wellness services, New York City ensures that staying healthy and fit while on vacation is not only possible but also enjoyable.

For travelers who prefer to maintain their fitness routine indoors, New York City boasts an extensive selection of gyms and fitness centers, many of which offer day passes or short-term memberships perfect for visitors. One popular option is Equinox, a high-end fitness club with multiple locations throughout the city, including spots in Midtown, the Upper West Side, and SoHo. Equinox is known for its state-of-the-art equipment, a wide variety of fitness classes, and luxurious amenities such as steam rooms and saunas. To visit Equinox, you can purchase a day pass online or inquire directly at any location. Getting to these locations is straightforward: for example, the Midtown location at 97 Greenwich Avenue is easily accessible via the 14th Street–Union Square subway station (4, 5, 6, L, N, Q, R, W trains).

Another excellent option for fitness enthusiasts is Blink Fitness, which offers a more budget-friendly alternative without compromising on quality. Blink Fitness has numerous locations across the city, including Manhattan, Brooklyn, and Queens. The gyms are well-equipped with cardio machines, strength training equipment, and free weights. Blink Fitness also emphasizes a welcoming and non-intimidating atmosphere, making it a great choice for travelers of all fitness levels. Day passes can be purchased online or directly at the gym. For instance, the Blink Fitness location in Times Square at 321 W 44th Street is conveniently located near the Times Square–42nd Street subway station (1, 2, 3, 7, N, Q, R, S, W trains), making it easy to access from anywhere in the city.

For those who prefer outdoor fitness activities, New York City's parks and public spaces offer a variety of options. Central Park is perhaps the most famous location for outdoor exercise, with miles of running and cycling paths, open fields for yoga or tai chi, and several designated workout areas with equipment. Whether you want to jog around the Reservoir, join a group fitness class on the Great Lawn, or rent a bike to explore the park's many scenic routes, Central Park provides a beautiful backdrop for staying active. To get to Central Park, you can take the subway to any of the stops along its perimeter, such as 59th Street–Columbus Circle (A, C, B, D, 1 trains) or 72nd Street (B, C trains).

Another excellent outdoor fitness option is the Hudson River Park, which stretches along the west side of Manhattan from Battery Park to 59th Street. This waterfront park offers stunning views of the Hudson River and features running and cycling paths, outdoor gyms, and sports courts. The park also hosts free fitness classes during the warmer months, including yoga, Pilates, and boot camps. The Pier 25 area is particularly popular for its workout facilities, including a miniature golf course, beach volleyball courts, and an outdoor gym. Hudson River Park is accessible via several subway stations, depending on which section you want to visit. For example, the Canal Street station (A, C, E trains) provides easy access to the southern end of the park, while the 14th

Street station (A, C, E, L trains) is convenient for the central section.

In addition to gyms and outdoor activities, New York City offers a wealth of wellness and spa services that can help you unwind and rejuvenate after a day of exploring the city. One of the most luxurious options is the Aire Ancient Baths, located in Tribeca at 88 Franklin Street. This serene spa is inspired by ancient Roman, Greek, and Ottoman bathing traditions and features a series of thermal baths, a flotarium, and a saltwater pool. Aire also offers a range of massages and wellness treatments, making it an ideal destination for relaxation. To get to Aire Ancient Baths, you can take the subway to the Franklin Street station (1, 2 trains) or the Canal Street station (A, C, E trains).

Another top wellness destination is the Great Jones Spa, located in NoHo at 29 Great Jones Street. This spa is known for its extensive water lounge, which includes a thermal hot tub, cold plunge pool, river rock sauna, and chakra-light steam room. Great Jones Spa also offers a variety of massages, facials, and body treatments designed to soothe and revitalize both body and mind. The spa is easily accessible via the Bleecker Street subway station (4, 6 trains) or the Broadway–Lafayette Street station (B, D, F, M trains).

For travelers interested in combining fitness with wellness, Exhale Spa offers a unique blend of fitness classes and spa services. With locations in the Flatiron District and on the Upper East Side, Exhale Spa is renowned for its signature Core Fusion classes, which combine elements of barre, yoga, Pilates, and cardio. After a workout, you can indulge in one of the spa's many treatments, such as massages, facials, or acupuncture. The Flatiron location, at 19 West 21st Street, is conveniently located near the 23rd Street subway station (N, R, W trains) and the 6th Avenue station (F, M trains).

If you prefer to stay active while taking in the sights, consider joining a walking tour with a fitness focus. Companies like Fit Tours NYC offer guided fitness tours that combine sightseeing with exercise, such as running tours of Central Park or yoga sessions with a view of the city skyline. These tours provide a unique way to stay fit while experiencing New York's iconic landmarks.

Finally, for those seeking a more holistic approach to wellness, New York City is home to several wellness centers that offer services such as meditation, acupuncture, and nutritional counseling. The Open Center in Chelsea, located at 22 East 30th Street, is a leading holistic learning center offering classes and workshops in yoga, meditation, and healing arts. The center's peaceful atmosphere and knowledgeable instructors make it a great place to focus on your well-being during your stay in the city. The Open Center is accessible via the 28th Street subway station (R, W trains) or the 33rd Street station (6 train).

New York City offers a diverse array of health and fitness facilities that cater to every type of traveler. Whether you prefer the comfort of a well-equipped gym, the beauty of outdoor activities, or the luxury of spa services, you'll find plenty of options to stay active and rejuvenated during your visit. With convenient locations, accessible transportation, and a wide range of activities to choose from, maintaining your health and fitness routine while exploring the city has never been easier. Whether you're looking to break a sweat, relax and unwind, or simply enjoy the city's vibrant fitness culture, New York City has something to offer everyone.

CHAPTER 14

PHOTOGRAPHY TIPS AND BEST SPOTS

New York City is a paradise for photography enthusiasts, offering countless opportunities to capture stunning images that reflect the city's unique character. From its iconic skyline and historic landmarks to its vibrant neighborhoods and serene parks, there's no shortage of incredible scenes to photograph. Whether you're an experienced photographer or a beginner looking to capture some memorable shots, understanding the best places for photography in the city, learning how to take great photos of its famous landmarks, and mastering some basic photo editing tips can significantly enhance your photography experience.

One of the most iconic places to capture the essence of New York City is Central Park. This sprawling urban park offers a diverse range of scenes, from the serene landscapes of the Ramble to the bustling activity around Bethesda Terrace. In the spring and fall, the park comes alive with vibrant colors, making it an ideal location for nature photography. For a unique perspective, visit the Bow Bridge, which offers a picturesque view of the Manhattan skyline framed by the park's lush greenery. To reach Central Park, you can take the subway to any of the stations along its perimeter, such as 59th Street–Columbus Circle (A, C, B, D, 1 trains) or 72nd Street (B, C trains).

Another must-visit location for photographers is the Brooklyn Bridge. This architectural marvel not only connects

Manhattan and Brooklyn but also provides stunning views of the city's skyline, particularly at sunrise or sunset. Walking across the bridge allows you to capture both the intricate details of its design and the panoramic views of the East River and the surrounding cityscape. For the best results, try shooting during the golden hour, when the light is soft and warm. To get to the Brooklyn Bridge, you can take the subway to the Brooklyn Bridge–City Hall station (4, 5, 6 trains) or the High Street–Brooklyn Bridge station (A, C trains).

Times Square is another iconic spot that offers endless photography opportunities, especially for capturing the vibrant energy of New York City at night. The bright lights, towering billboards, and bustling crowds create a dynamic environment that's perfect for experimenting with long-exposure shots. To capture the full effect of the neon lights and fast-paced movement, consider using a tripod to keep your camera steady. Times Square is easily accessible via the Times Square–42nd Street subway station (1, 2, 3, 7, N, Q, R, S, W trains).

For breathtaking views of the entire city, the Top of the Rock Observation Deck at Rockefeller Center is a prime location. This vantage point offers unobstructed views of landmarks such as the Empire State Building, Central Park, and the Statue of Liberty. The observation deck's 70th floor provides a perfect spot for panoramic shots, especially during sunset when the city is bathed in golden light. To visit the Top of the Rock, you can take the subway to the 47-50 Streets–Rockefeller Center station (B, D, F, M trains).

If you're interested in capturing the architectural beauty of New York City, the Flatiron Building is a must-see. This historic landmark, with its unique triangular shape, stands out against the backdrop of modern skyscrapers. The best time to photograph the Flatiron Building is during the early morning or late afternoon when the light creates interesting shadows and highlights its intricate details. To get to the Flatiron Building, you can take the subway to the 23rd Street station (N, R, W trains) or the 23rd Street station (F, M trains).

Taking great photos of New York City's landmarks requires more than just pointing your camera and shooting. Understanding how to compose your shots, using the right settings, and paying attention to the light can make a significant difference in the quality of your photos. When photographing landmarks, try to include elements that convey a sense of place, such as people, street signs, or surrounding buildings. This adds context to your images and makes them more engaging.

Lighting is crucial in photography, and in a city like New York, natural light can change dramatically throughout the day. The golden hour—shortly after sunrise and before sunset—is often the best time for photography because the light is soft and warm, creating a flattering effect on your subjects. Midday sunlight, on the other hand, can be harsh and create strong shadows, so it's important to adjust your camera settings accordingly or seek out shaded areas to shoot.

When photographing landmarks, it's also important to consider different angles and perspectives. Instead of taking the same shot that everyone else takes, try finding a unique vantage point or experimenting with different compositions. For example, instead of shooting the Empire State Building from street level, consider capturing its reflection in a nearby glass building or framing it between two other structures.

After capturing your photos, editing them can help enhance their quality and bring out the best in your images. Simple adjustments such as cropping, straightening, and correcting exposure can make a significant difference. Many photo editing apps and software are available, ranging from beginner-friendly options like Adobe Lightroom Mobile to more advanced tools like Photoshop. When editing, focus on maintaining the natural look of your photos—adjusting contrast, brightness, and color saturation can help, but be careful not to overdo it.

One editing tip that can improve your photos is adjusting the white balance to ensure that the colors look natural. In cityscapes, different light sources, such as streetlights and neon signs, can create color casts that affect the overall tone of your image. Correcting the white balance can help achieve more accurate colors.

Finally, if you're planning to share your photos on social media or print them as souvenirs, consider resizing them for the intended purpose. For social media, lower resolution images work well, while for prints, you'll want to ensure that your images are high resolution to maintain quality.

New York City offers countless opportunities for photography, with its iconic landmarks, vibrant streets, and scenic parks providing a wealth of subjects to capture. By visiting the best photography spots, understanding how to take great photos of landmarks, and applying some basic editing techniques, you can create stunning images that reflect your experience in the city. Whether you're a seasoned photographer or just starting, New York City's dynamic environment will inspire you to capture its beauty in new and creative ways.

Photography and Drone Regulations

Photography in New York City is a popular activity for both tourists and locals alike. The city's diverse landscapes, iconic buildings, and vibrant street life provide endless opportunities for capturing memorable images. However, it's essential to be aware of the rules and regulations that govern photography in public spaces and the use of drones, to ensure that your photography activities are not only legal but also respectful to the people and places around you.

In New York City, photography in public spaces is generally allowed, and the city's streets, parks, and public landmarks are some of the most photographed areas in the world. Public spaces like Times Square, Central Park, and the Brooklyn Bridge are often filled with photographers capturing everything from sweeping landscapes to candid street scenes. However, while you are free to take photos in these areas, it's important to be mindful of certain rules that apply to photography in public spaces.

Firstly, when photographing people in public, it's important to be respectful of their privacy. While the law allows for photography in public places without needing permission from the people in your photos, it's a good practice to ask for consent, especially if you are taking close-up shots or photographing children. In many cases, people are happy to oblige, but being respectful of personal boundaries goes a long way in maintaining a positive experience for everyone.

Another key rule to remember is that while photography is allowed in most public spaces, there are restrictions in certain areas, particularly around government buildings, military sites, and areas with heightened security. For example, photographing bridges, tunnels, and airports may attract unwanted attention from security personnel, and in some cases, you may be asked to stop or delete your photos. It's important to be aware of your surroundings and avoid photographing areas that are clearly marked as restricted.

Moreover, if you are using a tripod or setting up professional photography equipment, you may need a permit, especially if you are shooting in busy or sensitive areas. The City of New York requires a permit for photography that involves more than a handheld camera, such as when using lights, reflectors, or a crew. Permits are also needed for commercial photography or filming. These permits can be obtained through the Mayor's Office of Media and Entertainment, and it's recommended to apply in advance to avoid any disruptions during your shoot.

When it comes to drone photography, New York City has very specific regulations that must be followed. Flying drones in the city is heavily restricted, and in most cases, it is illegal. The Federal Aviation Administration (FAA) prohibits the use of drones in New York City's five boroughs due to the dense population and the proximity to major airports. This means that flying a drone for recreational or commercial purposes is not allowed in places like Central Park, Times Square, or anywhere else within the city limits.

There are a few exceptions to this rule, particularly for licensed commercial drone operators who have obtained special permission from the FAA and the New York City Police Department (NYPD). These operators must follow strict guidelines, including maintaining a line of sight with the drone at all times, flying below 400 feet, and avoiding flying over people. However, for most tourists, it is unlikely that they will be able to use drones in New York City.

For those who are set on capturing aerial views of the city, there are alternatives to using drones. One option is to visit observation decks like the Top of the Rock at Rockefeller Center or the Empire State Building, which offer breathtaking views of the city's skyline without the need for a drone. Another option is to take a helicopter tour, which allows you to capture stunning aerial photos while adhering to the city's regulations.

In addition to following the legal guidelines, it's important to practice safe and respectful photography. This means being mindful of the people and environment around you. For example, when photographing in busy areas like Times Square, it's important to stay aware of your surroundings and avoid blocking walkways or inconveniencing others. Using a tripod in these areas can be particularly challenging, so consider using a handheld camera or finding a less crowded spot to set up your equipment.

When photographing in natural areas, such as Central Park or along the Hudson River, be sure to respect the environment by staying on designated paths and not disturbing wildlife. If you're shooting in a residential area, be aware that some people may not appreciate having their homes or private spaces photographed, so it's best to avoid pointing your camera directly into someone's window or yard.

Lastly, it's important to consider the cultural sensitivity of certain locations. For example, photographing religious sites, memorials, or areas with cultural significance should be done with care and respect. Some sites may have specific rules about photography, such as prohibiting flash photography or asking visitors to refrain from taking photos during certain times. Always look for signs or ask a staff member if you're unsure about the rules.

While New York City offers incredible opportunities for photography, it's crucial to be aware of the rules and regulations that govern photography in public spaces and the use of drones. By following these guidelines and practicing safe and respectful photography, you can capture the beauty of the city while ensuring that your activities are both legal and considerate of others. Whether you're photographing the bustling streets of Manhattan, the serene landscapes of Central Park, or the architectural wonders of the city, being informed and respectful will help you create stunning images while having a positive experience.

Road Trip Routes and Scenic Drives

A road trip starting from New York City offers a variety of scenic drives and day trips that are perfect for those looking to explore the natural beauty and historical landmarks beyond the hustle and bustle of the city. New York City, while rich in urban attractions, is also an excellent starting point for journeys into picturesque countryside, charming small towns, and breathtaking coastal areas. Planning a road trip from New York City requires careful consideration of the routes, attractions, and logistics, but the rewards are well worth the effort.

One of the most popular scenic drives from New York City is the journey up the Hudson River Valley. This route offers stunning views of the Hudson River, rolling hills, and quaint historic towns. To begin, you would head north on the Henry Hudson Parkway, which eventually merges into the scenic Route 9. As you drive along this route, you'll pass through picturesque towns such as Tarrytown, known for its historic sites like Lyndhurst Mansion and Sunnyside, the home of Washington Irving. Continuing north, you'll reach the village of Sleepy Hollow, famous for its connection to Irving's "The Legend of Sleepy Hollow." Here, you can explore the Sleepy Hollow Cemetery, where Irving himself is buried, and the Old Dutch Church, one of the oldest in the state.

As you continue up the Hudson Valley, you'll reach the town of Cold Spring, a popular spot for antiquing and dining. The village is set against the backdrop of the Hudson Highlands, providing breathtaking views of the river and surrounding mountains. Cold Spring also serves as a gateway to the Hudson Highlands State Park, where you can take a break from driving to hike up Breakneck Ridge or Bull Hill for panoramic views of the Hudson River. Continuing further north, you can visit the United States Military Academy at West Point, a site steeped in American history and offering guided tours of its impressive campus.

Another excellent road trip option from New York City is a drive out to Long Island's North Fork. Known for its vineyards, beaches, and charming small towns, the North Fork is a great destination for a day trip or weekend getaway. To get there, take the Long Island Expressway (I-495) east, and continue along Route 25. This drive will take you through the heart of Long Island's wine country, where you can stop at various wineries for tastings and tours. The North Fork is also home to charming towns like Greenport, where you can explore historic sites, enjoy fresh seafood, and take a ferry to Shelter Island for more scenic views and outdoor activities.

For those interested in a coastal drive, a trip down the New Jersey shore is another fantastic option. Starting from New York City, you can take the Garden State Parkway south, which will lead you through several coastal towns and beaches. Stop at Asbury Park, known for its vibrant arts scene, boardwalk, and historic venues like the Stone Pony. Further south, you can visit the charming Victorian town of

Cape May, which boasts beautiful beaches, historic homes, and a lighthouse offering stunning views of the Atlantic Ocean. This drive is particularly beautiful during the fall, when the foliage adds a splash of color to the landscape.

If you're looking for a road trip that takes you into the heart of nature, consider a drive to the Catskill Mountains. The Catskills are located about two hours north of New York City, making them an ideal destination for a day trip or weekend retreat. To get there, take the New York State Thruway (I-87) north, and exit at Kingston to enter the Catskill region. The drive offers scenic views of mountains, forests, and rivers, with plenty of opportunities for hiking, fishing, and exploring quaint mountain towns. In the fall, the Catskills are particularly popular for leaf-peeping, with vibrant autumn colors that attract visitors from all over.

When planning a road trip from New York City, it's important to consider the logistics of your journey. Ensure your vehicle is in good condition, with a full tank of gas, and be sure to carry a GPS or map, as some areas outside the city may have limited cell service. Pack snacks, water, and any other essentials you might need on the road. It's also a good idea to plan your route in advance, including stops for sightseeing, meals, and rest.

For those who prefer not to drive, there are still plenty of options for exploring scenic routes from New York City. Many tour companies offer day trips and guided tours to popular destinations like the Hudson Valley, Long Island, and the Catskills. These tours often include transportation, guided commentary, and admission to key attractions, making them a convenient option for those who want to experience the beauty of the region without the hassle of driving.

In addition to planning your route and logistics, consider what you want to see and do on your road trip. New York City's surrounding areas offer a wide range of attractions, from historic sites and museums to outdoor activities and scenic viewpoints. Whether you're interested in exploring small towns, hiking through forests, or relaxing on the beach, there's something for everyone.

For those interested in history, be sure to include stops at some of the region's historic landmarks, such as West Point, the Vanderbilt Mansion in Hyde Park, or the Sagamore Hill National Historic Site on Long Island, the former home of President Theodore Roosevelt. If you're a fan of the outdoors, plan to spend time hiking, kayaking, or fishing in one of the many state parks and nature reserves that surround the city. For wine lovers, a visit to the vineyards of the Hudson Valley or Long Island's North Fork is a must, where you can sample local wines and enjoy the beautiful countryside.

A road trip from New York City offers a wealth of opportunities for exploration, whether you're looking to escape the city for a day or embark on a longer journey. With careful planning and consideration of your route, attractions, and logistics, you can create a memorable road trip experience that showcases the natural beauty, history, and charm of the region. Whether you're driving along the Hudson River, exploring the vineyards of Long Island, or hiking in the

Catskills, the journey promises to be as rewarding as the destination.

Local History Museums

New York City, often celebrated as a global hub of culture, art, and finance, is also a treasure trove of history. The city's rich and multifaceted past is meticulously preserved in its many local history museums. These museums offer a deep dive into the city's evolution from a modest Dutch settlement to the bustling metropolis it is today. Visiting these institutions provides an opportunity not only to understand the events and people that shaped New York but also to connect with the stories that continue to influence the city's dynamic character.

One of the most significant museums dedicated to New York City's history is the Museum of the City of New York (MCNY). Located on Fifth Avenue at the northern end of Museum Mile, this museum is an essential stop for anyone looking to understand the city's past and its impact on the present. The museum's extensive collection includes over 750,000 items that chronicle New York's history from its founding to the present day. These items include photographs, prints, maps, costumes, and toys, as well as more modern artifacts that represent the city's evolution over time.

The permanent exhibition "New York at Its Core" is a must-see. It provides a comprehensive overview of the city's 400-year history through objects, multimedia displays, and immersive experiences. Divided into three chronological sections—"Port City: 1609-1898," "World City: 1898-2012," and "Future City Lab"—the exhibit takes visitors on a journey through the economic, social, and political developments that have shaped New York. To reach the Museum of the City of New York, visitors can take the 2 or 3 subway lines to 110th Street and walk east to Fifth Avenue, or the 6 train to 103rd Street and walk west.

Another institution that offers an in-depth look at New York's history is the New-York Historical Society, located at 170 Central Park West. Founded in 1804, it is the oldest museum in New York City and one of the country's oldest cultural institutions. The museum's collection features a vast array of historical artifacts, art, and documents that tell the story of New York and the nation. The permanent exhibition, "New York Rising," highlights key moments in the city's history, including the Revolutionary War, the abolitionist movement, and the development of modern New York. The museum also offers rotating exhibits that focus on various aspects of the city's history, such as immigration, the labor movement, and the impact of notable New Yorkers.

One exhibit not to miss at the New-York Historical Society is the "Gallery of Tiffany Lamps," which displays one of the world's largest and most comprehensive collections of Tiffany glass. The stunning craftsmanship of these pieces reflects both the artistic and industrial history of New York during the late 19th and early 20th centuries. Additionally, the museum houses the Patricia D. Klingenstein Library, one of the oldest and most comprehensive research libraries in the United States, making it an invaluable resource for anyone interested in delving deeper into the city's past. The New-York Historical Society is easily accessible via the B or C subway lines to 81st Street.

For those interested in the maritime history of New York, the South Street Seaport Museum offers a unique perspective on the city's development as a port. Located in the historic South Street Seaport district, the museum is dedicated to the preservation and interpretation of the city's maritime heritage. The museum's collection includes historic ships, artifacts, and documents that illustrate New York's role as a major port and gateway for immigrants. Visitors can explore the museum's exhibitions and then step aboard the tall ships moored at the seaport, such as the Wavertree, an 1885 iron-hulled sailing ship that has been meticulously restored.

The South Street Seaport Museum's exhibitions cover various aspects of New York's maritime history, including the rise of the port, the lives of sailors, and the impact of maritime trade on the city's economy and culture. One notable exhibit is "Millions: Migrants and Millionaires aboard the Great Liners, 1900-1914," which explores the experiences of immigrants arriving in New York and the wealthy passengers who traveled in luxury on the same ships. The museum is accessible by taking the 2, 3, 4, 5, J, or Z trains to Fulton Street, then walking east towards the waterfront.

For a more localized perspective, the Tenement Museum on the Lower East Side provides an intimate look at the lives of immigrants who settled in New York during the 19th and early 20th centuries. The museum is housed in a former tenement building at 97 Orchard Street, where visitors can explore restored apartments and learn about the families who lived there. Through guided tours, the museum tells the stories of Irish, Italian, Jewish, and German immigrants, among others, who faced the challenges of life in a new country while shaping the cultural fabric of the city.

The Tenement Museum offers various tours that focus on different aspects of immigrant life, such as "Hard Times," which explores the lives of two families during economic downturns, and "Under One Roof," which looks at the experiences of immigrants who lived in the building during the 20th century. Each tour provides a poignant reminder of the struggles and resilience of the city's immigrant communities. The museum is accessible by taking the F train to Delancey Street or the J, M, or Z trains to Essex Street.

Additionally, the Lower East Side Tenement Museum's "Shop Life" exhibit offers a unique glimpse into the commercial history of the neighborhood, showcasing the types of businesses that operated in the tenement building over the years. This exhibit illustrates how immigrant entrepreneurs contributed to the city's economic growth and cultural diversity.

For those interested in the broader context of New York's cultural and social history, the Museum of Chinese in America (MOCA) offers valuable insights into the experiences of Chinese immigrants and the development of Chinatown. Located at 215 Centre Street, MOCA explores the history, culture, and contributions of Chinese Americans through a variety of exhibits and programs. The museum's core exhibition, "With a Single Step: Stories in the Making of

America," traces the history of Chinese immigration to the United States, the challenges faced by the Chinese American community, and their significant impact on American society.

MOCA also hosts rotating exhibitions that focus on different aspects of Chinese American culture, such as art, photography, and community activism. The museum's programs, including walking tours of Chinatown and educational workshops, provide a deeper understanding of the neighborhood's history and its ongoing evolution. To reach MOCA, visitors can take the 6, N, Q, R, J, or Z trains to Canal Street, and then walk a short distance to Centre Street.

In addition to visiting these museums, there are several ways to engage with New York City's history beyond the exhibits. Many of the museums mentioned offer educational programs, lectures, and workshops that allow visitors to delve deeper into specific topics. The New-York Historical Society, for example, hosts regular talks by historians, authors, and scholars who discuss various aspects of the city's past. The Museum of the City of New York offers walking tours, where participants can explore historic neighborhoods and learn about the city's architectural and cultural heritage.

Exploring these museums not only provides a rich understanding of New York's history but also enhances one's appreciation of the city's vibrant culture and diversity. By immersing yourself in the stories of the past, you can gain a deeper connection to the city and its people, both past and present. Whether you're a history buff, a casual visitor, or someone who calls New York home, these museums offer an invaluable opportunity to learn about the forces that have shaped this iconic city.

New York City's local history museums are essential destinations for anyone interested in understanding the city's past and its impact on the present. From the comprehensive exhibits at the Museum of the City of New York and the New-York Historical Society to the intimate stories told at the Tenement Museum and the Museum of Chinese in America, these institutions offer a wealth of knowledge and insight. Visiting these museums not only enriches your understanding of New York's history but also provides a deeper appreciation for the city's diverse cultural heritage.

CONCLUSION

As you reach the end of this book, you are now equipped with the knowledge and insights needed to make the most of your time in New York City. From understanding the city's diverse neighborhoods and planning your itinerary to knowing the best spots for dining, shopping, and exploring, you have all the tools to create an unforgettable experience tailored to your interests and pace. This book was designed to empower you to navigate the city with confidence, offering practical tips and detailed information that go beyond the surface to provide real value for your trip.

Whether it's your first visit or you're returning to discover something new, the information provided here is meant to guide you toward making choices that will enrich your journey. New York City is a place where every corner has a story, every street has a vibe, and every experience can become a treasured memory. By taking the time to prepare and plan with the help of this book, you can ensure that your visit is not just another trip, but a truly personal adventure.

Remember, the most important aspect of any travel experience is how it resonates with you. This city offers something for everyone, and with the insights you've gained, you're now ready to explore it in a way that's meaningful to you. Enjoy your time in New York City, make the most of every moment, and carry the memories of this incredible place with you long after your journey ends.

CREATING YOUR OWN ITINERARY

Planning a trip to a city as vast and vibrant as New York City requires thoughtful preparation to ensure that you make the most of your time while experiencing the things that matter most to you. Crafting your own itinerary allows you to create a journey that reflects your unique interests, energy levels, and pace. Instead of following a rigid plan, you can design a flexible itinerary that accommodates spontaneous moments while still covering all the essentials you want to see and do. This approach not only makes your trip more enjoyable but also ensures that your experience feels personalized and fulfilling.

When creating your itinerary, start by considering what you hope to gain from your trip. Think about the things that excite you most about New York City—whether it's the cultural landmarks, the diverse neighborhoods, the art, the food, or the shopping. What are the must-see sights for you, and what experiences would make your visit unforgettable? This reflection will help you focus on what's most important and avoid getting overwhelmed by the sheer number of options the city offers.

Once you've identified your key interests, think about the time you have available. How many days will you be in the city, and how much can you realistically fit into each day without feeling rushed? New York City is filled with things to see and do, but trying to pack too much into each day can lead to fatigue and leave you feeling like you've missed out on the simple pleasure of soaking in the atmosphere. Instead, plan your days with a mix of must-see attractions and downtime, allowing yourself to explore and enjoy the city at a leisurely pace.

Next, consider the geography of New York City. The city is divided into five boroughs, each with its own character and attractions. Manhattan is home to many of the city's most famous landmarks, while Brooklyn offers a more laid-back, artsy vibe. Queens is known for its diverse food scene, the Bronx for its rich history and green spaces, and Staten Island for its suburban feel and scenic ferry ride. Grouping activities by neighborhood can save you time and energy, allowing you to explore one area thoroughly before moving on to the next.

Flexibility is another crucial aspect of a well-crafted itinerary. While it's important to have a plan, leaving room for spontaneity can lead to some of the most memorable moments of your trip. Maybe you'll stumble upon a hidden gem while wandering through a neighborhood or decide to spend extra time in a museum that captures your interest. Building in some free time each day allows you to adapt to the city's rhythm and your own energy levels.

As you sketch out your days, think about how you'll move around the city. New York City's public transportation system is extensive, but it can be crowded and overwhelming if you're not used to it. Factor in travel time between locations and consider walking when possible to experience the city at street level. If you're planning to visit several attractions in a single day, map out the most efficient routes to minimize backtracking.

Finally, keep in mind that not everything will go according to plan, and that's okay. Weather, crowds, and other factors can disrupt even the most carefully planned itineraries. Embrace these changes as part of the adventure, and be open to adjusting your plans as needed. The key to a successful trip is not how closely you follow a schedule, but how much you enjoy the experiences you have along the way.

To help you with this process, I'm including a free 14-page itinerary planner. This planner is designed to document each step of planning your trip, from setting your priorities and budgeting your time, to organizing your days and noting down essential information like transportation routes and dining options. With this planner, you'll have everything you need to create an itinerary that suits your needs and ensures that your trip to New York City is everything you want it to be.

Remember, the best itinerary is one that feels right for you. It should reflect your interests, accommodate your pace, and leave room for discovery and relaxation. By taking the time to plan your trip thoughtfully, you're setting yourself up for an experience that is not only enjoyable but also deeply personal and memorable. So, take your time, explore your options, and create a plan that will allow you to experience New York City in a way that's uniquely yours.

HOW TO ACCESS AND USE YOUR FREE TRAVEL PLANNER

Thank you for choosing this travel guide! To help you organize your trip efficiently, we're offering a **Free Travel Planner** that you can print out and use to document your plans.

Here's how you can access and print your planner:
1. **Locate the QR Code**: You'll find the QR code below this section.
2. **Scan the QR Code**: Use your smartphone's camera or a QR code reader app to scan the code.
3. **Download the Planner**: After scanning, you'll be directed to the download page. Follow the instructions to download the planner file.
4. **Print the Planner**: Print out the planner on your home printer or at a local print shop.
5. **Start Planning**: Use the printed planner to jot down your travel plans, organize your itinerary, and ensure a well-prepared trip.

SCAN THE QR CODE BELOW

Made in the USA
Monee, IL
02 April 2025